THE ELIZABETH KECKLEY READER
VOLUME TWO

Tyree Daye and Jeffrey Langley,
"Coined: Sonnet for Elizabeth Keckley"

The Elizabeth Keckley Reader

VOLUME TWO
ARTISTRY, CULTURE & COMMERCE

Dr. Sheila Smith McKoy, editor

The Elizabeth Keckley Reader: Volume Two
Editor Sheila Smith McKoy
© Eno Publishers 2017
All rights reserved

Each selection herein is the copyrighted property of its respective author or publisher, if so noted on the Permissions page, and appears in this volume by arrangement with the individual writer or publisher.

Eno Publishers
P.O. Box 158
Hillsborough, North Carolina 27278
www.enopublishers.org

ISBN: 978-0-9973144-4-1
Library of Congress Control Number: 2015960648
Frontispiece: "Coined: Sonnet for Elizabeth Keckley," by Tyree Daye and Jeffrey Langley.
Cover photograph of Elizabeth Keckley is courtesy of the photography collection of Moorland Spingarn Research Center at Howard University.

Design and production by Copperline Book Services, Hillsborough, North Carolina

The Elizabeth Keckley Reader series is made possible with a grant from the North Carolina Arts Council.

www.ncarts.org

EDITOR'S ACKNOWLEDGMENTS

This work would not have been possible without the rare grace and presence of Elizabeth Hobbs Keckley (Keckly), who continues to be a persistent presence in my life. As we celebrate her artistry in this volume, I remain thankful for the talent, business acumen, and dignity of Keckley, whose work has survived her, her detractors, and her supporters.

I thank Elizabeth Woodman from Eno Publishers for hatching the wonderful plan of creating a reader focused on the life and life's work of Keckley whose work has not received the critical attention it deserves and whose life is a telling cultural commentary on the politics of power. I extend a special thanks to Rinita Banerjee, our wonderful editorial assistant, who remained dedicated to the project after her official work on the *Elizabeth Keckley Reader* ended. I am also indebted to Eno Publishers' Madeline Farrow, Sophia Shaw, and John Fate Faherty whose work made this volume possible. I owe endless thanks to Laura Lacy, the marketing director at Eno Publishers, as well.

Thanks also to my colleagues at Kennesaw State University and North Carolina State University, especially to Juliana Nfah-Abbenyi and Marc Dudley; to Helen Houston, Sandra Govan, John Lowe, Barbara McCaskill, Jessie Carney Smith, Jerry Ward, Barbara Paul-Emile, my son, Raymond Smith McKoy, John Berard, and all of my family members—those related by blood and by love.

Above all, I thank those who generously contributed their scholarship and creative expertise to this volume. We have enabled Elizabeth Keckley to continue her work for yet another generation of scholars and creators.

CONTENTS

xi Introduction | Dr. Sheila Smith McKoy
    When Genius Meets Spirit: Artistry, Culture & Commerce

CRITICISM

1   ONE | Carme Manuel
    Elizabeth Keckley's Behind the Scenes
    or the "Colored Historian's" Resistance to the Technologies of Power
    in Postwar America

41 TWO | Carolyn Sorisio
    Unmasking the Genteel Performer
    Elizabeth Keckley's Behind the Scenes and the Politics of Public Wrath

71 THREE | Katherine Adams
    Freedom and Ballgowns
    Elizabeth Keckley and the Work of Domesticity

113 FOUR | Xiomara Santamarina
    Behind the Scenes of Black Labor
    Elizabeth Keckley and the Scandal of Publicity

141 FIVE | Sarah Blackwood
    "Making Good Use of Our Eyes"
    Nineteenth-Century African Americans Write Visual Culture

167 SIX | Steve Criniti
    Thirty Years a Slave, and Four Years a Fairy Godmother
    Dress-Making as Self-Making in Elizabeth Keckley's Autobiography

187 SEVEN | Lisa Shawn Hogan
    Exposing Mary Lincoln
    Elizabeth Keckley and the Rhetroic of Intimate Disclosure

DRAMA

217 EIGHT | Tazewell Thompson
A scene from "Mary T. and Lizzy K."

225 NINE | Maureen Quilligan and Michael Malone
Scenes from "Behind the Scenes"

POETRY

233 TEN | Jaki Shelton Green
"a feast of whispers"

236 ELEVEN | Zelda Lockhart
"Posthumous"

241 TWELVE | Gideon Young
"what is it i hide from myself"

242 THIRTEEN | L. Teresa Church
"Woman of the Cloth"

243 FOURTEEN | Melvin E. Lewis
"The Modiste in Séance
For the Spiritualist in Elizabeth Hobbs Keckley"

245 FIFTEEN | Diane Judge
"Needlework and Names"

246 SIXTEEN | Lenard D. Moore
"Dear Elizabeth Keckley"

247 Elizabeth Hobbs Keckley Timeline

251 Further Reading

255 About the Editor

257 About the Contributors

261 Permissions & Acknowledgments

263 Index

INTRODUCTION

SHEILA SMITH McKOY

When Genius Meets Spirit
Artistry, Culture, and Commerce

"I must do something for myself, Mrs. Douglas, so I have come back to Washington to open my shop."
   The next day I collected my assistants, and my business went on as usual. Orders came in more rapidly than I could fill them. (223)
—Elizabeth Keckley, *Behind the Scenes:*
   Or, Thirty Years a Slave, and Four Years in the White House

To-day, I had to be trusted for a few spools of thread with which to do my sewing. In the old days I employed upwards of 20 sewing girls. My credit was food for hundreds of dollars' worth of goods. My services were sought everywhere, and I was always busy.
—Smith D. Fry, "Lincoln Liked Her:
   The Story of Elizabeth Keckley, a White House Factotum"

AS I INDICATE IN the introduction to the first volume of *The Elizabeth Keckley Reader* series, *Writing Self, Writing Nation* (2016), Elizabeth Keckley's extraordinary journey in life took her from enslavement to freedom, from financial success to poverty, from public commentary on her life and work to nearly being erased from history. The first volume focuses in large part on the unfolding of Keckley's life alongside that of our nation before, during, and immediately after the Civil War. As well, it recounts the narrative of her connection to the Lincoln White House and to Mary Todd Lincoln, whose life story both elegantly and uneasily intersects that of Keckley. Most articulations of Keckley's history find it difficult to consider her accomplishments beyond her connection to Mary Todd Lincoln. However, this volume celebrates Keckley's extraordinary and abiding legacy beyond her connection to the Lincolns. It is a celebration of the artistry that made her "famous among famous women and more famous men, in a wonderful period of the history of the republic" (Fry).

The epigraphs that open this discussion provide a telling commentary on Keckley's experiences as a designer and dressmaker. As I write this reflection, one hundred and ten years after Keckley's death, I am grateful that her designs have survived. As indomitable as her spirit, these designs offer us a view into her creative genius, into the women and the public for which she designed, and into her entrepreneurial accomplishments. As an artist and artisan, a business owner and employer, Keckley pushed against the limitations of race, place, and gender.

As Keckley begins her memoir, *Behind the Scenes: Or, Thirty Years a Slave, and Four Years in the White House*, it is clear that her experiences as a dressmaker and businesswoman are extraordinary. She describes her life as one "so full of romance" that it might "sound like a dream to the matter-of-fact reader (xi)." As Keckley ends her narrative, we find her still "toiling by day with [her] needle, and writing by night," refusing to regret the "burdens" she has borne for "sweet friendship's sake" (330–31). She expresses these sentiments just before the letters of Mary Todd Lincoln, with their numerous pleas for Keckley's financial and personal assistance, are appended to the volume. It is worth noting that there is an interesting contradiction between Keckley's business endeavors and the "business" that Todd Lincoln involved her in, the former successful enough to sustain Keckley and her employees, and the latter, the "Old Clothes Scandal"—Todd Lincoln's attempt to sell her clothes and jewelry for an income—an abject failure. In contrast to this failure, even when she was enslaved, Keckley's business earned enough income to keep "bread in the mouths of seventeen persons for two years and five months" (45). Owing to the creation of her unique way of fitting dresses, her St. Louis-based business was successful enough that she repaid the female benefactors who loaned her $1,200 to purchase freedom for her and for her son, George. Further, after her years creating gowns as the modiste of Todd Lincoln, she established her business in Washington employing young women to meet the demands of her work. To borrow from Keckley's own description of her work, "The months passed, and my business prospered" (225).

Making her living as an artist and artisan, Keckley was able to live as a free woman in a racially stratified America. She could afford to pay the requisite fees—the earliest form of "black tax"—that municipalities charged free blacks to live and work within their jurisdictions. Keckley was financially well-positioned enough to pay these fees in St. Louis. When she arrived in Washington, DC, she connected with members of the elite there, who assisted her in having the fees waived.[1] In considering Keckley's financial ability to live within these jurisdictions in order that she could work, one cannot underestimate the impact of her ability to support herself as an independent dressmaker and fashion designer. In her memoir, Keckley notes that she had her own "... system of cutting and fitting dresses" (64). This system gained her access to the wealthy women for whom she created in St. Louis as well as for the politically well-positioned women—the wives of congressmen and party leaders from both sides of the Confederate-Union divide in Washington, DC. It is ironic, then, that her talents as a seamstress and a designer, honed from skills she learned from her enslaved mother, enabled her to live as a modiste and a free African American businesswoman.

Perhaps the most effective way to describe Keckley's position, then, is to recognize that she lived in a space of cultural hybridity between enslavement and freedom, between her white patrons and her life as an African American woman, and between membership in the rising African American artisan class and her status in an America that failed to resolve "race question." Keckley's artistry offered her a different kind of freedom, one that was defined by the public consumption of her iconic designs during a time in our history when her entrepreneurial opportunities were heightened, rather than limited by, her status as free African American woman.

As a free female entrepreneur, Keckley was also positioned at the intersection of several identities that were not clearly defined in her America. Keckley had the opportunity to contribute to growing black middle class that maintained their own churches, created their educational institutions, and sustained their own businesses. As a business owner and an artist, Keckley was also an anomaly in this growing African American middle-class community: She supported herself financially outside of the confines of marriage, without the oversight of a father, and outside the confines of domestic servitude. Having married a man who "persisted in dissipation," Keckley divorced him and started her life anew and was able to support herself outside of the other familial bonds that defined most women of her era. As a single, independent woman, Keckley might easily have been defined as a social pariah, pushing against the definitions of womanhood that were celebrated during her lifetime.

Despite being vulnerable to attack from proponents of white supremacy and patriarchy, Keckley was integrated into both white and black societies. Had Keckley been an unmarried white woman, choosing an occupation over marriage would have been perceived as unseemly since domesticity was the ideal state of womanhood. On the contrary, we learn from Francis J. Grimké—her eulogist and pastor—that Keckley was both integrated into her society and accepted as "the very personification of grace and dignity . . ." (Grimké 20 November 1935)[2]

Keckley thrived in the space of cultural hybridity even though she was neither constrained by marriage, family, or the vagaries of race. She was a successful entrepreneur and refused to be a "proper" woman by embracing marriage to achieve social status. Yet, she contributed to the project of racial uplift embraced by the class-conscious social strivers in nineteenth- and early twentieth-century African American society.

Unlike most nineteenth-century artisans, Keckley was not amongst the "laboring poor" (Wilentz 34; see also 332). Her work not only positioned her for upward social mobility, but it also provided income for the women she trained in her craft. Making a living by her "needle" provided Keckley with a social and significant mobility that enabled her to travel. A survivor of rape during her enslavement, Keckley was also free from the brutal realities of white male patriarchy as a self-employed woman working largely for other women. Her talent as a designer and artist freed her; she was unbound by the limitations faced by most women of her era, irrespective of race. She was also well-positioned financially, at least until she published her book that, in her own words, "made some enemies for me who should have always been my friends" (Fry). Nonetheless, Keckley created and designed fashions for women who depended upon her work to create and sustain their public images. As the contributors in this volume note, Keckley was as adept with her needle as with the creation of her brand. In fact, her work made the process of public commentary about fashion and the public image of American First Ladies possible. Because several of her creations have survived, contemporary audiences understand her value as a designer and an artist. There is an indelible line of descent from Keckley's enslaved foremothers to her legacy. There is also a direct relationship between the politicization of the black female body in the nineteenth century and its counterpart in fashion, the full, bell-shaped skirt that defines clothing of the era. Keckley's designs bear the mark of history.

That said, her legacy and her art continue to inspire us in myriad ways. Thus, *The Elizabeth Keckley Reader, Volume Two,* includes critical essays that capture Keckley's unique place as a designer and artisan. As important, her life and her artistry provide the inspiration for poetry, drama, and visual art, some of it also included in this volume. This work grew out of the writers' fascination with Keckley's extraordinarily determined life; others were inspired by her invincible spirit. This collection is an homage to Keckley's spirit of invention and her insistence on living an exceptional life.

NOTES

1. Keckley writes, "I left Baltimore with scarcely money enough to pay my fare to Washington. Arriving in the capital, I sought and obtained work at two dollars and a half per day. However, as I was notified that I could only remain in the city ten days without obtaining a license to do so, such being the law, and as I did not know whom to apply for assistance, I was sorely troubled. I also had to have some one vouch to the authorities that I was a free woman. My means were too scanty, and my profession too precarious to warrant my purchasing license. In my perplexity I called on a lady for whom I was sewing, Miss Ringold, a member of Gen. Mason's family, from Virginia. I stated my case, and she kindly volunteered to render me all the assistance in her power. She called on Mayor Burritt with me, and Miss Ringold succeeded in making an arrangement for me to remain in Washington without paying the sum required for a license; moreover, I was not to be molested" (*Behind the Scenes* 65).

2. Grimké writes this letter to contest assertions that Keckley was a "purely fictitious" character.

WORKS CITED

Fry, Smith D. "Lincoln Liked Her: The Story of Elizabeth Keckley, a White House Factotum." *Minneapolis Register,* 6 July 1901, accessed 20 June 2015. https://archive.org/stream/marytoddlincolnlinc_11/marytoddlincolnlinc_11_djvu.txt.

Grimké, Francis J. "Letter to the Editor." 20 November 1935.

Keckley, Elizabeth. *Behind the Scenes: Or, Thirty Years a Slave, and Four Years in the White House* (1868). Hillsborough, N.C.: Eno Publishers, 2016.

Smith McKoy, Sheila. "Writing Self, Writing Nation: Reconsidering Thirty Years a Slave and Four Years in the White House." *The Elizabeth Keckley Reader, Volume 1: Writing Self, Writing Nation*. Hillsborough, N.C.: Eno Publishers, 2016.

Wilentz, Sean. *Chants Democratic: New York City and the Rise of the American Working Class, 1788–1850*. New York: Oxford University Press, 2004.

VOLUME 2: ARTISTRY, COMMERCE & CULTURE

CRITICISM

CHAPTER ONE

CARME MANUEL

Elizabeth Keckley's *Behind the Scene*s;
or, the "Colored Historian's" Resistance to the Technologies of Power in Postwar America

BEHIND THE SCENES: OR, *Thirty Years a Slave, and Four Years in the White House*, by Elizabeth Keckley, "an unabashed and often plainly self-congratulatory success story" (Andrews, "Changing" 234), encountered brutal hostility at its publication. The reasons for this were due mainly to the political events taking place in the country after Lincoln's death. Mrs. Lincoln's "Old Clothes Scandal" was just a distraction designed to convey unpalatable critiques of white America.[1] But Keckley's principal aim was to question white conceptions of American identity as defined in the Fourteenth Amendment. Thus, what Barbara Foley calls "the narrative illusion of historicity" (390) is exploited in *Behind the Scenes* for a variety of political ends. In fact, it was Mary Lincoln who, after reading the book, disparaged her former employee as "the colored historian." As did many other significant female and male black writers who wished to explore the tribulations of both slavery and post-Civil War racism, Keckley chose what might be labeled a "his/herstorical discourse"—that is, a hybridized narration in which the gendered male/female self can be appraised only as a historical entity in order to engage in political action.[2] There are three elements which made it possible for her to do so at the time of the composition of her text: her status as a free middle-class black woman before the war and her involvement during these years in liberatory black politics; the political optimism that early Reconstruction years encapsulated for blacks; and the new social approach to the rising power of the press and the visual media. Keckley depended on the potential of referentiality that written and visual media presented to expose both her version of her life and of American history from a radical, female, middle-class, and African American point of view.

It is crucial to note that Keckley was part of the black social elite that had developed in Washington and other large cities based, according to Leon Litwack, on "deeply rooted distinctions . . . of class, education, income, occupation, and acculturation to white society" (513).[3] As a dressmaker in the South throughout the 1850s who had arrived in the capital in the early 1860s, Keckley fits into the group of free Negroes that Ira Berlin refers to when he explains that "the 1850s were also a time of unprecedented prosperity" (343). Keckley's rise to notoriety is already embedded in the authorial information on the front page of her book: "Formerly a Slave, but More Recently *Modiste*, and Friend to Mrs. Lincoln." Her self-presentation is balanced on two poles that are made to appear extreme: "slave" and "*modiste* and friend" to Lincoln's widow. The French word she uses to describe her labor echoes the prestige that this profession had for Americans at the time. In a period where feminine fashion was ruled by publications such as *Godey's Lady's Book* and was reverential to prescriptions by French royalty, an African American woman's being both a "modiste" and "friend to Mrs. Lincoln" meant to be on the top rungs of the black social and vocational ladder.[4] In a way similar to that described by Clare H. Crowston, who discusses the emergence of the eighteenth-century *couturière* in France (3), it can be argued that Keckley emerged from the intersection of two distinct forces: first, from cultural conceptions of black femininity that cast needlework as an appropriate black female trade and encouraged black women to work for white clients of their own sex; second, from gendered and raced divisions of labor in America that accepted black women in this type of work. Yet, as a *black* modiste, Keckley had an influence that was more crucial than the importance Crowston assigns to the figure of the seamstress in French culture. In a presentation of self as a professional mantua-maker with a workshop in Washington and a number of employees under her responsibility, this black woman stood both as a teacher and a surrogate mother to other black women, two roles represented by her being a commanding mistress seamstress. Also, within her own social world, Keckley transmitted to her apprentices the professional and cultural skills they needed to survive in a rigidly segregated society where black women's access to labor was tragically confined to a limited number of jobs. If French mistress seamstresses, for both client and apprentice, provided "one of the most important rites of passage from rough nature to civilized culture" (Crowston 4), Mistress Keckley taught her black apprentices how to enter the labor market in postwar America and to become economically independent.[5] In fact, the economic autonomy provided by her dressing enterprise had made it possible for her to leave her husband and purchase her son's and her own freedom from slavery in St. Louis for $1,200. By emphasizing her financial self-sufficiency and the reality of upward social mobility through the sewing trade, this former "slave entrepreneur" (Walker 368) offered an unexpected example of free African American women's entrepreneurship in both prewar and postwar America.

Together with improvements in labor conditions among African Americans, "a new militance" appeared (Berlin 345). This "awakening of the free Negro's political consciousness" (346), which increased as the sectional crisis developed, made whites feel that the freemen's presence was becoming increasingly obnoxious. Berlin explains that among those who saw an opportunity to profit from the new attacks on free black liberty were white wage earners, who openly challenged their black competitors in occupations where free blacks had long gone unchallenged. By the late 1850s, for example, free blacks had monopolized the caulking trade in Baltimore for more than a decade. Exasperated by black success, whites determined to drive them off by force. Beginning in 1858, gangs of white "Tigers" roamed the Baltimore docks, beating black caulkers and harassing shipyards that employed them. Within the next two years, whites broke the free black monopoly and obliged many blacks to seek employment in other cities. "Before long, the example of the Tigers' success incited white workers in other trades to drive out blacks" (349).

These events should be related directly to Keckley's experience as a free black working woman in Baltimore, as this is a period that is cloaked in complete mystery and obscurity in *Behind the Scenes* and in biographical accounts by critics. Her likely involvement in some sort of promotional activity within the city's black community, however, is made clear by another outstanding black woman, Maria W. Stewart. In her *Sufferings during the War*, Stewart writes: "I was told on my way that Washington had become a perfect Paradise for the colored people since President Lincoln had taken his seat.... There was a lady, Mrs. Keckley, I knew, formerly from Baltimore, who proved to be an ardent friend to me in my great emergency which took place afterward" (Richardson 102). She later adds that "[T]wo Presbyterian ladies, Mrs. Slade and Keckley, came to my help; and they did not say 'Be ye warmed and be ye fed' without affording the means; and one of them was the lady I was acquainted with in Baltimore. The other was a resident here" (108). Stewart's references to the help granted to her by Keckley stand as unquestionable testimony of the underground activities in which she was engaged within the African American community during prewar times and her rising status among her own people some years before she became Mrs. Lincoln's modiste. In fact, Keckley's political commitment deepened during and after the war. In about September 1862, as a result of the waves of freedmen arriving in Washington, she and several others created the Contraband Relief Association, and in 1863, as she herself reports, she was re-elected president, an office which she continued to hold at the time of writing *Behind the Scenes*.

Keckley's activities were further encouraged by the intrinsic meaning of the Civil War. Historians understand that the conflict was fundamentally a struggle for the nation's future. African Americans, in the aftermath of the controversy, were aware that its conclusion had started a process of modernization that would lead to the redefinition of American citizenship so that all Americans became subjects of the *national* state.[6] *Behind the Scenes* is a political text emanating from the situation of these early postwar years.[7] It highlights a crucial moment in which "black women shared in the political mobilization" (Foner, "Rights" 878).[8] Keckley was encouraged in this moment to write and publish a text that, cloaked beneath the veil of a literary defense of Mary Lincoln, supported, cherished and struggled to fortify the racial politics prized by Radical Republicanism.[9]

Between the end of the Civil War and the printing of *Behind the Scenes* in April 1868, two Constitutional Amendments were passed which changed the status of blacks and created a "constitutional revolution" (Pyne and Sesso 479). The Thirteenth Amendment formally freed the slaves, and the Fourteenth Amendment bestowed citizenship. The latter was the outcome of a compromise between moderate and Radical Republicans, transforming black Americans into citizens both of the United States and in their states of residence.[10] Even if historians approach the interpretation of Reconstruction differently, they agree that compelling Radical Reconstruction was the conviction that "the freedmen must be granted certain rights and protected in their exercise, in order to preserve the fruits of victory and pay the debt owed the Negro for his aid in saving the Union" (Fredrickson 178).[11]

Behind the Scenes shows Keckley's alliance with Radical Republicanism. One of the most striking features of this period is "the remarkable political mobilization of the black community" (Foner, "Reconstruction Revisited" 89). As did black male Republican politicians, Keckley tried to construct a text including "values emanating from slavery and traditional American ideals... such as the dignity of labor, messianic religion, and, especially, the quest for full incorporation as citizens of the republic" (90). Consequently, *Behind the Scenes* can best be understood as Keckley's (R)adical appropriation of the available postwar technologies of power in order to forge an expression of the aspirations of African Americans; among these new technologies are both the visual image and the press.

Behind the Scenes can be interpreted as an act of black textual signifying on the visual world as created by white America in the early postwar years, a world which was defined as *the* American history. Hence the text derives its meaning from the background of intertextual visual fictions produced after the end of the Civil War and during the early Reconstruction period. Keckley draws on these sources to address a main theme: the representation of the new emancipated black self. As an African American woman belonging to the black elite and as an American citizen as defined by the Fourteenth Amendment, she recasts historical discourse by imposing an inclusive black documentary presence where earlier there was none, or if it existed, was deeply distorted. *Behind the Scenes* refashions the visual, and rewrites history to include a dignified female black presence long denied the stage and unknown to the public.

The war brought about a transition in American life, which established changes in the mode of social perception. Daguerreotypes, photographs, and cartoons were related to the emergence of new practices of observation and national identity formation. These new techniques of representation and regulation were central to the restructuring of the national state as white and to the exclusion of blacks. Following Michel Foucault's ideas in *Discipline and Punish*, we could contend that this production of a new sense of Americanness released new effects of power, just as new forms of the exercise of power yielded new knowledge of the social body that was to be altered. Similarly, in John Tagg's rendering of British society at the time, what characterized the American postwar period in which photographic evidence emerged was a social and racial division "between the power and privilege of *producing and possessing* and the burden of *being* meaning" (6; original emphasis); that is to say, a contrast between those who had the capacity to define reality through the camera and those who were stood submissively in front of it. Keckley was as concerned with political and economic events as well as she was with "one of those moments of transformation which render the roots of social experience socially visible or invisible" (Tagg 171). *Behind the Scenes* revolts against "the burden of *being* meaning." Keckley deals with a set of circumstances in which the logic that gave expression to postwar American reality collapsed and was replaced by the new, *radically reconstructed* logic of social perception. That her book failed and was received with unprecedented scorn is indicative of power and its challenge to her textual "alterations." *Behind the Scenes* shows, then, the formation of socially new ways of seeing black America.

Keckley uses a twofold strategy to accomplish her ends. She first grants authenticity/realism to her "black and blackened behind-the-scenes" through the many interpolated documentary particulars and guarantees of veracity that were central to the political effectiveness of the fugitive-slave narrative as a genre. Yet, in these postwar years, Keckley—as Booker T. Washington did later—aims at authenticity through an overwhelming inclusion of press documents and letters with references to herself. Her text stands as an instrument of persuasion, and to that purpose, she uses corroborative devices to secure an effect of immediate historicity and reliability.[12]

At the same time, she goes well beyond the mere insertion of these textual pieces of evidence. As an alert witness to the profound social changes of her society, Keckley was deeply aware of the power of the visual to create truth and cause a political impact. What defines and creates "truth" in any society is a system of more or less ordered procedures for the production, regulation, distribution, and circulation of statements. Tagg writes that "[t]hrough these procedures 'truth' is bound in a circular relation to systems of power which produce and sustain it, and to the effects of power which it induces and which, in turn, redirect it." It is this dialectical relation that constitutes what Foucault calls "a régime of truth." "This brings Foucault to the view that the problem is one of changing not people's 'consciousness' but the political, economic, and institutional régime of the production of truth—or, at least, of showing that it is possible to construct a new politics of truth" (173). For nineteenth-century Americans, mechanically reproduced images carried the weight of truth and transparency. The visual representation of the self and of marginalized others (blacks, immigrants, Native Americans, prostitutes, prisoners, etc.) was instrumental in the creation and diffusion of notions of class, race, and American identity. Keckley reinserts new forms of knowledge through manipulating the status of the visual as evidence of the neutral and the given, and thus struggles to detach the power of truth from the specific forms of white hegemony.[13]

Also, Alan Trachtenberg writes that "[t]he paucity of blacks in [war albums and the photographic record of America], their appearance on the margin of scenes, parallels their status within the mental pictures that screened the mind from the full social and political facts of the war" (*Reading* 80). On the whole, "the photographic record tends to banish blacks to the margin of visibility—their presence unacknowledged even when plainly there" (110).[14] As Richard Rudisill argues, as reproductions of the real world, daguerreotypes and photographs served as symbols in the quest for the American national character. In *Behind the Scenes*, Keckley rewrites popular visual representations of blacks and restores their visibility in order to construct a new politics of historical truth.

Roland Barthes's notions on the different sensations viewers have when observing photographs are useful in understanding the modes in which Keckley conveys her carefully selected images from America's recent past of slavery and war. Barthes explains that the viewer experiences two kinds of sensations when looking at a picture. He calls the first one the *studium*, that is, simple human interest. The second feeling, the *punctum*, breaks through the *studium* felt by the conscience of the watcher, rushes the stage and *pierces* him/her (Barthes 64–65).[15] Keckley's position as a marginalized subject in postwar America facilitates her gaze into her own (her)storical past, which goes beyond the *studium*, the general knowledge accessible to all spectators. As an African American woman belonging to Washington's black elite, Keckley's *punctum* reinterprets "American *scenes*" as "*Black* American scenes," that is to say, as "American *behind-the-scenes*." This implies that the way she presents her narrative images is connected to her capacity to obtain unexpected and unlooked-for meanings. The result is an experience that radically contrasts with the evident meanings, while apparently fitting them, which is the experience the generally accepted *studium* presents.

The first important visual material included graphically in *Behind the Scenes* is an engraving of her on the book's 1868 frontispiece.[16] Tagg explains that the history of photography is "a model of capitalist growth in the nineteenth century," and this is most evident "in the rise of the photographic portrait which belongs to a particular stage of social evolution: the rise of the middle and lower-middle classes toward greater social, economic and political importance." That signified that "[t]o 'have one's portrait done' was one of the symbolic acts by which individuals from the rising social classes made their ascent visible to themselves and others and classed themselves among those who enjoyed social status" (Tagg 37).[17] In America, daguerreotypes emphasized democratic personality and the pictures promoted a sense of national identity in reproducing the common things in American life. Keckley's portraits showing her attired with fine clothes are therefore signs of her political purpose. They both assert her presence in American visual representation and imbue her with a new social and political identity. This is the reason that *Behind the Scenes* appeared to be extremely presumptuous to many readers but for this fact was, ultimately, subversive.

Keckley's involvement in the clothing profession in *Behind the Scenes* is, as discussed above, more than just a way to earn her living. Her status as a black modiste should be compared with her past as a slave, both in terms of social and visual uplift. Eugene Genovese explains how the ruling class in the antebellum South understood the importance of dress as an index of social position and how South Carolina's slave code of 1740 strictly regulated dress (559). Accordingly, the importance given to clothing by African Americans was a natural reaction to the general deprivations suffered throughout slavery.

Keckley's engraving and photographs as a black bourgeoise would have limited significance if not contrasted with those of Mrs. Lincoln, however, especially those photographs taken by Mathew Brady in which Mrs. Lincoln appears dressed in Keckley's own designs (Fig. 1). The most crucial meanings of Keckley's visual representations thus emerge from their powerful significations on the white image, as these recast Keckley as a dignified, respectable middle-class black woman and American citizen in her own right.

In fact, *Behind the Scenes* bears witness to the fact that Keckley's ambitions went well beyond the restrictions of the dressmaking profession. Her position as a careful drafter and remaker of scenes—her *punctum*, or what might be called "her textual alterations"—attests to her desire to become "the colored national historian" in a way which mirrors the career of Brady, the most famous photographer of the time. Brady had issued an "Address to the Public" in the New York *Tribune* of April 10, 1854, vindicating photography as a "true art" (qtd. in Trachtenberg, *Reading* 26). Similarly, Keckley did not want to be considered a simple dressmaker (i.e., skillful in her ability to control the mechanics of sewing), but rather a *modiste* (an artist who emphasized her special way of cutting, who could be an arbiter of tastes, etc.). Additionally, as an artistic work, her *Behind the Scenes* appeals to middle-class tastes and respectability since it refashions the new technologies of representation in its rendering of personal and public portraits (Fig. 2). As Trachtenberg writes, "[I]n the crafting of the mythos of the public portrait, which included a public image of the image maker, no American played a greater role than Mathew Brady.... More than any other American, Brady shaped the role of the photographer as *a national historian,* one who keeps records of the famous and the eminent, as well as the run-of-the-mill citizen" (*Reading* 33; emphasis added).[18] In 1850, Brady had published *The Gallery of Illustrious Americans,* which presents an "illusion of unity... founded on values represented by white male leaders and achievers." Yet in this book, "Black Americans held in slavery... remain voiceless, unseen, unillustrated. Just as their invisibility haunted the rhetoric of a 'virtuous' republic, so the aura of virtue in *The Gallery of Illustrious Americans* veiled the fear at the heart of the book—fear of disunion descending into fratricide" (*Reading* 52). *Behind the Scenes* stands as Keckley's *Gallery of Illustrious Americans* as re-visioned by an African American woman.

Among the vast assortment of visual material published during the war and the early postwar years, Becky Rutberg chooses to include a remarkable image in her biographical account of Keckley, which she titles "Caricature on miscegenation mocking Mrs. Lincoln's friendship with Lizzie and forecasting the nature of future relationships between black and white people" (Rutberg 87). "Lizzie's relationship with Mrs. Lincoln," Rutberg writes, "attracted the poison pen of the press. Many people—even several abolitionists—disapproved of Mary Lincoln's selection of a black woman as her best friend. A cartoon appeared in the newspaper that depicted their friendship as beginning a trend of miscegenation" (88). Originally, the picture bore the title of *Miscegenation or the Millennium of Abolitionism* (Fig. 3). James Lively writes that "[b]y 1860 political cartoons had come to be an important form of political expression" (Lively 99), and he argues that "[a]bolition was repeatedly attacked with special emphasis upon the dire effects of miscegenation" (103). Even though there is nothing definitive in this caricature that points to a direct relation between Mrs. Lincoln and Keckley, Rutberg's reading of this image is meaningful here.[19] Abraham Lincoln was in fact the first person to recognize the relevance of the new visual media in disseminating power and changing agency. Brady's first portrait of Lincoln was taken on February 27, 1860, at the time of his famous

Cooper Union address. This print was distributed by the thousands and numerous lithographs were made of it by Currier & Ives. Returning to this image, Lincoln said: "Brady and the Cooper Institute made me President" (Horan 130). Writing at a time when blacks seemed to enjoy certain political favors, Keckley sought to legitimize them as participants in American society by dressing them up. Through her "insights," she also fashioned her own textual Reconstruction into scenes known and unknown for postwar whites in order to rewrite Brady's gallery of illustrious characters.

While *Behind the Scenes* does deal with Keckley's relationship with the famous Mrs. Lincoln, this is not the main focus of the author's attention. To achieve her radical purposes, Keckley had to distance herself from the textually and visually slandered First Lady and connect herself to the only immaculate character in America's contemporary historical tableau—Abraham Lincoln. Elevated to the category of martyr, the character of the assassinated president lent itself to any type of interpretation that best fit the historian's understanding of America past and present. In *Behind the Scenes,* Lincoln represents the aborted dream of racial justice as well as the acceptance of the Radical Reconstructionists' political agenda.

There are three moments of obvious historical manipulation in *Behind the Scenes* that are linked to Lincoln's role as caring president to the black nation: the death of Keckley's son, the jarring omission of the New York Draft Riots, and the meeting between Lincoln and Frederick Douglass. Keckley's *punctum* on these occasions is to join a long list of black and white commentators on the dead president's role for the progress of racial relationships. Kenneth Stampp writes that as late as 1862, in the second year of the Civil War and of his presidency, Lincoln defended the view that blacks and whites were different races and favored colonization.[20] Keeping in mind Lincoln's ideas about blacks, the first thing to take into account to understand Keckley's portrait of the president in *Behind the Scenes* is the timing of her text's composition. She started to write the book after Lincoln's death, when black Americans then and "in the years to follow, lifted the fallen martyr into sainthood" (McFeely 240). She was well aware that her text would serve more practical purposes if written as a eulogy which could run up against the countless others produced by Americans, both black and white, at the time.[21] Keckley's domestic images of Lincoln and his family represented a tremendous novelty in the literature about the doomed president. Her firsthand descriptions of the "man at home" not only completed the political dimensions of his public image but also expressed him in sentimental terms that embodied the attractiveness of the democratic American. Most important, however, was Keckley's strategic mythologizing of Lincoln for her own self-aggrandizement as well as for the foregrounding of her black community.

In Chapter Six, Keckley tells us that before Willie Lincoln's death, she had lost her own son, George W.D. Kirkland, on 10 August 1861 at the battle of Wilson's Creek in Missouri. What Keckley does not say is that George had enlisted in the Union Army's First Missouri Volunteers as a white man since he looked white enough to pass. Jennifer Fleischner credits this silence to Keckley's "self-control and pride" (*Mrs. Lincoln* 223).[22] Similarly, Rafia Zafar believes that "Keckley's relative silence could also confirm her in white eyes as a successful performer, one who could be judged socially deserving, and worthy of higher status" (177). But if her main objective in the text is considered, this black mother's dignified restraint of maternal despair seems to obey to a more technical intention. Keckley sacrifices her pride on her son's martyred heroism because she had no way to link coherently her personal scene of mourning to Lincoln's public racial politics. This is one of the many cases in the text where Keckley's unveiling what Zafar calls "the black back regions" (179) would necessarily have distorted her own strategies of self-legitimization as tied to white characters. This omission must be interpreted then as part and parcel of Keckley's effort to secure an apparent apolitical relationship toward the president.

Her son's enlistment as a black man in the Union Army had been prohibited by Lincoln's politics on black conscription.[23] No wonder then that Keckley comments so little on her *black* son's death, since she found it impossible to reconcile Lincoln's politics at that time with her son's patriotism. Yet she uses the scene to recast herself as a contained *stabat mater* in contrast to Mrs. Lincoln hysterical mourning for her beloved, and to exhibit herself as a grieving black mother who had sacrificed her only offspring's life for the nation.

The second "alteration" which Keckley performs refers to what Herbert Asbury, in his *Gangs of New York*, calls "the battle of Six Days," which took place in New York City on 13 July 1863; draft riots also broke out in other Northern cities. White men, furious about the federal government's new conscription of troops—from which the wealthy could exempt themselves by paying a substitute—took vengeance on the people for whom they were called to risk their lives, the blacks for whom the war was being fought. Leslie Harris writes that the riots provided the justification to expel blacks not only from interracial employment, but also from living and leisure spaces; that they definitely helped restrict the access of blacks to jobs where there were whites; that they legitimized white superiority; and that they showed the success of racist campaigns against miscegenation promoted by the sensationalist press during the 1840s and 1850s (279–88).

Despite the formidable importance of these events and the consequences they spawned, *Behind the Scenes* is surprisingly silent about them. While Keckley does not include a single comment or reference to the riots throughout her text, Rutberg does mention Keckley's involvement in these events when she writes that "[T]he Visiting Committee of Lizzie's First Black Contraband Relief Organization distributed groceries and clothing to many homeless black people whose homes were destroyed in the riot" (83). This absence in Keckley's text may be due to the fact that she once again had no way to comment on these scenes triumphantly. The New York riots demonstrated that Lincoln's racial agenda, no matter how moderate and conservative, meant a reversal of power that white Democratic workers would not tolerate.[24] If she had used these images in her text, she would have had to recognize black vulnerability in a world that would employ deadly violence to restore the nation's traditional racial situation. For Keckley, discussing black humiliation or reversal implied minimizing her teleological role as black historian. In fact, she seems ready to resort to any strategy to avoid presenting such scenes.[25] Nowhere in the text does Keckley manipulate historical data so skillfully to serve these purposes of black elevation as in chapter ten. Here she tells how Lincoln met Douglass on 4 March 1865. Douglass was under the ban prohibiting blacks from entering the White House. But Lincoln did graciously let him in and expressed his admiration for his commitment to racial uplift (119–20). This scene is not corroborated by historical evidence. Douglass had already had two interviews with Lincoln—the first one in the summer of 1863 and the second on 19 August 1864. They discussed, among other things, the recruitment of black soldiers for the Union Army and the future of Southern slaves in the event that peace be concluded while they remained within Confederate lines.[26] Douglass himself, however, would recreate these events from a more self-enhancing perspective in his *Life and Times of Frederick Douglass, Written by Himself* (1892).[27]

Keckley's and Douglass's different renderings of the same event—their diverse *puncta*—show clearly the way these African American autobiographers appropriated and manipulated history to legitimize themselves not only as witnesses, but as active protagonists who were deprived of a place in the contemporary space of American history. There are no visual records perpetuating the image of Abraham Lincoln with any black leader, Douglass included. Thomas Nast, the staunch supporter of Lincoln's politics, had helped to glorify the president's crowning achievement related to African Americans—the Emancipation Proclamation in 1 January 1863—with a double-page cartoon, "The Emancipation of the Negro, 1863, The Past and the Future," in *Harper's Weekly* on 24 January 1863 (56–57) (Fig. 4). Nast renders black uplift in terms similar to those of the generic antebellum slave narrative.

In this illustration, the figure of Columbia stands at the top and in the midst of the word "Emancipation." On the left the torments of slavery are graphically shown. The centerpiece illustrates a reunited family of former slaves living now on terms similar to those of the white middle-classes, under Lincoln's protective portrait, which presides over the room and their lives. In the small centerpiece below, Father Time holds the Baby New Year, who unshackles a black man. On the right, Nast recreates several scenes announcing some of the fruits of emancipation: Black children enjoy the benefits of public schooling and black adults are transformed into paid employees. Yet the picture underlines the fact that these newly emancipated Americans, no matter how respectable and self-reliant, will continue to play the same role as before as they remove their hats in subordination to their white superiors. Lynn Domina explains that Keckley, far from identifying herself with the mass of blacks, "introduces class distinctions among the members of her race, identifying herself if only by association with the 'well-to-do colored people' rather than with 'suffering blacks'" (140). Nast's illustration precludes any type of differentiation among African Americans and erases the success of blacks with whom Keckley identifies in *Behind the Scenes*. Keckley's class-dissociation movement thus expands Nast's imagining of the meaning of Emancipation to include Lincoln's recognition of black hierarchies and the leading role of women such as herself, and that of men, such as Frederick Douglass.

Keckley's erasure of images from her past throughout her text are also noteworthy since they follow a paradigm recurrent in other African American women writers.[28] She is careful never to lose sight of her ultimate aim: to enhance a political public agenda of black vindication. To this end, there

*Figure 1: Mathew B. Brady, Mary Todd Lincoln. 1861.
Image courtesy: Library of Congress.*

are other points in the text where Keckley inserts her voice and her presence. These scenes, however, attest to her overwhelming desire to step out of the White House's domestic sphere and involve herself in the political circles of the nation. What I believe to be the climax of the narrative takes place when Keckley legitimizes herself as a participant in her own right in the scenes that reconstruct the mythical moments after the death of the president.

Keckley's consciousness of exclusion from visual and civic manifestations that recreated the progress of the nation appears consistently in many written accounts by these black women writers.[29] Faced with marginalization from all American political spaces, Keckley, in her role as "colored historian," wedged the African American presence into the culminating moment of the reestab-

Figure 2: Elizabeth Keckley. Photographic print, ca. 1860.

lishment and consolidation of American identity in these postwar years: the death of Abraham Lincoln as a moment of national reunification, as it was interpreted by the press and visual media, especially in numerous symbolically charged illustrations. On 29 April 1865, *Harper's Weekly* published one of the first and most graphically emblematic images of the president's death, Thomas Nast's "Abraham Lincoln's coffin."

"The greatest American master of political cartooning" believed, according to Morton Keller, that he had a moral duty to his community (Vinson 338). Lincoln had recognized the extraordinary importance of Nast's work when he had said that the cartoonist was the best sergeant the Union had for recruiting soldiers.[30] "Abraham Lincoln's coffin" shows Columbia, or Lady Liberty, weeping over the stateman's coffin, as well as a grieving Union soldier and a Union Navy man mourning the president's loss. What is most striking, however, is the literal and consequently symbolical invisibility of the cause for which Lincoln was at that moment glorified by millions of Americans: his leading role as the Great Emancipator, the long expected Moses of black American slaves. The complete absence of his redeeming role as represented in this illustration can be seen as one of the reasons for Keckley's black appropriation of the body and symbolical potential of Lincoln in chapter nine ("The Assassination of President Lincoln"):

> When I entered the room, the members of the Cabinet and many distinguished officers of the army were grouped around the body of their fallen chief. They made room for me, and, approaching the body, I lifted the white cloth from the white face of the man that I had worshipped as an idol—looked upon as a demi-god. . . . I gazed long at the face, and turned away with tears in my eyes and a choking sensation in my throat. Ah! never was man so widely mourned before. The whole world bowed their heads in grief when Abraham Lincoln died. (140–41)

For Elizabeth Young, the ritual of public display of Lincoln's body "sanctified the martyred president and elevated his viewing audience, uniting them as members of the Lincolns' national 'family' mourning his death." On the other hand, for "newly emancipated African Americans, access to Lincoln's dead body served as a vital test of their membership in this family" (Young 131). Keckley's description of this moment of close contact with Lincoln "testifies to her power" (Melba Joyce Boyd qtd. in Young 131).[31] From her privileged position within the Lincoln household, and thus from the behind-the-scenes White House, Keckley's right to partake of the intimacy and sacredness of the moment is recognized by the "many distinguished officers of the army" who "were grouped around the body of their fallen chief." Hence, she carves herself a niche into this extraordinary historical tableau. Keckley re-visualizes Nast's conception of the moment with a *punctum* which places her next to the white Northern soldiers to mourn in public the lost myth and to leave testimony of her own *memento mori*. Tom Lutz explains how the romantic revision of sensibility transformed the body into an evident representation of truth. Tears, he claims, acquired a greater meaning than words to express the truth (55). The tears wept by Keckley when contemplating the dead Lincoln transform her into a black Columbia whose crying and choking are a glorious revelation and legitimization of the African American inclusion into the definitions of both American citizenship and American identity.[32]

Keckley's process of self-aggrandizement through the manipulation of the documentary mode and challenge of its veracity does not stop here. Her name-dropping technique also ventures into the realm of the era's Southern elites: First, she links herself to the president of the Confederacy through her sartorial skills and refashions one of the most popular postwar Northern visual and narrative legends on Southern manhood; second, she recreates the interregional reconciliation motif inserting herself as the main protagonist.

One month after Lee's surrender to Grant at Appomattox, the ex-Confederate president and Keckley's former employer, Jefferson Davis, was captured by Union troops. The rumor was that he was disguised as a woman in crinoline. Similar to stories about Lincoln's passage through Baltimore disguised in a Scotch cap and ulster, Davis's escape offered juicy material for cartoonists (Lively 105). Nina Silber explains that his capture "helped crystallize Northern men's ideas about unmanly Southern men and disruptive Southern women." The newspapers published reports stating that he had been caught disguised in one of Mrs. Davis's dresses. Historians have questioned the truth of this information, even if most of them concur that Davis "donned some form of disguise that may have belonged to his wife—most likely a cloak or shawl (or both) which were commonly worn by both men and women" (Silber 625).[33] Keckley resorts to the motif of a disguised Davis in chapter four. She tells the following:

> In the winter of 1865 I was in Chicago, and one day visited the great charity fair held for the benefit of the families of those soldiers who were killed or wounded during the war. In one part of the building was a wax figure of Jefferson Davis, wearing over his other garments the dress in which it was reported that he was captured. There was always a great crowd around this figure, and I was naturally attracted toward it. I worked my way to the figure, and in examining the dress made the pleasing discovery that it was one of the chintz wrappers that I had made for Mrs. Davis, a short time before she departed from Washington for the South. When

Figure 3: Anon., "Miscegenation or the Millennium of Abolitionism," lithograph. New York: Bromley & Co., 1864.

it was announced that I recognized the dress as one that I had made for the wife of the late Confederate President there was great cheering and excitement, and I at once became an object of the deepest curiosity. Great crowds followed me, and in order to escape from the embarrassing situation I left the building. (50–51)[34]

Keckley is recognized in Chicago as the maker of the piece of clothing which cast the ex-Confederate president into ridicule, and as such, the most important participant in "the metaphorical unmanning of Southern aristocracy" (Silber 630). For Young, Keckley "uses the imagery of feminization to humiliate Davis" (133). She adds that "it is the female ex-slave, not the male slaveholder, who shapes the political discourse surrounding slavery. As with her own account of Lincoln, Keckley's relation to Davis's clothing underscores her own role in the making of political iconography. The scene highlights Keckley's own power, placing her at the center of a drama of authentication in which she plays a starring role" (134). It is important to note that, even though her only way to contribute to the legend of Davis's capture is from the realm of domesticity (as a dressmaker), Keckley is nevertheless acclaimed by the public because she is successful in bridging the gap between the political world of action and the feminine domestic sphere, aligns herself with triumphant Northern political rhetoric, and transforms her recognition by the Northern public into a visual subversion.

The victory of Northern masculinity, however, went well beyond the boundaries of the Confederate political elite. The conquering North relied on the traditional image of a feminized South to establish its regional and political superiority. This gendered image took the form of an interracial marriage in popular culture. The reconciliation motif, however, between Federal and Confederate spheres, depended upon Northern dominance. The postwar North-South encounter was represented both in written and visual iconography as the reunion between a magnanimous victor and a vanquished, proud, yet repentant South. Keckley must also be held responsible for being one of the first African American writers to exploit this popular theme running through the postwar years. She manipulates the reconciliation theme to elevate her status before her distrusting white Northern readers by presenting the unexpected. Far from showing any attitude of open vindictiveness against her former owners, Keckley reshapes herself into the figure of a pardoning and morally superior black female. Two main moments in the text rewrite the relationship between the ex-slave and white Southerners for a postwar Northern audience eager to soften the rough edges of Reconstruction.

The first scene exhibits Keckley's most important silence on her personal life. Frances Smith Foster calls attention to the fact that Keckley "chose to omit many 'strange passages' of her personal history and instead to concentrate upon 'the most important incidents' that 'influenced the moulding of [her] character.' Among the missing elements are some surprising details, such as her family history, her date of birth, her physical appearance, and her education" ("Historical" xvii). She was born a slave in Virginia and her biological father was her mother's owner, Armistead Burwell. When she was about twenty years old, she endured sexual abuse by a man named Alexander Kirkland, and bore a son she named George, after her slave father. When her son was eighteen months old, she was sent to live with Burwell's daughter Ann and her husband. Ann was, in fact, her white sister. Keckley describes her new home in terms of terrible poverty. Hugh A. Garland, a lawyer and merchant, had had financial difficulties and moved the family to St. Louis, Missouri. Keckley's economic self-reliance is first shown in her reaction toward Garland's decision to rent her mother, Agnes Hobbs. This is the moment for both her entry into the sewing trade and her reversal of the nineteenth-century cult of heroic motherhood. Keckley's successful initiation into the labor market is rooted in her feelings of filial outrage. Yet her laudable devotion to the welfare of her mother is highlighted by her toil to "keep bread in the mouths of seventeen persons for two years and five months," since the patriarch of the family, lawyer Garland, was unable to provide for them. What is striking here is the contrast between Garland and Keckley in terms of force of work, and that Keckley's *punctum* when observing these years can be felt via one of the nation's great antebellum dramas: the Dred Scott case. Garland was the attorney for the defendant, and his role in the case was crucial since he challenged the legal decision that Scott was not a citizen because he was a "negro of African descent." Thus, *Behind the Scenes*, as Foster explains, can be read as Keckley's "offering her testimony to a passel of Hugh A. Garlands, who advocated restricting citizenship for freed slaves, arguing, as did Keckley's first mistress, that they were not fit for equality, that they were not (and might not ever be) 'worth [their] salt'" ("Historical" lxvi).

The second scene has to do with Keckley's reunion with her white Southern family in Chapter Fourteen, entitled "Old Friends." William Andrews writes that antebellum black writers affirm that slavery is a tomb from which they can be resurrected only with outright rebellion, whereas for postwar writers it was a school of useful teachings ("Reunion," *passim*). Keckley's conciliatory view of slavery in *Behind the Scenes* cannot be interpreted either as cowardly abandonment of her radical historical revision or as an act of capitulation to white readers, but as an element of that "immodesty of the modiste," and as Foster explains, as the basic element of "subversive ennobling" of the narrative voice ("Romance" 119). What must be taken into consideration, however, is the opening of Chapter Fourteen and the scene in which Keckley is visited and encouraged to go to her Southern family by Mrs. Longstreet, formerly Bettie Garland. The fact that James Longstreet's wife triggers Keckley's journey into the South, both physically and emotionally, is most crucial to understanding the aims of this "colored historian." Kenneth Stampp describes Lieutenant General James A. Longstreet of the Confederate Army as a "distinguished scalawag" (160).[35] Longstreet's example, set at the beginning of Keckley's account of her trip South, provides not only the interpretative clue to her apparent surrender to Southern mores, but also the rereading of the Northerners' good will toward the defeated proslavery Confederates and anti-Negro Democrats. Throughout this chapter, Keckley underlines that the past is past, that even the most recalcitrant Confederate can join the Radical Republican political agenda of racial equality.

One year before her actual visit to her Southern "family"—which caused the general shock of her free black Washington friends—on 5 August 1865, Thomas Nast had published a double-page political cartoon in *Harper's Weekly* (488–89). On the left-hand illustration, and under the caption "Pardon," Columbia asks: "Shall I trust these men...?" The question continues in the frame on the right under the legend "Franchise": "and not this man?" The cartoon on the left shows Confederate politicians and generals applying for pardons (among these kneels General Robert E. Lee in the foreground), which may allow them the right to vote and hold office. These outstanding Southern men are contrasted with a black Union soldier who has been maimed in the war and has still not been granted the right of suffrage. Written at a time when the Congress had deprived Confederate leaders of the right to hold office but had not yet guaranteed the right to vote to freed blacks, Keckley's chapter on her "old friends" is resonant with conciliatory echoes. Once more, Keckley emerges from the mass of African Americans and even progressive white Washingtonians, and displaces the white Columbia by becoming a black female Christ who, influenced by her nostalgic childhood memories, forgives past physical injuries and spiritual humiliations.

As a matter of fact, her conciliatory attitude is underlined (*i.e.*, punctated) from the beginning of *Behind the Scenes* when she recalls her relationship with Jefferson Davis and dismisses him from her textual space with the following words: "The years have brought many changes; and in view of these terrible changes even I, who was once a slave, who have been punished with the cruel lash, who have experienced the heart and soul tortures of a slave's life, can say to Mr. Jefferson Davis, 'Peace! you have suffered! Go in peace'" (49).[36] Keckley's words reverberate with these biblical tones. In a most arrogant rhetorical gesture, she appropriates Christ's exact words to exhibit her superior moral stature to the Confederate leader and legitimize her petition of full citizenship and franchise. In a way similar to Lincoln's reconciliation policies after the Federal victory as described in the book, Keckley assumes here a patronizing attitude that diminishes slavery, "a choice perceived as necessary if former slaves were to participate in the American Dream" (Domina 147).

Related to this idyllic rendering of the relationship between the ex-slave and her former masters are Keckley's omissions regarding her association with members of the black community.[37] Just as African Americans exhibited differences in their religious affiliations, so did they along class, cultural, historical, and regional lines. As mentioned earlier, Keckley organized a branch of the First Black Contraband Relief Organization. As a woman activist deeply engaged in the racial cause both during the prewar and postwar years, Keckley is concerned with highlighting her relationship with contemporary well-known male black leaders, such as Frederick Douglass, Henry Highland Garnet, and Daniel Payne. She also mentions her bonds with the elitist Fifteenth Street Presbyterian Church and her stay at the Walker Lewises. Nothing is mentioned, however, of other black women engaged in antislavery or racial uplift causes. Indeed, Nell Irvin Painter writes that "Keckley's autobiography said much about the Lincolns but nothing about Sojourner Truth" (204).[38]

Painter also discusses Frederick Douglass's impressions of President Lincoln: "Twelve years after Truth went to see the President, Douglass said that 'in his interests, in his associations, in his habits of thought, and in his prejudices, [Abraham Lincoln] was a white man.... But Douglass sometimes presented Lincoln as innocent of racial prejudice" (207). Painter remarks that African Americans had grounded reasons for drawing such a benign picture of Lincoln at the time: "One was a reason of state: Whatever Lincoln's personal limitations, his politics were the best to be had. The other was more personal: When Lincoln patronized them, he violated Truth and Douglass's self-presentation as people commanding respect. The narrowness of Lincoln's spirit threatened to diminish their stature as well" (207).[39] Painter's representations also illuminate Keckley's textual construction of Lincoln and her constant signifying on American historical figures and scenes in *Behind the Scenes*.[40] Keckley discards the examples that link her to the black world since the book's ideal white readership would not be interested in these more intimate aspects of her experience. She instead culls her narrative from sources that would have greater resonance with this postwar Northern white audience; her vindication is thus textually rendered both by statements and by omissions.

Keckley's control of information is amply displayed not so much in what she shows but what she deliberately keeps "behind the scenes," and her most extraordinary omission is her own first published biographical testimony.

It is Lizzie who fashioned those splendid costumes of Mrs. Lincoln, whose artistic elegance have been so highly praised during the past winter. It was she who "dressed" Mrs. Lincoln for "the party," and for every grand occasion. Stately carriages stand before her door, whose haughty owners sit before Lizzie docile as lambs while she tells them what to wear. Lizzie is an artist, and has such a genius for making women look pretty, that not one thinks of disputing her decrees. Thus she forgets her sorrow, interesting herself to serve each one who comes, as if to dress her was the chief business of her existence.

But to the woman who stretched out her hand to her as a sister, she broke into passionate tears, saying: "I am alone in the world. I have nothing to live for any longer. I try to interest myself in these things, but cannot." Lizzie has her rooms in a neatly furnished, handsome brick house owned by a colored man, who first bought his own freedom, then that of his wife and children. This house and several others in the city, which bring him in handsome rents, are the result of his own industry and economy. A woman of thought and refinement, a woman of deep affection and high aspiration, she stands alone in her womanhood, alone in the universe.

According to Jennifer Fleischner (*Mrs. Lincoln* 236–37, 244–45), white journalist Mary Clemmer Ames ("Life in Washington. Stories of the Late Slaves," 18 April 1862, New York *Evening Post*) "signaled [Keckley's] crossing a threshold into visibility few women of her background managed in their lifetime" (*Mrs. Lincoln* 244). Yet if this had indeed been so, why in *Behind the Scenes* did Keckley not include a single reference to what Fleischner reads as a notorious tribute?

Contrary to Keckley's political project, Ames's article mimics the dynamics of a dictated slave narrative. Keckley's political agenda in 1868 was radically at odds with Ames's intentions in 1862. Keckley was most concerned in bridging the gap between the North and the South, and in contributing to the national ideal of a united people. Ames, however, writing in 1862, prior to the Emancipation Proclamation and as a supporter of the Republicans, aimed at exacerbating sectional divisions and at drawing the sympathy of Northerners toward the iniquity of the Confederate cause. To this effect, the journalist diminishes the potential of "Elizabeth Keckley" and brings her into "visibility" transformed into "Lizzie," a tragic mulatta. Ames's "Lizzie" metamorphoses from a "ruined young maid" to a battered Cinderella, and from this to a sacrificial mother. Her portrait emphasizes

Figure 4: Thomas Nast, "The Emancipation of the Negroes, January 1863—The Past and the Future," wood engraving. Harper's Weekly 7 (24 Jan. 1863): 56–57.

the black woman's sexual vulnerability, passivity, and abandonment.[41] Keckley's self-reliant image in *Behind the Scenes* is submerged here in the heart-rending depiction of a bereaved black mother who pathetically cries out her pain to the world and "stands alone in the universe" (Ames, "Life" 1).

What emerges in the Ames article is a portrait that less describes Keckley's talents and successes than it reinforces the lifelong effects of having been a slave. For good measure, Ames also sandwiches Keckley's portrait between the descriptions of some more pitiable slaves.[42] Keckley, who shows herself as separated from the mass of ex-slaves in Washington and draws fine distinctions of class and refinement throughout *Behind the Scenes*, must have been profoundly disturbed by Ames's text. This journalist's article and her ostensibly sympathetic portrayal of "Lizzie" as a "late slave in Washington" is compromised by competing claims that bear their own overt logic and testify to Ames's and her era's ambivalence about both blacks and women.

There is a further reason for Keckley's not mentioning this white journalist's "eulogy." Mary Todd Lincoln was neither a celebrated figure at the time Keckley published her book, nor at the moment of the president's death. From the very

Figure 5: Thomas Nast, "This Is a White Man's Government," wood engraving. Harper's Weekly 12 (5 Sept. 1868): 568.

beginning of her removal to Washington, Mrs. Lincoln had acquired a reputation for being snobbish, indecent, and a perversion of the true woman. Ames was partly responsible for this reputation, having written disparagingly about the First Lady and would crown her as the White House villain in her *Ten Years in Washington: Life and Scenes in the National Capital, as a Woman Sees Them* (1873).[43] Ames defended women as moral and intellectual forces in politics, but at the same time urged them to exercise their power as true angels of the house. Ineluctably, Mrs. Lincoln and her involvement in public life were thus excoriated:

> But just as if there were no national peril, no monstrous national debt, no rivers of blood flowing, she seemed chiefly intent upon pleasure, personal flattery and adulation; upon extravagant dress and ceaseless self gratification.
>
> Vain, seeking admiration, the men who fed her weakness for their own political ends were sure of her favor. Thus, while daily disgracing the State by her own example, she still sought to meddle in its affairs. Woe to Mr. Lincoln if he did not appoint her favorites. (Ames, *Ten Years* 238)[44]

Ames's opinion of Mrs. Lincoln made it impossible for Keckley to elevate herself and the journalist responsible for her elevation without downgrading the same subject she was purportedly redeeming from guilt in *Behind the Scenes*. Keckley's reference to Ames and to the type of *punctum* "A Stylish Black Woman" had offered her would have seriously compromised her goal to present herself as a self-reliant American citizen and as Mary Lincoln's confidante.

Unfortunately, for all of Keckley's efforts to rewrite the representation of American history, her text did not achieve the impact she expected, and a coarse parody was published soon thereafter. Her use of the documentary mode partly explains the reasons for the hostile reception of the book. Keckley was unaware of what John Tagg calls "the crucial relation of meaning to questions of practice and power." If her text sought to represent a reality that was different from the text itself, then this representation could only have been possible through "an act of negation." Nonetheless, the documentary mode "cannot achieve this because it is already implicated in the historically developed techniques of observation-domination and because it remains imprisoned within an historical form of the regime of truth and sense. Both these bind it fundamentally to the very order which it seeks to subvert" (Tagg 102). As it alludes to national events in postwar America, *Behind the Scenes* claims a civic function for black Americans as American citizens by overthrowing racist stereotypes and inserting (R)econstructed images into the political scene. Keckley's exuberant "mood of optimism" (Andrews, "Reunion" 8) breached the frontiers raised not only by cultural and social racial assumptions, but also, most crucially, by postwar political laws. The text met disapproval and scorn because it was deemed too subversive an effort against these frontiers (Foster, "Historical" xiv).

Behind the Scenes argues that the black written word inscribes a sense of African American identity onto the history told by the white photographical and press archive. Embedded in its pages was not only a black "herstory" of personal success—what Barthes would call Keckley's "biographism" (79)—but a fiercely outspoken rewriting of contemporary American visual and journalistic history, which claimed racial pride as part of American citizenry. Richard Bushman declares that "[o]f all black people, aspiring blacks were the most threatening" (439). As Eric Foner writes of African Americans after the war, Keckley's elaborated conception of herself as an equal citizen of the American republic galvanized her political and social activity during Reconstruction, and her *Behind the Scenes* "challenged the nation to live up to . . . its democratic creed" ("Rights" 863). This African American modiste "learned too late of the social death waiting for a black woman who would forthrightly discard the nonpersonhood of her race and sex" (Zafar 183). Keckley's "alternative iconographies" (Young 111) signified on white political representation of nationhood and identity. Some months after the publication of *Behind the Scenes*, Thomas Nast offered the above cartoon in the 5 September 1868 *Harper's Weekly*, which read: "'This Is a White Man's Government.' We regard the Reconstruction Acts (so called) of Congress as usurpations, and unconstitutional, revolutionary, and void'—Democratic Platform" (568; Fig. 5). Nast's illustration is instrumental in understanding the political climate that reigned in postwar America, a climate that was bound to stifle perilous voices and critical *puncta* such as Keckley's.[45]

"The needle and the sword cannot be manipulated by the same hands" (qtd. in Crowston 1), wrote Jean-Jacques Rousseau in his *Emile* in 1762. An emasculating occupation for men, needlework was a natural and appropriate vocation for women. Yet Elizabeth Keckley stands prominently in a long lineage of African American workers whose labor effectively struck for and defended new identities for blacks in segregated America.

NOTES

1. *Behind the Scenes* is far from being merely a book about Mary Todd Lincoln's clothing scandal. Crowston explains that clothing held a particular political importance in Old Regime France. Women's clothing, in particular, had formed the center of a heated debate since eighteenth-century France, with philosophers from Montesquieu to Rousseau criticizing women's extravagant attires (see Karen Halttunen, *Confidence Men and Painted Women: A Study of Middle-Class Culture in America, 1830–1870* [New Haven: Yale University Press, 1982], 56–91). Similarly, given the democratic nature of American republican ideology, in which the president literally embodied the people, his appearance and that of his wife held enormous political symbolism as visual displays of the vitality and glory of the nation. Taking into account Crowston's research into French vestimentary culture, Mary T. Lincoln's "Old Clothes Scandal" was not new. In fact, Crowston describes how recent historical studies have shown that the delegitimization of the Old Regime in the 1770s and 1780s took place at least in part through an attack on female courtiers, and specifically through open criticism on the queen's supposedly extravagant lifestyle (30). Thus, political criticisms and social attacks on Mary T. Lincoln's clothing expenses reproduced accusations that had been leveled at upper-class women for decades. At the same time, however, these criticisms against Mrs. Lincoln also served to condemn her husband's politics during the confrontations between Whigs and Radical Republicans in the early postwar period.

2. In this respect, Domina prefers to consider Keckley's text an "autobiography," since her "relation to the public world establishes her primary textual identity as American and her community as Americans" (141).

3. Sterling sums up the situation of blacks by the 1860s, when Keckley's reputation became widespread (215–16).

4. Keckley uses the word "modiste" to describe herself in Chapter Four ("Learning that Mrs. Davis wanted a modiste, I presented myself, and was employed by her on the recommendation of one of my patrons and her intimate friend, Mrs. Captain Hetsill" [43–44]); Chapter Five ("I became the regular modiste of Mrs. Lincoln. I made fifteen or sixteen dresses for her during the spring and early part of the summer, when she left Washington" [65]); and Chapter Six ("As soon as it was known that I was the modiste of Mrs. Lincoln, parties crowded around and affected friendship for me" [67]). For Andrew Johnson's daughter, she is just a "dressmaker" (Chapter Twelve), and at the end of her narrative in Chapter Fifteen, she is compelled "to take in sewing to pay for my daily bread" (233).

5. Walker explains that business participation of the slave entrepreneurs was viewed "not only as a means of escape from the degrading poverty of their lives, but a basis for improving the socio-economic status of the race as well" (370). In the same vein, Andrews declares that Keckley's discourse can be seen "to have invited her readers, particularly those who were black and female, to buy into an economy of selfhood consistent with the interests of the newly emerging capitalist order in the postwar North" ("Changing" 237).

6. Vidal recreates Mary Lincoln's first meeting with Keckley in a surprising way, since he seems to capture Keckley's political commitment to her race. After the "well-dressed mulatto woman" introduces herself to the First Lady and is asked several questions about her prices, Mrs. Lincoln inquires directly about her reasons for not having accompanied Mrs. Jefferson Davis on her trip home to the South. "I am colored," responds Keckley. "But free," retorts Mrs. Lincoln. "Even so, I could never live in a slave state. I am an abolitionist. In fact, I must warn you, Mrs. Lincoln, I am very political," Keckley answers (Vidal 90). Vidal devotes three pages of his novel to this first encounter between the two women and seems to have summed up the essence of Keckley's narrative.

7. Foner writes that "in 1867, politics emerged as the principal focus of black aspirations" and African Americans "probably considered themselves more fully American then than at any time in the nineteenth century" ("Rights" 874, 876).

8. Zafar also highlights this point when commenting that *Behind the Scenes* "appeared during the Reconstruction period, at a time when optimism for the cause of civil rights could still be justified, if less optimistically than in 1865" (157).

9. Unlike Sorisio, I do not think one of Keckley's "primary goals was to defend herself and Mary Todd Lincoln from public ridicule." Nor do I believe that "we have little reason to doubt her affection for Lincoln or overt motivation for writing her book" (19). As an African American woman in Reconstructionist America, Keckley was acutely aware of the literary possibilities open to her for promoting black uplift. *Behind the Scenes* does in fact ridicule Mary Lincoln, and redeems outstanding

Republican leaders who were being pilloried for helping her. It also shows Keckley's alliance with the Radicals in distancing herself from the daughters of Andrew Johnson, whom the Republicans sought to impeach in 1868.

10. Kaczorowski writes that "[t]he fundamental rights of citizens were now defined as rights pertaining to U.S. citizenship, and, as such, were recognized by the Constitution and laws of the United States" (67). Yet, for a larger number of loyal Northerners, "the question of Negro rights was, from first to last, clearly subordinate to the more fundamental aim of ensuring national hegemony for Northern political, social, and economic institutions" (Fredrickson 165). Thus, the vast majority of Northerners approached Reconstruction with "their basic racial prejudices largely intact. The Negro was appreciated as an amiable being with some good qualities, whose innate submissiveness had served—and might continue to serve—Northern purposes. But he was expected to remain in his 'place'"(174).

11. Similarly, Stampp writes that "[f]or a few years after Lincoln's death, a combination of Northern humanitarians and radical Republicans overturned this conservative plan of Reconstruction and came near imposing upon the South a far-reaching social revolution, particularly in the relations of the two races"(49). "The radicals of the Reconstruction era were either the reformers of the prewar years or men who had been strongly influenced by their moral imperatives. In fact, radical Reconstruction ought to be viewed in part as the last great crusade of the nineteenth-century romantic reformers" (101).

12. In Chapter Fifteen of *Behind the Scenes*, Keckley clarifies that as the First Lady's friend, she had already tried to counteract the accusations made against her at the precise time they were taking place: "So many erroneous reports were circulated, that I made a correct statement to one of the editors of the New York *Evening News*. The article based upon the memoranda furnished by me appeared in the *News* of 12 Oct. 1867" (221). In addition, she reproduces "a portion of it in this connection" in her book. The extract she presents to the reader of *Behind the Scenes* is long enough to see how she had interpreted the affair and the strategies she had used to redeem Mrs. Lincoln's damaged reputation. Keckley's words of friendly defense are indeed a supreme exercise in both self-aggrandizement and commendation for the black community. She is not so much concerned with revealing Mrs. Lincoln's allegedly innocent goodwill as she is with stressing the crucial roles that she and some important African American figures had played in helping Lincoln's widow and with legitimizing them as true American patriots.

13. Harriet Jacobs had already commented sarcastically on her Aunt Nancy's funeral—the "tribute of respect to the humble dead as a beautiful feature in the 'patriarchal institution'"—and had emphasized that "We could have told them a different story" (146–47).

14. According to Trachtenberg, "the presence of black laborers in the pictures is incidental." The stereotype of the black servant "would survive the war and provide

a new rallying cry for union of North and South.... It appears scattered among the Civil War photographs at large. So do clusters of black refugees on the edge of Union Army camps, 'contraband' (as former slaves freed by Union forces were known) gathered at depots, and portraits of black Union soldiers" (*Reading* 110). This relationship of what Trachtenberg calls "invisible presences" and "visible absences" ("Albums of War" 3) has as a consequence that "the visibility of the war" depended upon "the invisibility of exactly the uncanny relation" represented in these images (29).

15. In Barthes's analysis, the specificity of time and place that the first photographers searched for could only be attained if this specificity inspired an answer from the spectator. This particular answer is the *punctum*, which contrasts with the *studium*, accessible to all spectators. He offers two versions of the *punctum*: the irrational preference for a detail in the photograph and in the term's meaning of wound, the powerful and unexpected feeling provoked by something in the photograph. The spectator—for whom the *punctum* establishes the way memory connects with the paths of the subconscious—is what brings these meanings into the photograph. It is something that the watcher projects onto the image; it is independent from the photographer's intention and exists completely on the connotative level.

16. Modern editions of the text include more pictures of her such as the photograph taken in New York City in the 1860s (Foster, "Romance" 113) and the daguerreotype by Nicholas H. Sheperd (Rutberg 71).

17. On the topic of poses, Tagg writes that "the change from a profile representation to a full-face involved more than expediency and taste. It summoned up a complex historical iconography and elaborate codes of pose and posture readily understood within the societies in which such portrait images had currency. The head-on stare, so characteristic of simple portrait photography, was a pose which would have been read in contrast to the cultivated asymmetries of aristocratic posture.... Rigid frontality signified the bluntness and 'naturalness' of a culturally unsophisticated class and had a history which predated photography" (35–36).

18. "Like his predecessors among painters at royal courts, Brady sought and gained prestige, a reflected glory, from the eminence of his clients, adopting the practice of European aristocratic art to a new medium and a republican society. With the public portrait, Mathew Brady defined the first significant public role for American photographs" (Trachtenberg, *Reading* 34). Brady had photographed a diversity of people (abolitionists, scholars, soldiers, politicians, priests, merchants, authors, actors, etc.) and his place "corresponded to an idea of American society shared by the established and the rising classes. And the work of the place, the making of portraits, was to embody that idea in visual form, to launch images into the world as tokens of an ideology so secure as to seem natural: the ideology of American success" (38).

19. "The artist conjures up a ludicrous vision of the supposed consequences of racial equality in America in this attack on the Republican espousal of equal rights. The scene takes place in a park-like setting with a fountain in the shape of a boy on a dolphin and a large bridge in the background. A black woman (left), 'Miss Dinah,

Arabella, Aramintha Squash,' is presented by abolitionist senator Charles Sumner to President Lincoln. Lincoln bows and says, 'I shall be proud to number among my intimate friends any member of the Squash family, especially the little Squashes.' The woman responds, 'Ise 'quainted wid Missus Linkum I is, washed for her 'fore de hebenly Miscegenation times was cum. Dont do nuffin now but gallevant 'round wid de white gemmen!...' A second mixed couple sit at a small table (center) eating ice cream. The black woman says, 'Ah! Horace its-its-its bully 'specially de cream.' Her companion, Republican editor Horace Greeley, answers, 'Ah! my dear Miss Snowball we have at last reached our political and social Paradise. Isn't it extatic?' To the right a white woman embraces a black dandy, saying, 'Oh! You dear creature. I am so agitated! Go and ask Pa.' He replies, 'Lubly Julia Anna, name de day, when Brodder Beecher [abolitionist clergyman Henry Ward Beecher] shall make us one!' At the far right a second white woman sits on the lap of a plump black man reminding him, 'Adolphus, now you'll be sure to come to my lecture tomorrow night, wont you?' He assures her, 'Ill be there Honey, on de front seat, sure!' A German onlooker (far right) remarks, 'Mine Got. vat a guntry, vat a beebles!' A well-dressed man with a monocle exclaims, 'Most hextwadinary! Aw neva witnessed the like in all me life, if I did dem me!' An Irishwoman pulls a carriage holding a black baby and complains, 'And is it to drag naggur babies that I left old Ireland? Bad luck to me.' In the center a Negro family rides in a carriage driven by a white man with two white footmen. The father lifts his hat and says, 'Phillis de-ah dars Sumner. We must not cut him if he is walking.' Their driver comments, 'Gla-a-ang there 240s! White driver, white footmen, niggers inside, my heys! I wanted a sitiwation when I took this one.' The term 'miscegenation' was coined during the 1864 presidential campaign to discredit the Republicans, who were charged with fostering the intermingling of the races. In the lower margin are prices and instructions for ordering various numbers of copies of the print. A single copy cost twenty-five cents 'post paid'" ("Cartoon Corner" n. pag.).

20. According to Stampp, "[i]t would appear, then, that Lincoln approached the problem of reconstruction with three assumptions regarding the American Negro: (1) emancipation from slavery must be gradual; (2) colonization was the ideal solution to the race problem; and (3) colonization failing, the free Negro would have to accept an inferior status in American society" (35). "Had Lincoln lived to the end of his second administration," Stampp believes, "he would have been forced to accept the presence of the Negro in his country as a permanent fact" (48). Lincoln's attitude toward African Americans, then, was hardly encouraging and far from idealistic. In fact, this historian concludes with the opinion that "in some respects the radical leaders, rather than Lincoln, proved to be the sentimental idealists and the inept politicians; while Lincoln, rather than the radicals, was not only the hardheaded realist but the most skillful politicians of them all" (49).

21. Some of the best-known works published before *Behind the Scenes* were Josiah G. Holland's *Life of Abraham Lincoln* (Springfield, MA: Gurdon Bill, 1866) and Isaac Arnold's *History of Abraham Lincoln and the Overthrow of Slavery* (Chicago: Clarke,

1866). According to Barry Schwartz, both depicted Lincoln as semi-godlike. For a study of the crystallization of Lincoln's image as an icon for racial justice, see Barry Schwartz, "Collective Memory and History: How Abraham Lincoln Became a Symbol of Racial Equality," *Sociological Quarterly* 38.3 (Summer 1997): 469–96.

22. Fleischner reads this scene from a different point of view. She explains that Keckley's silence concerning her son's loss within the context of Mrs. Lincoln's mourning of her own son, "entails a form of internalized aggression, a redirecting of anger away from the more powerful external objects of white authority and back against the self" (Fleischner, *Mastering Slavery* 114).

23. According to historians, during the first year of the war Lincoln refused to interfere with slavery, and gave no sign that he would make its abolition a condition of reconstruction (Stampp 43). On two occasions, he countermanded the orders of military officers who proposed to free the slaves of Confederate sympathizers in their districts; he failed to enforce the emancipation clause of the Confiscation Act; and he refused to accept Negro volunteers in the Union Army for months after Congress authorized him to do so. In fact, on 19 August 1862, New York *Tribune* editor Horace Greeley, the staunch abolitionist who is revered throughout *Behind the Scenes*, published a public letter to Lincoln titled "The Prayer of Twenty Millions," which gained national notoriety. In it, he complained bitterly about the policy the president was pursuing in regard to the slaves and about his failure to execute the Second Confiscation Act of 17 July 1862, which freed all Southern slaves coming under Union military jurisdiction. On 22 August Lincoln responded to Greeley, also in a public letter, which was published in the 6 September issue of *Harper's Weekly*. In it, he asserted that his main objective was to save the Union. "If I could save the Union without freeing any slave I would do it, and if I could save the Union by freeing all the slaves I would do it" (Lincoln 563).

24. Lincoln and other moderate or conservative Republicans had welcomed the idea of eliminating the black problem through colonization or emigration, but efforts to establish black colonies in Chiriquí (Panama) and Haiti were utter failures. Fredrickson explains: "One aspect of the administration's program of racial containment was the recruitment and use of black troops in the South. But there was an even more pressing reason to enlist ex-slaves as soldiers: The military manpower shortage, acute by 1863, was only partially relieved by a conscription policy that was controversial and difficult to implement." The effect of the decision to enlist blacks in the Union Army "was to mitigate Northern racial prejudice and to dispel rather dramatically any lingering sentiment in favor of government-sponsored colonization" (Fredrickson 167).

25. Domina reads Keckley's comments on Tad Lincoln's reading difficulties in a way similar to my interpretation of these scenes. She asserts that "if a colored boy appears dull, his dullness embraces Keckley, who has struggled throughout the text to establish her own individuality, her own ability to enflesh the great American characteristic of self-reliance" (144).

26. Their first conversation—"one that has been given enormous importance in the history of black Americans" (McFeely 229)—is documented by Douglass himself in his *Life and Times of Frederick Douglass* (1881):"I shall never forget my first interview with this great man" (347). He was received cordially and began the conversation by telling Lincoln the object of his visit: He "was assisting to raise colored troops" (348). Douglass left and felt "so well satisfied with the man and with the educating tendency of the conflict, I determined to go on with the recruiting" (349). On the second occasion, the following year, Lincoln asked him "to consult with other black leaders and tell them that something should be speedily done to inform the slaves in the Rebel States of the state of affairs in relation to them, and to warn them as to what will be their probable condition should peace be concluded while they remain within the Rebel lines; And more especially to urge upon them the necessity of making their escape" (qtd. in McFeely 233).

27. After describing his problems in being admitted into the White House and concluding that the officers were simply "complying with an old custom, the outgrowth of slavery" (366), Douglass relates the following: "*Recognising* me, even before I reached him, he exclaimed, so that all around could hear him, 'Here comes my friend Douglass.' Taking me by the hand, he said, 'I am glad to see you. I saw you in the crowd to-day, listening to my inaugural address; how did you like it?' I said, 'Mr. Lincoln, I must not detain you with my poor opinion, when there are thousands waiting to shake hands with you.' 'No, no,' he said, 'you must stop a little, Douglass; there is no man in the country whose opinion I value more than yours. I want to know what you think of it?' I replied, 'Mr. Lincoln, that was a sacred effort.' 'I am glad you liked it!' he said, and I passed on, feeling that any man, however distinguished, might well regard himself honoured by such expressions, from such a man" (366; emphasis added).

28. Barthelemy explains the reasons behind Nancy Prince's apparent slip in her *A Narrative of the Life and Travels of Mrs. Nancy Prince* (1853), when she fails to mention her central role in expelling a slaveholder who was hunting fugitive slaves in 1847 from the black Boston neighborhood of Smith Court. These silences, similar to the ones Keckley practices in *Behind the Scenes*, should not disappoint modern readers or make them feel that these women were "ashamed" of their behaviors. Instead, these omissions should lead them to think how Prince and Keckley "had to weigh the effect" of their stories "on the marketplace" (Barthelemy xxviii).

29. Two entries in Frances Anne Rollin's diary help us to understand this feeling. In the first one (1 January 1868), she comments on her visit to an antislavery fair at the Horticultural Hall in Boston, where a painting titled "John Brown" was exhibited at Child's Gallery. Rollin's *punctum* when writing on her contemplation of the picture cannot be more significant: "I do not like the painter's license. He is blessing instead of kissing the Negro child" (qtd. in Sterling 455). As Sterling explains, the story that the "antislavery martyr" had kissed a black child while on his way to the gallows had been invented by a New York *Tribune* reporter and had become history

when John Greenleaf Whittier had incorporated it into his poem, "Brown of Osawatomie," some of the lines of which Rollin noted down in her entry. In the second entry, dated 22 February 1868—around the same time Keckley was finishing off *Behind the Scenes*—Rollin tells about the importance of her own writing and the ways she feels excluded from what she calls "the body Politic" (qtd. in Sterling 456).

30. For a discussion of the importance of Nast's political cartoons and pictures throughout the Civil War and during Grant's presidential election, see Wendy W. Reaves, "Thomas Nast and the President," *American Art Journal* 19.1 (Winter 1987): 60–71. Pyne and Sesso believe that one "useful source for reviewing popular stereotypes of African Americans during Reconstruction is to analyze the cartoons of Thomas Nast," since this study provides "an excellent means of analyzing changing Northern opinions about Reconstruction, as well as changing perceptions of African Americans' fitness for voting and engaging in political activities" (483).

31. Young describes the first moments after the assassination, in which blacks were not permitted to see Lincoln's body and how this prohibition changed in response to the protests of Frances E.W. Harper. This fact confirms Keckley as an African American with privileged access to the political space of the White House and American history.

32. Contrary to my analysis, Santamarina interprets the fusion of gendered labor and sentiment in Keckley's status as sole witness to Mary Lincoln's grief after the president's assassination. Santamarina argues that Keckley recasts her relationship to the First Lady "as a form of recognized participation in political affect" and foregrounds "her privilege in the structure of fictive kinship that the whole nation bears in relation to the country's First Family" (528).

33. According to Silber, "Davis certainly never wore a petticoat or a hoopskirt, yet these were the frequently mentioned adornments to the Confederate disguise" (625). These garments were mentioned because "[s]uch decorations, obviously more feminine than a simple shawl or cloak, allowed artists and songwriters to thoroughly delineate Davis's unmanly demeanor and get a good laugh out of it as well" (626). Davis's capture appeared in songs, poetic accounts and magazines, and was recreated theatrically in private farms and museums throughout the North. Countless cartoons and prints were published in journals such as *Harper's Weekly* and *Frank Leslie's News,* and even sold as single prints, and were welcome by a broad audience in the North. For Silber, these exhibitions represented "the symbolic display of Northerners' view of Southern gender confusion at the close of the war" (626).

34. Keckley's date in *Behind the Scenes* for her visit to the fair (winter 1865) does not match with the statement published in the Chicago *Evening Journal,* 7 June 1865 (51). She certifies that she visited Trophy Hall, where the figure of Jefferson Davis was on exhibition, on 6 June. This date coincides, however, with Silber's explanation that "The United States Sanitary Commission presented a wax figure of Davis dressed in the clothes of an old woman at their June fund-raising fair in Chicago" (626).

35. Moreover, Longstreet's case illustrates "the inadequacy of any simple gener-

alization about the character or origin of this class of radicals. . . . Longstreet . . . [was] a graduate of West Point and one of Lee's ablest corps commanders. After the war Longstreet moved to New Orleans and became a partner in a cotton factorage business and head of an insurance firm. In 1867, arguing that the vanquished must accept the terms of the victors, he joined the Republican party and endorsed radical reconstruction. In 1868, he supported Grant for president, and in subsequent years Republican administrations gave him a variety of offices in the federal civil service" (Stampp 160). According to Foner, his case "inspired some Confederate veterans to follow in his footsteps" (*Reconstruction* 297). Yet it seems the Southern democrats never forgave his betrayal and took their symbolic vengeance on him after his death in 1903. In fact, the United Daughters of the Confederacy voted not to send flowers to his funeral, and unlike other Confederate military officials, no statues of Longstreet were erected as memorials (Connelly and Bellows 34–37).

36. In the New Testament, Jesus pronounces this farewell on two occasions: Mark 5:34 and Luke 7:48–50. In Luke, Jesus comes into Simon's house and a woman recognises the Lord and washes his feet with her tears and anoints his head with oil. He then says: "Your sins are forgiven" (7:48) and bids her farewell with the words: "Go in peace" (7:50).

37. Richardson explains how Maria W. Stewart indulges in what she calls "caste consciousness" and how she textually "establish[es] her status as a free black who, however humble her origins, was at a remove from the more than 40,000 newly freed contrabands who poured into Washington in the latter days of the war" (131).

38. Painter writes the following about the meeting: "In Washington, Truth discovered that the 'Libyan Sibyl' was not sufficiently prominent to enter the White House. Someone with influence had to open the way even for her to wait outside Lincoln's office. That someone was Elizabeth Keckley. . . . Keckley encountered everyone in Washington working in freedpeople's relief. Unlike Truth, Keckley and other middle-class black Washingtonians did not work closely with the various freedpeople's aid associations chartered by white abolitionists. Middle-class black people and middle-class white people could not work together, even toward the same end. They did, however, make each other's acquaintance enough for Truth's friend Lucy Colman to secure Keckley's aid in taking Truth to meet the President" (203–04). Truth visited the President with the white abolitionist Colman at 8 am on Saturday, 29 October 1864, and she felt delighted with the man. Yet Colman's rendition of the visit is "closer to prevailing attitudes and scholarly appraisals of Lincoln's racial consciousness," affirms Painter (206). "'Being loved as the Great Emancipator irritated Lincoln.' Colman realized: 'He believed in the white race, not in the colored, and did not want them put on an equality'" (207).

39. According to Painter, Truth was "a celebrity in Washington among the antislavery social workers and their constituents. She held several meetings, including two well-attended benefits for the Colored Soldiers' Aid Society in the Reverend Henry Highland Garnet's Presbyterian Church. There she doubtless encountered

Washington's black bourgeoisie and philanthropists, such as Elizabeth Keckley and Harriet Jacobs.... No record remains of Truth's interactions with Washington's black bourgeoisie." The explanation, according to Painter, which lies closer to home is that "[b]y her own lights, Truth may not have valued exchanges with African-American colleagues enough to have them recorded" (212).

40. Keckley's purpose of reconstituting American history as including blackness can be detected even in minor scenes such as the one where Lincoln and Senator Charles Sumner (Massachusetts) discuss the meaning of the term "tote" in Chapter Ten. According to Tagg, "[a] crucial part of the attempt of the emergent bourgeoisie to establish its hegemony in the eighteenth and nineteenth centuries was the creation of several institutions of language.... It was across such institutions that the realist convention was installed and ceased to be visible as convention, becoming natural—identical with reality" (100). Keckley's inclusion of this linguistic discussion reveals, once more, her intention to stress what Genovese calls "[t]he duality of the black experience both within and without the American national experience, and the contribution of different classes and strata of the black community to that duality" (431). This duality that had first appeared in the kind of English spoken on rural slave areas and then it has spread to the urban Southern centers and then to the rest of the nation.

41. In 1859 Ames had moved to New York, where she lived with the sisters and writers Alice and Phoebe Cary, who introduced her to Horace Greeley and other editors. She started her career in journalism and would gain national reputation from 1866 to 1884 for her column in the New York City *Independent*, "A Woman's Letter from Washington." Ames's gift for an irony both gendered and raced is evident here, as throughout the article she lauds Keckley's persistence toward freedom precisely as much as she suggests her condign subservience and isolation:

> It is Lizzie who fashioned those splendid costumes of Mrs. Lincoln, whose artistic elegance have been so highly praised during the past winter. It was she who "dressed" Mrs. Lincoln for "the party," and for every grand occasion. Stately carriages stand before her door, whose haughty owners sit before Lizzie docile as lambs while she tells them what to wear. Lizzie is an artist, and has such a genius for making women look pretty, that not one thinks of disputing her decrees. Thus she forgets her sorrow, interesting herself to serve each one who comes, as if to dress her was the chief business of her existence.
>
> But to the woman who stretched out her hand to her as a sister, she broke into passionate tears, saying: "I am alone in the world. I have nothing to live for any longer. I try to interest myself in these things, but cannot." Lizzie has her rooms in a neatly furnished, handsome brick house owned by a colored man, who first bought his own freedom, then that of his wife and children. This house and several others in the city, which bring him in handsome rents, are the result of his own industry and economy. A woman of thought and refine-

ment, a woman of deep affection and high aspiration, she stands alone in her womanhood, alone in the universe.

42. Preceding the text on Keckley, Ames writes in "A Slave-Girl's Story" about "a cunning little nig; the oddest and the jolliest little Congo" she has ever seen. Bena is described after the fashion of Harriet Beecher Stowe's Topsy in *Uncle Tom's Cabin*, even if the character here stands as a self-sufficient individual who is ironically dwarfed by the burden of slavery. The next sketch, "A Slave 'Boy' and his Family," tells about Albert, a young mulatto, who has a baby he has not seen in eighteen weeks. His wife is a slave and both she and the child are at the mercy of their mistress. The abolition of slavery in the District of Columbia will involve the "injustice" of their self-ownership. Then comes Keckley's sketch, and following that, "A Sorrowful Tale" about George who, desirous of his freedom, pays part of the money to his mistress and is cheated out of his own purchase by a Union officer. Ames thus exposes the immorality of possessing human beings. The next story, "Wealthy Negroes," explains that some of the wealthiest men in Washington are colored and free, and reveals the cruelty of a system that does not let individuals enjoy the fruits of their labor. "Society in Washington" is a piece on the rich of the city and their reunions and closes Ames's report.

43. Rutberg refers twice to Ames's opinions in her *Mary Lincoln's Dressmaker* (1995). Even if she never acknowledges the original sources of her references, the first one (57) belongs to "Life in Washington. Stories of the Late Slaves" and the second (62–63) to *Ten Years in Washington* (237). According to A.C.C., Sandburg's portions of the White House narrative in his *Mary Lincoln: Wife and Widow, Part I* (New York: Harcourt, Brace, 1932) "draw largely upon such reminiscent material as that of Mary Clemmer Ames" (99).

44. For other values of Ames's text, see Claussen, who draws on *Ten Years in Washington* to show that this journalist "was apparently the first feminist voice to address the issue of women in civil service" (233).

45. See McPherson, who from his post-revisionist position on Reconstruction explains: "The Republican commitment to black rights had never been very deep. Only the party's radical wing had supported racial equality with genuine conviction, and by 1874 the convictions of some had been shaken. The revolutionaries achievements of the war and reconstruction—emancipation, civil equality, Negro suffrage, black participation in Southern governments—owed more to anti-Southern than to pro-black motivation. They sprang primarily from the military exigencies of war and the political exigencies of peace, rather than from a considered social purpose" (593).

WORKS CITED

A.C.C. Rev. of *Mary Lincoln: Wife and Widow, Part I*, by Carl Sandburg; *Mary Lincoln: Wife and Widow, Part II: Letters, Documents and Appendix*, by Paul M. Angle; *Mrs.*

Abraham Lincoln: A Study of Her Personality and Her Influence on Lincoln, by W.A. Evans. *Mississippi Valley Historical Review* 21.1 (June 1934): 98–99.

Ames, Mary Clemmer. "Life in Washington: Stories of the Late Slaves." *Evening Post* 18 April 1862: 1.

———. *Ten Years in Washington: Life and Scenes in the National Capital, as a Woman Sees Them.* Hartford: A.D. Worthington, 1873.

Andrews, William L. "The Changing Moral Discourse of Nineteenth-Century African American Women's Autobiography: Harriet Jacobs and Elizabeth Keckley." *De/Colonizing the Subject: The Politics of Gender in Women's Autobiography.* Eds. Sidonie Smith and Julia Watson. Minneapolis: University of Minnesota Press, 1992. 225–41.

———. "Reunion in the Postbellum Slave Narrative: Frederick Douglass and Elizabeth Keckley." *Black American Literature Forum* 23.1 (Spring 1989): 5–16.

Asbury, Herbert. *Gangs de Nueva York.* 1927, 1928. Trad. Carme Font. Barcelona: Edhasa, 2003.

Barthelemy, Anthony G. Introduction. *Collected Black Women's Narratives: N. Prince, L. Picquet, B. Veney, S.K. Taylor.* New York: Oxford University Press, 1988. xxix–xlviii.

Barthes, Roland. *La Cámara Lúcida.* 1980. Trans. Joaquim Sala-Sanahuja. Barcelona: Paidós, 1995.

Berlin, Ira. *Slaves without Masters: The Free Negro in the Antebellum South.* New York: Pantheon Books, 1974.

Bushman, Richard L. *The Refinement of America: Persons, Houses, Cities.* New York: Knopf, 1992.

Claussen, Cathryn L. "Gendered Merit: Women of the Merit Concept in Federal Employment, 1864–1944." *American Journal of Legal History* 40.3 (July 1996): 229–52.

"Cartoon Corner." The Lincoln Institute Presents: Abraham's Lincoln's Classroom. n.d. Web. 20 Jan. 2008.

Connelly, Thomas L., and Barbara L. Bellows. *God and General Longstreet: The Lost Cause and the Southern Mind.* Baton Rouge: Louisiana State University Press, 1982.

Crowston, Clare Haru. *Fabricating Women: The Seamstresses of Old Regime France, 1675–1791.* Durham: Duke University Press, 2001.

Domina, Lynn. "I Was Re-Elected President: Elizabeth Keckley as Quintessential Patriot in *Behind the Scenes: Or, Thirty Years a Slave, and Four Years in the White House.*" *Women's Life-Writing: Finding Voice/Building Community.* Ed. Linda Coleman. Bowling Green: Bowling Green State University Popular Press, 1997. 139–51.

Douglass, Frederick. *The Life and Times of Frederick Douglass, Written by Himself.* 1892. London: Collier Macmillan, 1962.

Fleischner, Jennifer. *Mastering Slavery: Memory, Family, and Identity in Women's Slave Narratives.* New York: New York University Press, 1996.

———. *Mrs. Lincoln and Mrs. Keckly: The Remarkable Story of the Friendship between a First Lady and a Former Slave.* New York: Broadway Books, 2003.
Foley, Barbara. "History, Fiction, and the Ground Between: The Uses of the Documentary Mode in Black Literature." *PMLA* 95.3 (May 1980): 389–403.
Foner, Eric. *Reconstruction: America's Unfinished Revolution, 1863–1877.* New York: Harper Perennial, 1987.
———. "Reconstruction Revisited." *Reviews in American History* 10.4 (December 1982): 82–100.
———. "Rights and the Constitution in Black Life during the Civil War and Reconstruction." *Journal of American History* 74.3 (December 1987): 863–83.
Foster, Frances Smith. "Historical Introduction." Keckley ix–lxvii.
———. "Romance and Scandal in a Postbellum Slave Narrative: Elizabeth Keckley's *Behind the Scenes.*" *Written by Herself: Literary Production by African American Women, 1746–1892.* Bloomington: Indiana University Press, 1993. 117–30.
Foucault, Michel. *Discipline and Punish: The Birth of the Prison.* 1975. London: Allen Lane, 1977.
Fredrickson, George M. *The Black Image in the White Mind: The Debate on Afro-American Character and Destiny, 1817–1914.* New York: Harper & Row, 1971.
Genovese, Eugene D. *Roll, Jordan, Roll: The World the Slaves Made.* New York: Vintage Books, 1976.
Harris, Leslie M. *In the Shadow of Slavery: African Americans in New York City, 1626–1863.* Chicago: University of Chicago Press, 2003.
Horan, James D. *Mathew Brady: Historian with a Camera.* New York: Crown, 1955.
Jacobs, Harriet A. *Incidents in the Life of a Slave Girl: Written by Herself.* 1861. Ed. Jean Fagan Yellin. Cambridge: Harvard University Press, 1987.
Kaczorowski, Robert J. "To Begin the Nation Anew: Congress, Citizenship, and Civil Rights after the Civil War." *American Historical Review* 92.1 (February 1987): 45–68.
Keckley, Elizabeth. *Behind the Scenes: Or, Thirty Years a Slave, and Four Years in the White House.* 1868. Ed. Frances Smith Foster. Urbana: University of Illinois Press, 2001.
Keller, Morton. *The Art and Politics of Thomas Nast.* New York: Oxford University Press, 1968.
Litwack, Leon F. *Been in the Storm So Long: The Aftermath of Slavery.* New York: Random House, 1979.
Lutz, Tom. *El llanto: Historia Cultural de las Lágrimas.* 1999. Trad. Eunice Cortés Gutiérrez. Madrid: Taurus, 2001.
Lively, James K. "Propaganda Techniques of Civil War Cartoonists." *Public Opinion Quarterly* 6.1 (Spring 1942): 99–106.
McPherson, James M. *Ordeal by Fire: The Civil War and Reconstruction.* New York: Knopf, 1982.
McFeely, William S. *Frederick Douglass.* New York: W.W. Norton, 1995.
Painter, Nell Irvin. *Sojourner Truth: A Life, a Symbol.* New York: W.W. Norton, 1996.

Pyne, John, and Gloria Sesso. "A Humanities Approach for Teaching the Reconstruction Era: Encouraging Active Learning in the Classroom." *History Teacher* 31.4 (August 1998): 467–94.

Richardson, Marilyn, ed. Maria W. Stewart, *America's First Black Woman Political Writer: Essays and Speeches*. Bloomington: Indiana University Press, 1987.

Rudisill, Richard. *Mirror Image: The Influence of the Daguerreotype on American Culture*. Albuquerque: University of New Mexico Press, 1971.

Rutberg, Becky. *Mary Lincoln's Dressmaker: Elizabeth Keckley's Remarkable Rise from Slave to White House Confidante*. New York: Walker, 1995.

Santamarina, Xiomara. "Behind the Scenes of Black Labor: Elizabeth Keckley and the Scandal of Publicity." *Feminist Studies* 28.3 (Fall 2002): 514–37.

Silber, Nina. "Intemperate Men, Spiteful Women, and Jefferson Davis: Northern Views of the Defeated South." *American Quarterly* 41.4 (December 1989): 614–35.

Sorisio, Carolyn. "Unmasking the Genteel Performer: Elizabeth Keckley's *Behind the Scenes* and the Politics of Public Wrath." *African American Review* 34.1 (Spring 2000): 19–37.

Stampp, Kenneth M. *The Era of Reconstruction, 1865–1877*. New York: Vintage Books, 1967.

Sterling, Dorothy, ed. *We Are Your Sisters: Black Women in the Nineteenth Century*. New York: W.W. Norton, 1984.

Tagg, John. *The Burden of Representation: Essays on Photographies and Histories*. Minneapolis: University of Minnesota Press, 1993.

Trachtenberg, Alan. "Albums of War: On Reading Civil War Photographs." *Representations* 9 (Winter 1985): 1–32.

———. *Reading American Photographs: Images as History, Mathew Brady to Walker Evans*. New York: Hill & Wang and Noonday, 1989.

Vidal, Gore. *Lincoln: A Novel*. 1984. New York: Ballantine Books, 1985.

Vinson, J. Chal. "Thomas Nast and the American Political Scene." *American Quarterly* 9.3 (Fall 1957): 337–44.

Walker, Juliet E. K. "Racism, Slavery, and Free Enterprise: Black Entrepreneurship in the United States before the Civil War." *Business History Review* 60.3 (Autumn 1986): 343–82.

Young, Elizabeth. "Black Woman, White House: Race and Redress in Elizabeth Keckley's *Behind the Scenes*." *Disarming the Nation: Women's Writing and the American Civil War*. Chicago: University of Chicago Press, 1999. 109–48.

Zafar, Rafia. "Dressing Up and Dressing Down: Elizabeth Keckley's Behind the Scenes at the White House and Eliza Potter's A Hairdresser's Experience in High Life." *We Wear the Mask: African Americans Write American Literature, 1760–1870*. New York: Columbia University Press, 1997. 151–83.

CHAPTER TWO

CAROLYN SORISIO

Unmasking the Genteel Performer
Elizabeth Keckley's *Behind the Scenes*
and the Politics of Public Wrath

WHEN ELIZABETH KECKLEY WROTE her 1868 autobiography *Behind the Scenes; or, Thirty Years a Slave, and Four Years in the White House,* one of her primary goals was to defend herself and Mary Todd Lincoln from public ridicule. Because Keckley had "been most intimately associated with that lady in the most eventful periods of her life," she tells readers that her "own character, as well as the character of Mrs. Lincoln, is at stake" (xiv). Keckley was particularly concerned about public reaction to the "old clothes scandal," a scandal that erupted when the widowed Lincoln met Keckley in New York City and arranged to sell pieces of her wardrobe in what quickly degenerated into an event reminiscent of a circus sideshow.[1] Keckley thought that by providing more information she could demonstrate Mrs. Lincoln's positive characteristics and pure intentions, and, from what we know about Keckley, we have little reason to doubt her affection for Lincoln or overt motivation for writing her book.[2]

Despite Keckley's sincere intentions, *Behind the Scenes* was met with public ridicule and the media's wrath. *Putnam's Magazine,* for example, called it the "latest, and decidedly weakest production of the sensational press," which "ought never to have been written or published" and could not be read by "any sensible" person "with pleasure or profit" (119). *The New York Times* questioned Keckley's authorship and said she would have been better off to "have stuck to her needle" as "the disclosures made in" her book were "gross violations of confidence" (10).[3] Perhaps nowhere is the wrath against Keckley more evident than in the vicious parody spawned by her text, *Behind the Seams; by a Nigger Woman Who Took in Work from Mrs. Lincoln and Mrs. Davis.*[4] This parody reveals the author's anxiety over an African American woman's rising in class and social status, and is intent on proving that, even if Keckley were no longer a slave, she would always be a "nigger" (a word that appears six times in the first paragraph alone). In Keckley's personal and social circles, the response to *Behind the Scenes* was not much better. Mary Todd Lincoln read the book in early May and "thereafter renounced the 'colored historian' as friend and confidant" (Baker 280). Later in her life, Keckley attempted to talk with Robert Lincoln (who reportedly requested that the book be removed from circulation), but he refused to see her because *Behind the Scenes* reprinted his mother's private letters to Keckley, a decision that was made, apparently, without Keckley's consent (Washington 241).[5] Within the African American community, according to Frances Smith Foster, some believed Keckley "had been victimized but most were angered by their fear that the backlash from her actions would jeopardize their own positions" (129). For a combination of reasons, Foster notes that the book was eventually withdrawn from stores, and Keckley was left to earn her living by sewing and from a small pension she received for her son's death in the Civil War.[6]

As the reviews, parody, and community's reaction reveal, the attacks on Keckley were so severe that her life was never the same after she published *Behind the Scenes*. Why, we might ask, was the public so outraged by Keckley's decision to write about Mrs. Lincoln? Certainly, the censure was not the result of the public's excessive love for Abraham Lincoln's grieving widow. By the time the book was published, Mary Todd Lincoln was considered by many to be extravagant and improper in her dress, manners, and actions.[7] Nor can we argue that Keckley's public discussion of Lincoln was unprecedented. As Keckley notes in her preface, Lincoln had already "forced herself into notoriety" by stepping "beyond the formal lines which hedge about a private life, and invited public criticism" (xiii). She comments:

> I do not forget, before the public journals vilified Mrs. Lincoln, that ladies who moved in the Washington circle in which she moved, freely canvassed her [Lincoln's] character among themselves. They gloated over many a tale of scandal that grew out of gossip in their own circle. If these ladies could say everything bad of the wife of the President, why should I not be permitted to lay her secret history bare, especially when that history plainly shows that her life, like all lives, has its good side as well as its bad side? (xv)

In this and other passages, Keckley represents herself as joining (relatively late) an already public conversation about Mary Todd Lincoln, one that began in the social circles of the capital and continued in the media. She insists that, had "Mrs. Lincoln's acts never become public property," she "should not have published to the world the secret chapters of her life" (xv).

Even if Keckley (rightfully) argues that she did not initiate public debate, her prefatory justifications indicate that she understood she might be accused of indecorum in writing about Mary Todd Lincoln. Nonetheless, she could not have been prepared for the extent of the furor her book aroused, and, indeed, she told people late in her life that the public's reaction caused her much sorrow (Washington 221). Why, we might ask again, did her book cause so much outrage? Although reasons for the anger Keckley faced are many, this essay argues that one significant basis for the wrath was the means by which Keckley's memoir jeopardizes the increasingly delicate self-construction of the white American middle class, what Karen Halttunen calls their "genteel performance." When the *New York Citizen* declared that Keckley's offense was "of the same grade as opening other people's letters" and "listening at keyholes" (qtd. in Foster 128), it revealed what Halttunen describes as a deep-rooted fear of many middle-class Americans that any "vulgar boor" could suddenly "rip the fragile mask of the manner from the genteel performer and expose the would-be social climber in all his or her own underlying vulgarity" (116). The fact that Keckley was an African American woman writing about Lincoln intensified this fear, because the middle class's self-fashioning relied on an implicit juxtaposition of white and black womanhood. Keckley's text, intentionally or not, splinters the fragile veneer of middle-class culture in mid-nineteenth-century America, revealing and challenging the racial, gendered, and class ideologies that were inextricably tied to the middle class's increasingly precarious social status.

While the primary intent of this article is to explore Keckley's challenge to the white middle class's self-fashioning, a related goal is to examine the book's unique narrative structure. The work intertwines narratives of Keckley's enslavement, her rise to prominence as a businesswoman in Washington, DC, and her extensive and at times exclusive contact with Abraham and Mary Todd Lincoln. Without an understanding of the connections between the slave narrative elements of Keckley's work and the revelations about Mary Todd Lincoln's life, *Behind the Scenes* seems disunified, even to the point of being taken over by Mary Todd Lincoln's story for the majority of the text. However, the seemingly disparate sections of Keckley's narrative reveal a structural logic (one based on juxtaposition) when they are considered in relation to the roles of African American and white women in the postbellum era.

In the decade Keckley wrote and published her book, anxieties about the future status of all Americans were paramount. As the nation began its path toward what many hoped would be a radical reconstruction, Keckley's book carves out a space for herself as an African American woman claiming her right to participate in the public postbellum commodity culture not as property, but as proprietor. To understand better this aspect of the text, the first section of this essay examines Keckley's representations of commodity culture. Although it was essential for Keckley to claim a proprietary role in what she and other former slave narrators assumed would be a new era in American life, it was also important for her to assert her right to privacy and gentility, as these privileges were commonly associated with the domestic space and traditionally denied to African American women. Therefore, the second section of this essay examines Keckley's representations of gentility in relation to conceptions of race and womanhood in the Civil War era, arguing that Keckley's claims to gentility threatened some readers' sense of their own class status, and thus generated the backlash that greeted her book. Yet when we investigate the rules of gentility that Keckley draws upon to fashion herself as genteel, we begin to understand how, by writing her book, she violated those very rules in such a profound way as to destabilize her claim to a genteel self. Why would Keckley, a woman concerned about appearing genteel, ultimately write a book that threatened her own genteel status and outraged a friend she cared about? As my conclusion suggests, we can interpret Keckley's work as exposing the underlying anger, the unconscious or covert wrath, she may have felt for Mary Todd Lincoln in particular or for white ladies in general. If the public's wrath against Keckley is overt, Keckley's wrath against some members of the public may be covert and private. *Behind the Scenes* becomes, then, among other things, a means by which Keckley can go public with her anger.

Keckley and Commodity Culture

Foster argues that postbellum former slave protagonists "could be characterized as the epitome of the American Dream, surpassing Benjamin Franklin's rise from poverty to power by moving from being property to becoming proprietors" (119). Because narrators writing shortly after the war wrote in what William L. Andrews describes as "a mood of optimism" ("Reunion" 8), authors such as Keckley could portray themselves as climbing the social ladder to new financial and personal heights. Therefore, a significant portion of Keckley's narrative is a success story, tracing her rise from a slave to a businesswoman who employed numerous workers and was requested by Washington's elite. On the one hand, Keckley's adherence to the American motif of social and economic mobility would have appealed to readers who may have had similar desires and goals. On the other hand, the fact that Keckley was a former slave woman may have led some readers to question how extensive social and economic mobility should be. Would Keckley's success somehow cheapen their claim to a higher social and/or class status? Such questions were especially pertinent given the anxiety over class and social status that preoccupied many mid-nineteenth-century middle-class Americans. As Halttunen explains, although antebellum Americans "threw themselves into the cult of self-improvement, many nonetheless expressed anxiety about the American pursuit of the main chance" (32).

In part, this anxiety manifested itself racially. The parody of *Behind the Scenes* makes it clear that Keckley's decision to enter into the public sphere of commodity as author and modiste threatened some whites, as it repeatedly attacks Keckley for supposedly lying to make money, and ends by deriding her entrance into commodity culture. Mocking her endeavors as author and modiste, the parody echoes the language common to nineteenth-century advertisement with the words "Publishers and ladies please take notice. Terms moderate," but follows this supposed advertisement with the signature: "Betsey Kickley, (Nigger,)" signed with an "*X*" for her mark (*Behind the Seams* 24). To the parody's author, Keckley's entrance into the commodified sphere of authorship and dressmaking improperly transgressed racial lines. Therefore, s/he undercuts Keckley's newly claimed role by relegating her to the racialized category of "nigger"—a status that, as the inclusion of the "*X*" reminds readers, is (and presumably should be) associated with a level of illiteracy that makes African American participation in the post-war economy in any role but laborer difficult if not impossible.

Despite the fact that many perceived her new role as threatening class and race structures, Keckley embraced capitalism and upward mobility. Early in her work she tells readers she selected "the most important incidents which I believe influenced the moulding of my character" (18). Of these, she mentions almost immediately that she was "repeatedly told, when even fourteen years old, that I would never be worth my salt" (21). This criticism bothers Keckley throughout her life, and, perhaps as a result, she often defines her self-worth through the market value of her labor. For example, when Keckley's financially struggling master threatens to place her mother out for service, Keckley receives permission to work for her mother and her owner's family. By sewing, she manages to feed seventeen people for more than two years. She reflects that, while she "was working so hard that others might live in comparative comfort, and move in those circles of society to which their birth gave them entrance, the thought often occurred to me whether I was really worth my salt or no; and then perhaps the lips curled with a bitter sneer" (45–46). As these comments suggest, commodity culture is not so threatening to Keckley as it may have been to antebellum narrators, because she is no longer capable of being defined by law as property. In Keckley's world view, slavery does not represent the logical extension of an exploitative and masculine marketplace, as it did to authors such as Harriet Beecher Stowe in *Uncle Tom's Cabin* in the antebellum era.[8] Rather, she portrays slavery as a "hardy school" in which she learned "youth's important lesson of self-reliance" (19–20).

    The contrast of Keckley's postbellum position on slavery and commodity with an antebellum work such as Harriet Jacobs's 1861 *Incidents in the Life of a Slave Girl, Written by Herself* demonstrates the extent of Keckley's optimistic embrace of capitalism. Unlike Jacobs, who objects to her friends buying her out of slavery because "to pay money to those who had so grievously oppressed" her "seemed like taking from" her "sufferings the glory of triumph" (Jacobs 199), Keckley enlists the financial help of several white people in order to secure freedom legally for herself and her son. At one point, she plans to make a journey to New York City to appeal for help in securing funds. However, her owner tells her that she has to find six gentlemen who will vouch for her return and be financially responsible if she escapes. Asking one such man for his pledge, Keckley becomes "sick at heart" when he suggests she will go to New York, be influenced by abolitionists, and never return to St. Louis. "Slavery, eternal slavery," Keckley vows, "rather than be regarded with distrust by those whose respect I esteemed" (53). To avoid the financial humiliation she associates with failing to pay the loans raised to buy herself and her son, she works "in earnest, and in a short time paid every cent that was so kindly advanced" by her "lady patrons of St. Louis" (63).

Keckley's concern over her financial status, as Andrews notes, contrasts dramatically with Jacobs's narrative, as Keckley is far more troubled about her economic reputation than her sexual one. At this point in Keckley's narrative, we have been told about her son, who was born out of wedlock and fathered by a white man. Keckley tells readers that she does not "care to dwell upon this subject, for it is one that is fraught with pain. Suffice it to say, that he persecuted me for four years, and I—I became a mother" (39). Unlike Jacobs, who dwells on her sexual choices at some length and asks readers to "pity" and "pardon" her for having children with a white man to escape the persecution of her owner (54), Keckley rejects any guilt or blame, saying that if her son suffered the humiliation of his birth, "he must blame the edicts of that society which deemed it no crime to undermine the virtue of girls in my then position" (39). Keckley not only rejects blame, but also, through her use of "my then" position, suggests that she simply cannot be held to a morality that did not apply during slavery. As Andrews points out, no one, "least of all Keckley herself, is concerned about this slave woman's sexual respectability." Instead, her "financial reputation" is at issue, and "we may be sure that she wanted her *postbellum* audience to know of her unswerving fealty to the ethics of the marketplace" ("Changing" 233).

These passages reveal Keckley's self-presentation as a businesswoman willing to follow the rules governing the marketplace, even if those rules once defined her as chattel or are unjust. Interestingly, it is through the language of the marketplace that Keckley attempts to put the issue of slavery to rest. Speaking from a successful postbellum position, Keckley says with regard to slavery that, "as in all things pertaining to life," she "can afford to be charitable" (xiii). It is as if her role of successful capitalist affords her the luxury of forgiveness. Clearly, Keckley wants to represent slavery as a regrettable national sin, but one which, nonetheless, prepared her to be worth "her salt" in the postbellum economy. By contrast, the white women whom Keckley represents are pitifully ill-prepared for the post-war era. We get an early glimpse of white women's apparent ineptness in the person of Mrs. Burwell, a mistress of Keckley's whom she describes as "helpless" (31) and for whom she has to do the work of "three servants" (32). Throughout the narrative, Keckley is astonished not by white women who are unproductive and/or inept, but by any white woman who is productive or resourceful. This is evident in Keckley's short-lived work in the White House during President Andrew Johnson's administration. When Keckley visits the White House to make a dress for President Johnson's daughter, she notes that the sight of the President's daughter "busily at work with a sewing-machine" was "a novel one," as she could not "recollect ever having seen" Mary Todd Lincoln "with a needle in her hand" (225).

Keckley's subtle comparison of the preparedness that women from different races showed in the postbellum era is particularly noticeable in her representation of reunions with her former owners after the war. Keckley's reunion scenes shape her as an active participant in reconstruction history, and we can understand them as genuine attempts to revisit her past and salvage what was useful from it.[9] However, they also highlight her economic success, and juxtapose this success with the status of her former mistresses. For example, when Keckley's former mistress, Miss Ann, asks her if she always feels "kindly" toward her, Keckley answers that the only thing she holds against her is that she "did not give me the advantages of a good education." Miss Ann agrees, but goes on to comment that Keckley has "not suffered much on this score" since she gets "along in the world better than we who enjoyed every educational advantage in childhood" (257). Although this scene is designed to create a mood of reconciliation, Keckley's former mistress's comments reveal that the education Southern ladies received was virtually worthless in the postbellum economy. Keckley underscores her success when one of her former master's daughters comes to see her and is surprised to find Keckley "so comfortably fixed" (259). Likewise, she ends the chapter that contains these reunions with a letter from one of her former master's daughters, who has been forced to take up teaching and is suffering through a Massachusetts winter. The writer laments that none of the children Keckley worked for were "cut out for 'school marms' . . . I am sure I was only made to ride in my carriage, and play on the piano. Don't you think so?" (265–66). But Keckley does not answer this question explicitly. Rather, she leaves it up to the reader to conclude that her former charge is not so competent as Keckley in thriving in the social order surfacing after the war.

Nowhere is the juxtaposition between former slaves and former "ladies" more evident than in Keckley's representation of Mary Todd Lincoln's financial excesses. It is in this example that we can explore further the text's narrative pattern of juxtaposition. Keckley calls upon readers to consider the logic structuring her narrative early in her work, when in her preface she discusses slavery, saying that, if she has "portrayed the dark side of slavery," she has also "painted the bright side" (xi). Just a few pages later, after Keckley has shifted from a discussion of slavery to a justification for writing about Mary Todd Lincoln, she echoes her earlier language, arguing that "history plainly shows that her [Lincoln's] life, like all lives, has its good side as well as its bad side" (xv). Keckley's use of similar language invites the reader to compare the two subjects of her study—the story of her life in slavery and the story of Mary Todd Lincoln—in order to identify connections. Just as her preface attempts to integrate the different parts of her narrative, so too do individual chapters often reveal a similar pattern of juxtaposition. In effect, we can read some chapters as a synecdoche for the overall structure of the book, as Keckley often intertwines seemingly disparate but actually relevant topics with one another. Such is the case in Chapter Nine, which functions to compare ironically Mary Todd Lincoln with the Contraband population in Washington. Keckley begins by describing the freedmen and women who arrive in Washington with "exaggerated ideas of liberty" (139), particularly one "good old, simple-minded woman" who was "fresh from a life of servitude" and seemed to think that "the President and his wife had nothing to do but to supply the extravagant wants of every one that applied to them" (141–42). However, Keckley clarifies that this woman's wants were in fact "not very extravagant," that the freed woman was only upset because Mrs. Lincoln had not given her the standard present of two sets of undergarments that mistresses often provided for their slaves each year.

What is particularly interesting about Keckley's descriptions of the freed woman whose "extravagant" demands include two pairs of undergarments is that it appears in the same chapter that introduces the topic of Mary Todd Lincoln's debts. Keckley notes that the First Lady, "in endeavoring to make a display becoming to her exalted position," had to incur many expenses that she kept hidden from her husband. All totaled, Keckley claims these debts to amount to the staggering sum of $27,000. The irony of Mary Todd Lincoln's extravagance in the face of the freed woman's simple request is left to speak for itself. Keckley proceeds to include Mary Todd Lincoln's comment that there was "more at stake" in the reelection than Abraham Lincoln dreamed of, because if he were not reelected her debts would come to light (149). The inclusion of these comments might give readers pause, especially as they follow descriptions of former slaves in Washington. How could Mary Todd Lincoln compare the great needs of the Union during the devastation of the war with her personal debt? How could there be any more "at stake" in the war than the future of the slaves and the future of the nation? A reader could certainly question who was really more fit for freedom, the former slave woman or the former First Lady.

While the subject of slavery seems more historically profound than any scandal Mary Todd Lincoln could momentarily stir up, through her text's pattern of juxtaposing the narratives of white and African American women, Keckley demonstrates the importance of interrogating the relationship between white and black womanhood in the reconstructing nation. The two central topics of Keckley's narrative, then, are connected by more than just the historical fact that she worked for Mary Todd Lincoln; they interrogate the racial and symbolic order that justified enslavement and defined class and social status in postbellum America. One way she does so, as I describe below, is by claiming her own gentility and unmasking the genteel performance of white women such as Mary Todd Lincoln. However, as my above description of Keckley's embrace of capitalism indicates, Keckley also altered the perceived roles of white and African American women in the postbellum period through her representation of herself as a successful proprietor. As *Behind the Scenes* demonstrates, slavery forced most African American women into the commodified realm, while at the same time relegating many white women (at least symbolically or ideally) to the home, a sphere envisioned as removed from the marketplace and crowned with sincerity and gentility.[10] This twist of history, Keckley suggests throughout her narrative, left African American women particularly well-suited for an economic role in postbellum culture.

However, if Keckley carves a place for former slaves and African American women in the public sphere by juxtaposing her resourcefulness with the ineptitude of white "ladies," she still has to struggle with stereotypical and harmful associations of the African American woman as ungenteel and publicly accessible. After all, many antebellum Americans considered slave and free African American women's bodies as public property. The perception of their public status, all too often interconnected with harmful stereotypes of their alleged sexual availability, made any claims to true womanhood, to a private self, difficult to maintain. Therefore, *Behind the Scenes* cannot be read solely as an unproblematic representation of Keckley's triumphant rise from property to proprietor. Rather, Keckley points at times to her discomfort with certain aspects of commodification in the public realm, and her desire to distance herself from an uninterrogated acceptance of public commodity culture. Although Keckley certainly embraces capitalism, she develops strategies to enter into the public space of authorship and proprietorship while asserting a private, non-commodified, and genteel self.

This delicate balancing act that Keckley undertakes—the representation of herself as a public proprietor and a private lady—is exemplified in a revealing section of her book involving Keckley's work for President Johnson's family. When Keckley is asked by friends if she sent her business card to Johnson's family, she answers that she "had no desire to work for the President's family," as "Mr. Johnson was no friend to Mr. Lincoln" and "had failed to treat Mrs. Lincoln, in the hour of her greatest sorrow, with even common courtesy" (221). As we read elsewhere in Keckley's narrative, Johnson did not fulfill the expectations associated with genteel sympathy, neglecting to call or send a letter of condolence after Abraham Lincoln's death. Therefore, Keckley's reluctance to accept business from his family marks her as someone who upholds the genteel rules governing mourning practices and the extension of genteel sympathy. Indeed, Keckley's decision not to send her business *card* brings to mind the social calling *card*, thus aligning Keckley's refusal to seek Johnson's acquaintance to the process of social selection that Halttunen describes as essential to ante- and postbellum rules of gentility (112). Keckley's grounds for refusing to seek work from the Johnson White House differ from the opinions of the women she employs, who have their own reasons for not wanting to sew for Johnson's family. Although Keckley does not actively seek work from the Johnsons, when she is visited by Johnson's daughter, she takes an order for a dress. Upon learning of the order, one of Keckley's workers remarks that she fears "Johnson will prove a poor Moses," and that she "would not work for any of the family." None of her workers, Keckley comments, "appeared to like Mr. Lincoln's successor" (224–25).

In contrast to Keckley's seemingly apolitical and genteel reasons for initially refusing to seek work from the Johnson family, her employees express political, and specifically racial, motivations for wanting to refuse the dress order. Nonetheless, the lines that follow Keckley's description of her workers' dissatisfaction with Johnson are as follows: "I finished the dress for Mrs. Patterson, and it gave satisfaction. I afterwards learned that both Mrs. Patterson and Mrs. Stover were kind-hearted, plain, unassuming women, making no pretensions to elegance" (225). Here, in addition to showing how her desire to participate in the marketplace economy overrode her initial concerns (and the objections of her workers), Keckley continues to mark herself as genteel. Despite Johnson's reconstruction policies, she represents his daughters as the epitome of gentility, describing them as sentimentally sincere, making no hypocritical or overly theatrical "pretensions" to a false gentility. Therefore, Keckley claims gentility as a woman working within the marketplace, a move that puts her at odds with the middle-class culture that Halttunen describes. Rather than dividing business and home into separate spheres and charging women with the task of maintaining the family's gentility through a display of sincerity in the domestic and social space of the parlor, Keckley applies rules of gentility to the marketplace, thus asserting the dual roles of businesswoman and genteel lady that are crucial to her self-representation. Doing so, she blurs the boundaries between the domestic and public spheres, and, like Jacobs just seven years earlier, redefines conceptions of nineteenth-century womanhood. Yet, as the remainder of this essay argues, Keckley's representations of herself as genteel rely upon a precarious juxtaposition of her own life with Lincoln's, a juxtaposition that ultimately forces her to break the very expectations of gentility that were so important to her self-fashioning.

The Mask of Gentility

The juxtaposition of Keckley's and Lincoln's lives becomes more evident when one considers the tension between privacy and revelation in *Behind the Scenes*. Scholars note Keckley's seeming reticence about disclosing the personal facts of her life in slavery and after emancipation. In an argument relevant to my own, Rafia Zafar investigates Keckley's crafting of a "literary veil" to protect "the black female narrator from any scrutiny save one suitable for a black woman conscious of her tenuous status within middle-class American society" (153).[11] Indeed, Keckley tells us in the first paragraph of her Preface that "much has been omitted, but nothing has been exaggerated" (xi). That Keckley has selected facts and events to omit is significant enough for her to repeat in the first chapter, when she says that because she "cannot condense," she "must omit many strange passages in" her history (18). By asserting her power to omit, Keckley claims the dual roles of author and editor; she indicates that she has final say over what she will reveal in her text and what she will leave veiled. Doing so, she reverses rhetorically the racial dynamic of textual exposure that often appeared in antebellum antislavery texts. Much antislavery rhetoric written by white women was based on the dynamic similar to that described by Lydia Maria Child in her editor's preface to Jacobs's *Incidents*. Here, Child assumes responsibility for "presenting" the "monstrous features" of slavery to readers with the "veil withdrawn." But what she reveals is the corporeal secrets of Jacobs's personal history. By contrast, Keckley takes it upon herself to insist that the "veil of mystery must be drawn aside" from Mary Todd Lincoln's actions (xiv). Rather than unveiling the secrets of African American or slave women, Keckley withdraws the veil from the face of Mary Todd Lincoln's false gentility, exposing her to the public's gaze.

Keckley's awareness of the power of an author to veil and reveal is also evident when she describes her husband, a man who misrepresented himself to Keckley and led a life of "dissipation." In a move characteristic of her reluctance to reveal aspects of her personal life, Keckley tells very little about him, commenting that "he had his faults, but over these faults death has *drawn a veil*" (64; emphasis mine). But of course it is Keckley who has the power to let the veil remain intact or to rip it away. In this case, because it involves her own life and, perhaps, because it involves an African American, she elects nondisclosure. As Zafar argues, *Behind the Scenes* contains an "intriguing double-veiling" that can be found in the writing of other African American women, as the authors "withdraw the veil from the frivolous and self-centered nature of their white women employers at the same time they draw the veil over their own lives" (154). Examples of Keckley's unwillingness to reveal herself to the public's view can be found throughout her narrative, and a few suffice to demonstrate what we can identify as her strategic reticence. Chapter Two, "Girlhood and its Sorrows," divulges the most corporeally specific details about Keckley's life in slavery. In this chapter, Keckley reveals the cruel treatment she received at the home of Mr. Burwell, a man whom she identifies as a Presbyterian minister. Although she describes some of the beatings she received at Mrs. Burwell's prompting, she tells readers that she "will not dwell on the bitter anguish" of the hours after her beatings, "for even the thought of them now makes me shudder" (38). Just as Keckley refuses to "dwell" on her torture, so too does she "not care to dwell upon" the subject of the sexual abuse that resulted in her son. That Keckley refuses to comment in depth (or apologize at all) for her son is typical of her representations of him throughout her text, which are scarcely present and always reserved.

By veiling her private life and emotions, Keckley marks herself in mid-nineteenth-century terms as sincere and genteel. When she unveils, or unmasks, the white ladies she represents, she exposes them as ungenteel. To understand better the process of veiling and unveiling in relation to gentility, a brief summary of Halttunen's work is necessary. According to Halttunen, the ideal of social mobility, combined with urbanization, generated an enormous amount of anxiety among the American middle class in ante- and postbellum America. As middle-class Americans left their communities to pursue social mobility and wealth in urban areas, they struggled with how to "secure success among strangers without stooping to . . . manipulating appearance and conduct" (34). This conflict between "sentimental sincerity and genteel self-restraint" was resolved in what Halttunen calls the "genteel performance, a system of polite conduct that demanded a flawless self-discipline practiced within an apparently easy, natural, sincere manner" (93). From its inception, the genteel performance was connected with ideologies of gender, particularly the ideal of true womanhood. Halttunen explains how middle-class Americans, unable "to understand the historical forces at work modernizing their society," generally "identified the problem in simplistic, moral terms: American were becoming hypocrites." She continues: "The solution easily followed: the most naturally sincere portion of the population, women, were to ensure that hypocrisy was barred from polite middle-class social intercourse. The problem of hypocrisy, which had arisen in the streets and marketplaces of the world of strangers, would be confronted and resolved in the parlor of the middle-class home" (60). As Halttunen indicates, women were thought to be naturally inclined toward sincerity, although they were still capable of corruption. Therefore, women were important to a family's claim to gentility, as they embodied sincerity and worked to ensure that their home, particularly the parlor, was a place that would banish the hypocrisy that infested the marketplace and urban society.

Although Halttunen does not pursue the question of race in relation to the American middle class in much detail, to assess Keckley's work we need to consider the idea of the sentimental, sincere woman in terms of the racial binaries of womanhood at work in the nineteenth century. As Hazel V. Carby argues, any "historical investigation of the ideological boundaries of the cult of true womanhood is a sterile field without a recognition of the dialectical relationship with the alternative sexual code associated with the black woman," because black female sexuality was used to define the "boundaries" of true womanhood (30). If white women of the middle and upper class were often coded as private, sentimental, genteel, and passionless, black women were considered public, unsentimental, ungenteel, and passionate.[12] In effect, the sentimental, genteel culture represented by the ideal white woman was a racialized method of defining class status. Therefore, when Keckley marked herself as genteel through the methods that I analyze below, she threatened to dismantle the racialized binary of true womanhood that the genteel performance partially relied upon. Such a move was not to be tolerated by middle-class Americans. As the reviews and parody I quote in my introduction indicate, many believed that Keckley would have been better off to "have stuck to her needle" and remained a "woman who took in work" from white ladies.

But Keckley refuses to acknowledge her prescribed place in society, and therefore complicates the codes of gentility that dominated her time. One way of understanding the full extent of her challenge is to situate her book in relation to the major components of the genteel performance. Because the "line between true gentility and false etiquette was perilously thin," the genteel performance was only made possible by hundreds of rules that Halttunen divides into three areas: "the laws of polite social geography, the laws of tact, and the laws of acquaintanceship" (101). Additionally, as Halttunen explains, the rules governing mourning were increasingly important to the genteel performance as the century progressed. All four of these aspects of the genteel performance are critical to understanding the backlash toward Keckley's work. The first, "the laws of polite social geography," functioned to establish the parlor "as the stage upon which the genteel performance was enacted." Drawing upon the work of Erving Goffman, Halttunen argues that, in "societies built on the promise of social mobility, high demands for control over bodily and facial expressiveness made necessary a division of living space into front regions and back regions." In the front region, the social actor is "onstage or 'in character,'" but in the "back regions" a genteel performer could momentarily relax. The daunting task of the genteel hostess was to "keep all private domestic arrangements from intruding upon the genteel performance," particularly her servants, as hostesses' "own gentility rested in part on" their servants' "ability to remain inconspicuous" (104–06). One manual, *Etiquette at Washington: and*

Complete Guide through the Metropolis and its Environs, published eleven years before *Behind the Scenes*, instructed readers in what Halttunen calls an "unusually explicit statement of the theatrical nature" of the hostess's task that "the internal machinery of a household, like that portion of the theater '*behind the scenes*,' should . . . be studiously kept out of view" (qtd. in Halttunen 105).

When one considers "the laws of polite social geography" in general and the idea that the household's machinery was to be kept *behind the scenes* in particular, one begins to realize the subversive implications of Keckley's title. How could a genteel lady ensure her family's status by keeping the domestic machinery *behind the scenes* if her friends and/or servants could at any moment lift the curtain and reveal the messy, emotional, unrestrained actions that took place in the back regions? It is not so much, then, that Keckley revealed Mary Todd Lincoln's secrets but, rather, that this revelation demonstrated just how fragile the theatrical performance of parlor etiquette was for the typical middle-class aspirant. Seven years earlier, Jacobs told readers that, if "the secret memoirs of many members of Congress should be published, curious details would be unfolded" (142). Now, rather than threatening to go public with private sexual information involving African American women and white men, Keckley went public with private, domestic information involving, primarily, white women. True, what we learn is not all that scandalous in relation to nineteenth-century journalism. However, Keckley's revelations about Mary Todd Lincoln are threatening because they unmask a white woman's genteel performance.

Interestingly, Keckley deflects her decision to go *behind the scenes* and reveal the private, domestic life of Mary Todd and Abraham Lincoln by describing the seemingly inappropriate desires of others to do something quite similar. At one point, Keckley tells readers that she "soon learned that some people had an intense desire to penetrate the inner circle of the White House," especially because Abraham Lincoln had "grown up in the wilds of the West," a fact that shocked the polite world and "intensified curiosity." In fact, one woman, whom Keckley pointedly refuses to call a lady, asks Keckley for her assistance in introducing her to the "secrets of the domestic circle." Keckley refuses, and soon learns that the woman was an actress who wished to "publish a scandal to the world" (92–95). In this exchange, the anxiety over theatricality, class, and penetration of the back regions is evidenced on several levels. First, the Lincolns appear as ungenteel social climbers, as their roots in the West subject them to scrutiny from the seemingly more genteel, polite East.[13] Having read "patronizing newspaper comments about" the Lincolns' "supposed western vulgarity" before arriving in Washington to become First Lady, Mary Todd Lincoln was determined to assume the proper role of the genteel woman by flaunting appropriate fashions (Baker 165). Although the donning of correct clothes for a genteel role was hardly unique to Mary Todd Lincoln, her intense desire to wear the costume of gentility may have uncomfortably reminded many Americans of the theatricality underlying their own social status. Indeed, the ire directed toward Mary Todd Lincoln in one review of *Behind the Scenes* shows the anxiety generated by alleged social climbers. The editors of the *Cleveland Daily Plain Dealer* declared that they were pleased that Keckley's book was published, as it would serve as a warning "to those ladies whose husbands may be elevated to the position of the President of the United States ... not to put on *airs* and attempt to appear what their education, their habits of life and social position, and even personal appearance would not warrant" (1). Second, the woman who wishes to penetrate the White House is an actress, also underscoring the too close relationship between gentility and theatricality. Third, the actress planned to reveal the private, domestic aspects of the White House (presumably the Lincolns' lack of gentility) in the public realm of the marketplace for all to consume, thereby showing how perilously thin was the line between the genteel parlor and the ungenteel marketplace. Keckley, however, refuses to allow the actress access, thereby sparing Mary Todd Lincoln the embarrassment of having her "back regions" revealed.

Her willingness to shield Mary Todd Lincoln's domestic back regions from the public eye marks Keckley as genteel through her acquiescence to the second and third categories of rules that comprised the genteel performance, the laws of tact and acquaintanceship. Halttunen explains that the laws of tact "governed not the genteel performance itself, but its reception by those who witnessed it." In particular, the laws ensured "that members of the polite audience would assist, encourage, and honor a genteel performer's claims to gentility," especially by honoring "the sanctity of the back regions," a domain where a polite visitor "never intruded" (Halttunen 107). Because "lapses in gentility occurred," the performance could only be sustained "by the tact of the genteel audience" (111). Indeed, the "most tactless blunder a house guest could commit was to carry tales of her hostess's household" (108). Therefore, laws of tact relied upon the laws of acquaintanceship, a complex process of sorting out those who merited social invitation. Since "any ill-bred person . . . threatened to undermine everyone else's claims to gentility, such rudeness had to be banned from polite social intercourse" (111). By distinguishing her literary activity from the actress's inappropriate desire for scandal, Keckley represents herself as aware of, and adhering to, the genteel rules of tact and acquaintanceship, at least in this case.

Locating Keckley's and Mary Todd Lincoln's relationship within genteel rules of etiquette is difficult; their alliance is not easily definable because both blur the rigid social line between servants and acquaintances that gentility mandated. Keckley's title page identifies her as "formerly a slave, but more recently modiste, and friend to Mrs. Abraham Lincoln," thus indicating a certain progression—from chattel, to employee, to friend. Yet the book at times denies this linear progression, and places Keckley simultaneously as a friend and employee. A striking manifestation of this uncertainty comes near the end of the book, when Keckley relates her dealings with Mary Todd Lincoln in New York. Keckley includes a scene detailing her first night in the city with Lincoln, who is traveling under the guise of "Mrs. Clarke." When Keckley attempts to secure a meal in the hotel's dining room, she is ordered to leave, as the steward assumes that she is Mrs. Clarke's servant. The exchange is revealing:

"Are you not Mrs. Clarke's servant?" was his abrupt question.
"I am with Mrs. Clarke."
"It is all the same; servants are not allowed to eat in the large dining-room. Here, this way; you must take your dinner in the servants' hall." (280)

Granted, Keckley is trying to maintain Mary Todd Lincoln's anonymity and does not want to create conflict. Yet her ambivalent answer, "'I am with Mrs. Clarke,'" reveals her uncertainty as to just how to describe her role. After all, she requests and receives compensation from the United States government for her work when Mary Todd Lincoln cannot pay her, and therefore their relationship is located, to some extent, in the marketplace.[14]

Yet if we consider *Behind the Scenes* in relation to laws of acquaintanceship and to laws of tact, we see that Keckley has violated the rules of the genteel performance on both accounts. If readers of *Behind the Scenes* consider Keckley a servant, they would have reason for concern, as servants were to remain inconspicuous to ensure the gentility of the hostess. And if they considered Keckley an acquaintance of Mary Todd Lincoln, they could likewise be disturbed, as the foremost duty of an acquaintance was to help a friend maintain his or her mask of gentility. It is also fair to suggest that Keckley's blurring of the strict social categories necessary to the genteel performance could have hit a nerve in readers trying to maintain those illusive, but all-important, social distinctions. Certainly, when the editors of the *Cleveland Daily Plain Dealer* told readers that Keckley's book served as a lesson "not to make confidants of, or allow themselves to be duped by servants, *modistes*, or whatever they may be called, white or black, unless they wish to court notoriety by being held up by this class of people in a manner to disgrace" (1), they were revealing the perceived need to maintain the fabricated, yet necessary, genteel distinctions that Keckley and Mary Todd Lincoln's relationship challenged.

As the *Plain Dealer* indicates, instead of enabling Mary Todd Lincoln to maintain a mask of gentility, as a good servant or acquaintance would, Keckley reveals her in intense private moments. This is especially the case in relation to Mary Todd Lincoln's mourning for her son, Willie, and her husband. It is in the representations of mourning that we see the most pronounced juxtaposition between the gentility of Keckley and the ungenteel behavior of Mary Todd Lincoln. The contrast between Keckley's representation of deaths in her family and that of the Lincolns' mourning is striking. Indeed, nowhere is Keckley's strategic reticence more evident than in her representations of her own mourning, which may strike readers as significant, even odd. Although Keckley briefly refers to deaths in her family at various places in her narrative, they are eclipsed, in terms of space and emphasis, by the deaths in the Lincoln family. For example, after a detailed description of Willie's death, Keckley mentions her own son's death at the end of a paragraph about Willie and Mary Todd Lincoln:

> Previous to this I had lost my son. Leaving Wilberforce, he went to the battle-field with the three months troops, and was killed in Missouri—found his grave on the battlefield where the gallant General Lyon fell. It was a sad blow to me, and the kind womanly letter that Mrs. Lincoln wrote to me when she heard of my bereavement was full of golden words of comfort. (105)

As the sentence sequence of the above quote reveals, Keckley's son's death is subsumed into the narrative of Willie Lincoln. It is introduced in relation to Willie's death ("previous to this"), and the same sentence that comments on Keckley's reaction ("It was a sad blow for me") ends by emphasizing Mary Todd Lincoln's gentility in sending a letter of condolence. As if to downplay even further her son's importance to the narrative, Keckley follows this brief comment about his death with an extensive abstract of the "beautiful sketch" written by Nathaniel Parker Willis for Willie Lincoln, which ends the chapter.

When we consider Keckley's representations of mourning in relation to conceptions of gentility, *Behind the Scenes*' strategic reticence takes on an increased significance. For as the nineteenth century progressed, mourning practices increasingly became part of public, commodity culture (Halttunen 124–52). According to Keckley's representations, neither Keckley nor Mary Todd Lincoln participated in extensive public mourning rituals. Keckley wrote almost nothing about the deaths in her family, and Mary Todd Lincoln generally refused to attend the public functions in honor of her son's and husband's deaths. Therefore, in some respects, Keckley aligns herself and Mary Todd Lincoln with the sentimental idea that mourning is a solitary practice that is more sincere when private (Halttunen 132). However, by writing extensively and in detail about what many considered Mary Todd Lincoln's excessive and self-centered grief for Willie and Abraham, Keckley foists Mary Todd Lincoln into the public sphere while remaining private in her own grief. As Zafar notes (177), "Keckley's relative silence" about her grief could "confirm her in white eyes as a successful performer" within genteel culture because it demonstrated her emotional self-restraint.

To complicate matters, the details that Keckley reports about Mary Todd Lincoln's grief mark Lincoln as noticeably ungenteel. Although Mary Todd Lincoln's seclusion after the death of her son and husband could have signaled her sincere bereavement, her other actions belie a lack of gentility. In addition to the idea that sincere mourning was private, three components of sentimental, genteel mourning that Halttunen describes are particularly relevant to Keckley's representations of Mary Todd Lincoln. By analyzing each one in turn, we begin to see just how thoroughly *Behind the Scenes* unmasks Mary Todd Lincoln's performance. One rule of genteel mourning was that, although "middle-class men and women were encouraged to indulge 'the luxury of grief' as a mark of their sentimental sensibilities, they were instructed never to grieve excessively." Rather, mourning was to be "an occasion for discipline in emotional self-expression, for genteel self-improvement" (Halttunen 134). On all accounts, Keckley describes Mary Todd Lincoln as absolutely "inconsolable" (104), revealing an unacceptable level of emotional and physical abandonment. After the death of Willie, she describes Mary Todd Lincoln's "paroxysms of grief" as so severe that Abraham Lincoln warned that, if she did not control herself, she would be driven "mad" and might end up in an asylum (104–5). After Abraham Lincoln dies, Mary Todd Lincoln is found in "a new paroxysm of grief" with "the wails of a broken heart, the unearthly shrieks, the terrible convulsions, the wild, tempestuous outbursts of grief from the soul" (191). As Jennifer Fleischner points out (130), Keckley connects Mary Todd Lincoln's mourning with traits often assigned to African Americans (wild, childlike, passive, and weak), an association that underscores the racial reversal that *Behind the Scenes* enacts. Clearly, Mary Todd Lincoln fails to live up to the standards of genteel emotional self-restraint, standards that are racially coded as white.

Just as Mary Todd Lincoln is incapable of controlling her excessive grief, so too does she fail to channel it in the proper direction. The proper genteel mourner, according to Halttunen, feels "a rush of benevolence toward all men" at a certain point in the grieving process, a rush that manifests itself in a desire to "practice kindness toward all" and results in a restored and strengthened confidence among humankind (131). Mary Todd Lincoln's grief is noticeably devoid of any such communal response. Its intensity and excessiveness are shown to take over all aspects of her life, even her maternal role. Keckley tells readers that "Tad's grief at his father's death was as great as the grief of his mother, but her terrible outbursts awed the boy into silence" (192). Although Keckley does not linger upon this fact, the reader may be shocked that Mary Todd Lincoln, rather than being strong for her son, remained self-centered in her mourning. Additionally, her grief over Willie makes her object even more strenuously to Robert's entering the army. Keckley reports that, although Robert "was very anxious to quit school and enter the army," the "move was sternly opposed by his mother," because the Lincolns had "lost one son," and his loss was as much as Mary Todd Lincoln could "bear, without being called upon to make another sacrifice." To this, Abraham Lincoln would counter that "many a poor mother has given up all her sons" and "our son is not more dear to us than the sons of other people are to their mothers" (121). Although Mary Todd

Lincoln eventually relinquishes Robert to military service, this scene reveals that her grief for Willie did not manifest itself in compassion for other mothers or in larger societal concerns. As when she hopes her husband will be reelected so that her debts will not be revealed, she here seems incapable of manifesting a greater feeling of benevolence or social responsibility.

By contrast, Keckley, rather than becoming consumed by private grief upon the death of her son, uses her experience to sympathize more fully with Mary Todd Lincoln, thereby showing herself as sentimental in understanding another woman's pain. Even while Keckley criticizes Mary Todd Lincoln, saying, for example, that if she had been less secluded in her grief she might "have had many warmer friends to-day," she calls upon readers to be compassionate: "Could the ladies who called to condole with Mrs. Lincoln, after the death of her husband, and who were denied admittance to her chamber, have seen how completely prostrated she was with grief, they would have learned to speak more kindly of her" (196). Indeed, this passage seems to echo and reverse racially the quintessentially sentimental scene that appears in Chapter Nine of *Uncle Tom's Cabin*. In Stowe's novel, the fugitive slave Eliza Harris, in an effort to justify having fled her allegedly benevolent masters, asks Senator Bird's wife if she has "ever lost a child" (149). The Birds, who are mourning their son's death, are able to sympathize with Eliza due to their own suffering, and we are left to assume that the senator will act more benevolently and correctly in the public sphere in the future. In *Behind the Scenes*, it is Keckley who is shown to have empathy with Mary Todd Lincoln's grief and an overall desire to turn her own mourning into the actions needed to better humankind and relieve suffering. In the chapter following Keckley's descriptions of Mary Todd Lincoln's grief, and in the same chapter that we learn of Mary Todd Lincoln's reluctance to risk Robert in the war effort, Keckley reveals her creation of the Contraband Relief Association, a society designed to alleviate the sufferings of the recently freed slaves who were fleeing to Washington, DC, during the war. Although Keckley does not make the connection explicit, it appears that her grief over her son has led her to consider with more compassion others who have suffered, thereby leading to the association's formation. While it is true that Mary Todd Lincoln donates $200 to Keckley's charity, this gesture does not have the same resonance as Keckley's sentimental compassion and public benevolence, especially when one considers it in relation to the excessive debt Mary Todd Lincoln accumulates furnishing her wardrobe and the White House.

The final aspect of genteel mourning that is relevant to Keckley's work is that of the sentimental keepsake, the "reverence for the personal tokens or keepsakes left by the deceased" (Halttunen 133). As Joanne Dobson explains, in much nineteenth-century literature, "the sentimental keepsake constitutes a vivid symbolic embodiment of the primacy of human connection and the inevitability of human loss. Its use in numerous texts with varying (sometimes contrasting) intentions stems from a body of convention resonant with grief, loss of memory, consolation, and an acknowledgment of the fragility of human life" (273). In *Behind the Scenes,* the reactions of Keckley and Mary Todd Lincoln to sentimental keepsakes underscore their different mourning practices. To Keckley, the keepsake functions as an essential tie to those she has loved and lost. For example, at one point in her narrative, Keckley includes an abstract from an article in the *New York Evening News* based on information that Keckley provided to the reporter. In the article, the author writes that most "of the other articles that adorned Mrs. Lincoln on that fatal night became the property of Mrs. Keckley," who has "carefully stowed" them away and "intends keeping them during her life as mementos of a mournful event" (311). Here, Keckley represents herself to the reporter and to her readers as someone who longs genteelly to keep mementoes of Abraham Lincoln. Indeed, Keckley later makes it clear that the sentimental keepsake is an almost sacred object that should neither be neglected nor sold for profit. Although the cloak stained with Abraham Lincoln's blood could "not be purchased from" Keckley, she is willing to donate it to Wilberforce College, the institution that her son attended. By offering to donate the cloak to Wilberforce, Keckley shows, once again, that her private grief leads her to public benevolence, as she wishes to help the "cause of educating the four millions of slaves liberated by our President" (367). As Fleischner points out, despite Keckley's representation of herself as a proprietor, the "items Keckley accumulates are fundamentally unusable objects whose value is mostly sentimental and memorial, rather than pragmatic" (101).

Once again, Mary Todd Lincoln's behavior stands in stark contrast to Keckley's actions, as Lincoln rids herself and her home of almost all of Willie's and Abraham's possessions. After Willie's death, Mary Todd Lincoln "could not bear the sight of anything he loved" and "gave all of Willie's toys—everything connected with him—away" because she could not look upon them "without thinking of her poor dead boy" and to think of him in the grave was "maddening" (181–82). Likewise, when preparing to leave the White House, "Mrs. Lincoln gave away everything intimately connected with the President, as she said that she could not bear to be reminded of the past" (202). Mary Todd Lincoln's refusal to honor the genteel custom of the sentimental keepsake marks her as self-centered in her grief. Fleischner argues that her rejection of the sentimental keepsake is made all the more distasteful by her obsession with the mourning costume: "Keckley's depiction of Mrs. Lincoln's mourning . . . makes it the emotional equivalent of her materialism—all-consuming and self-directed. Mrs. Lincoln's impulse to get rid of everything connected to her dead while at the same time adding to her mourning wardrobe suggests that she experiences the death of loved ones as blows against herself, and not against another" (129). Unlike Keckley, whose experiences with death confirm her connections to humankind, Mary Todd Lincoln's obsessive behavior appears childlike, self-indulgent, and markedly ungenteel.

The contrast between Keckley's and Mary Todd Lincoln's mourning practices offers the most extreme example of the narrative juxtaposition that constitutes *Behind the Scenes*' logical structure. As a widowed and recently emancipated African American woman, Keckley had to carve a space for herself in the postbellum economy, and she does so by showing herself a competent businesswoman, one who has learned more than many white ladies because she endured the "hardy school" of slavery. Yet Keckley is also, no matter how much she refuses to "dwell" on the fact, a woman who suffered terrible sexual and physical abuse while a slave, at times at the prompting of white women. As a woman whose body was once considered chattel, it would make sense that she would feel a particular urgency about claiming privacy, and about considering herself deserving of the respect that accrues to genteel women. To assert these dual roles, Keckley contrasts her own life and character with those of several white women, most noticeably her friend Mary Todd Lincoln. Doing so, she challenges conceptions of gender, race, gentility, and commodity culture that were already in flux after the war.

Reading *Behind the Scenes*, this narrative juxtaposition is so pronounced that it almost seems impossible to accept Keckley's assertion of pure motives and good intentions when writing about Mary Todd Lincoln. Our information about Keckley indicates that she was a woman who held firm to genteel practices throughout her life. For example, one person who knew Keckley described her as "a woman of high ideals, character and dignity" who was "very reserved, refined, intelligent and unobtrusive" and had "certain rules of decorum" that she "always observed" (Washington 217). How, then, could she fail to observe the rules prohibiting any revelation of the messy material hidden *behind the scenes*? One answer to this difficult question is provided by Fleischner in her nuanced analysis of Keckley's psychological reaction to slavery. As Fleischner demonstrates, given "the nature of internalized prohibitions against self-assertion and self-expression—a likely legacy of actual enslavement—coupled with the external constraints against black candor in a white world, the unspoken, the masked, the ruptured, and the contradictory are palpable presences in slave narratives" (5). According to Fleischner, the "necessarily suppressed and repressed life of a mulatta woman serving in the White House in the 1860s" would surface in interesting ways (99). To this, I would add that the prohibitions against self-assertion and self-expression to which Fleischner refers would make it extremely difficult for Keckley to go public with her private wrath, or, perhaps, even to articulate that wrath to herself in a conscious manner. Certainly, one could argue that Keckley had sincere intentions, but like any author (especially, as Fleischner argues, one who has endured trauma) could not entirely control her text. Her unconscious or repressed wrath, either against Lincoln in particular or against the white women who authorized her abuse and whose claims to a genteel status rested on the denigration of African American women in general, may have caused a contradiction between intention and result. There are times when anger and other emotions surface and inform the text in ways that may have startled even the author herself.

We can also answer the question of how the gap between motivation and result may have widened by examining the social changes regarding gentility that were taking place as Keckley wrote and published. In Keckley's preface, she frames her work on the genteel premise of the sincerity of her intentions, saying that she was "prompted by the purest motive" to write, and her defense of Mary Todd Lincoln is based on the fact that Lincoln's intentions "were good" (xiii–xiv). The significance of inner character, intention, and motive dominates the prefatory justification, and points to the sentimental premise underlying Keckley's text. As Halttunen argues, sentimentalists believed that at its foundation good behavior "was not a matter of outward rules and ceremonies; it was simply the outpouring of right feelings from a right heart" (93). In its purest sense, to be genteel meant to be sincere. Therefore, even though Keckley is cognizant of her transgression of genteel etiquette, she justifies it by invoking the sentimental ideals that were supposed to be the foundation of the rules governing gentility, the belief that, if one's character were pure and motivation good, then outward actions would be judged accordingly. However, as Halttunen points out, by the 1860s, sentimental "anxieties about the hypocrisy of social disguise and formal ritual were yielding before a growing middle-class fascination with the theatrical arts of everyday life" (174), and many Americans were willing to accept the fact that "middle-class social life was itself a charade" (185). In this context, Americans were less concerned about the sincerity allegedly at the roots of genteel culture and more concerned about the outward forms of that culture itself. In fact, many Americans were able to laugh at their own theatricality, poking fun at the rules that governed their existence (Halttunen 153–90).

Yet even if white middle-class Americans in the 1860s gathered in parlors to mock their own theatricality, they clung to the privileges and the performance that accompanied their newly found genteel status and were far from prepared to have them challenged by an African American woman who was once a slave. Because their class status continued to rely partially upon an implicit juxtaposition between white and black womanhood, Keckley's challenge to these prescribed categories was particularly troublesome. Likewise, because their social status depended upon an idealized separation of the domestic and public spheres, and between those who would be servants and those who would be social equals, Keckley's claim to both privacy and proprietorship, to both service and friendship, transgressed boundaries that the white middle class wanted to uphold. When Keckley ripped away the curtain to expose the private behavior of a white middle-class woman in such a public forum, when she revealed what many readers wanted so desperately to keep *behind the scenes*, it was an unforgivable violation of gentility and an unacceptable assertion of racial worth. This combination was certain to, and indeed did, generate an enormous amount of wrath.

NOTES

1. In September 1867, the widowed Mary Todd Lincoln arrived in New York City to negotiate the sale of her clothes, where she was met by Keckley whom she had pleaded with to come. Although Lincoln claimed to want to remain anonymous and traveled under the guise of "Mrs. Clarke," she gave an appraiser a ring with her name inscribed on it. Once she was detected, the sale was widely known. In addition to drawing criticism for negotiating the sale, Lincoln also was criticized for her willingness to shame key Republican leaders into assisting her by going public with her financial needs in the press. Additionally, the dresses, many of which were given to Lincoln during her husband's first term in office, represented her willingness to exchange her access to the President for extravagant gifts during the war. For more information on the old clothes scandal, see Baker 271–80.

2. For example, late in her life, Keckley told Anna Eliza Williams (a woman who helped care for her) that she wrote *Behind the Scenes* because Lincoln had been a "true friend" and by selling the book she intended to help Lincoln, who was in "poor circumstances." Yet she lamented that the book caused so "much sorrow and loss of friends" and stated that she "never thought of injuring such a loyal friend" as Lincoln (Washington 221).

3. Although Keckley's book generated much anger, it was not universally condemned. For example, a review in *Hours at Home* indicated that the editors' "first impressions of the book" had "been greatly modified on reading it" as Keckley "writes with a straight-forwardness, a propriety, good sense, and grace and force of diction, that is not a little surprising, and which proves her true womanhood, notwithstanding she was born in slavery and passed thirty years of her life in bondage" (192). Also, although *The New York Times* condemned Keckley's writing of the text, its inclusion of a three-column review, complete with lengthy abstracts, belies the editors' supposed recoil from Keckley's revelations, as does a subsequent article on "Mrs. Lincoln's Wardrobe," which after only a paragraph written by the staff of the *Times* quotes extensively from Keckley's work.

4. The parody *Behind the Seams; by a Nigger Woman Who Took in Work from Mrs. Lincoln and Mrs. Davis* was republished by an anonymous "A. Lincoln Fann" in a limited edition in New York in 1945, and it is from that edition that I quote. I am grateful to Oberlin College for access to this text.

5. According to Washington (239), Keckley gave Mary Todd Lincoln's letters to James Redpath, who was helping to edit her book. Redpath promised that nothing would be printed that would in any way injure Mary Todd Lincoln, but then proceeded to include the letters with almost no editing.

6. Washington reports that Keckley "continued to sew for the best families in Washington" and "lived in the best colored homes" for many years after publishing *Behind the Scenes* (240). Although Keckley died in the Home for Destitute Colored Women and Children, she had enough in savings to leave some money to charity (215).

7. Before arriving in Washington as First Lady, Mary Todd Lincoln was causing a sensation; according to Baker, already "there was grumbling about her violation of female decorum" (166).

8. For an analysis of Harriet Beecher Stowe's *Uncle Tom's Cabin* in relation to the nineteenth-century conception of separate spheres, see Tompkins.

9. Andrews notes that postbellum reunion scenes have multiple functions, including representing the former slave as "demonstrating the moral leadership in such reunions" and therefore as "an active agent in the reconstruction of the South" ("Reunion" 12). Jennifer Fleischner argues that Keckley had to return to her past because personal "memory constitutes identity and is precious to the individual, no matter how it is conditioned by larger cultural and political forces of oppression" (117).

10. When referring to the Doctrine of Separate Spheres, I intend to indicate the ideal that was often held out to nineteenth-century middle-class Americans, not necessarily the reality of women's lives—white or African American—in this time period. As Cathy N. Davidson points out in her preface to the September 1998 Special Issue of *American Literature* (which is dedicated to interrogating the assumption of separate spheres), the "binaric version of nineteenth-century America is ultimately unsatisfactory because it is simply too crude an instrument—too rigid and totalizing—for understanding the different, complicated ways that nineteenth-century American society or literary production functioned" (445). But even if it was not a reality for many Americans, we can still argue that the rhetoric endorsing the home as a sacred, private realm ruled by a sentimental and sincere woman (coded white) was powerful enough to stimulate a response in writers such as Keckley. For an excellent overview of the concept of separate spheres in historical work, see Kerber.

11. As my use of Zafar's discussion of veiling and unveiling in African American women's texts indicates, Zafar's argument is, in some respects, similar to mine. In addition to exploring the relationship between revelation and concealment in African American women's autobiography, Zafar analyzes Keckley's representation of mourning in relation to Halttunen's work, arguing that Mary Todd Lincoln's mourning behavior was not consistent with proper genteel expectations and that, by contrast, Keckley's "relative silence" about her family members' deaths could confirm her as a successful genteel performer (see Zafar 177–80). Although we share these critical questions and strategies, my essay adds to Zafar's by exploring how Keckley's unveiling of Lincoln reveals the text's narrative logic of juxtaposition. Additionally, as I suggest, a discussion of Keckley's claims to gentility is enhanced by situating them in relation to Keckley's assertion of a place within postbellum commodity culture for African American women. Finally, my essay concentrates more upon the text's reception, both by addressing reviews of the work that I have not seen quoted in contemporary scholarship on Keckley, and by exploring the disparity between Keckley's sincerely benevolent intentions and the wrath that is evidenced in the book itself and in the book's reception.

12. Deborah Gray White explores the connections between reproduction and privacy in the slave community. "Just as with reproduction," she argues, "that which was private and personal became public and familiar" for slave women, whose bodies were often exposed or semi-exposed while they were working in the fields, being tortured, or sold on the auction block (27).

13. Mary Todd Lincoln is aware of her precarious status and justifies her extreme consumerism on the basis that she "must dress in costly materials" as the "people scrutinize every article" that she wears "with critical curiosity" because she grew up in the West (Keckley 149).

14. For information on Keckley's payment for her service to Lincoln, see Washington 225.

WORKS CITED

Andrews, William L. "The Changing Morel Discourse of Nineteenth-Century African American Women's Autobiography: Harriet Jacobs and Elizabeth Keckley." *De/Colonizing the Subject The Politics of Gender in Women's Autobiography.* Minneapolis: University of Minnesota Press, 1992. 225–41.

———. "Reunion in the Postbellum Slave Narrative: Frederick Douglass and Elizabeth Keckley." *Black American Literature Forum* 23 (1989): 5–16.

Baker, Jean H. *Mary Todd Lincoln: A Biography.* New York: W.W. Norton, 1987.

Behind the Seams; by a Nigger Woman Who Took in Work from Mrs. Lincoln and Mrs. Davis. 1868. New York, 1945.

Carby, Hazel V. *Reconstructing Womanhood: The Emergence of the Afro-American Woman Novelist.* New York: Oxford University Press, 1987.

Davidson, Cathy N. "Preface: No More Separate Spheres!" *American Literature* 70 (1998): 443–63.

Dobson, Joanne. "Reclaiming Sentimental Literature." *American Literature* 69 (1997): 263–88.

Fleischner, Jennifer. *Mastering Slavery: Memory, Family, and Identity in Women's Slave Narratives.* New York: New York University Press, 1996.

Foster, Frances Smith. *Written by Herself: Literary Productions by African American Women, 1746–1892.* Bloomington: Indiana University Press, 1993.

Halttunen, Karen. *Confidence Men and Painted Women: A Study of Middle-Class Culture in America, 1830–1870.* New Haven: Yale University Press, 1982.

Jacobs, Harriet. *Incidents in the Life of a Slave Girl, Written by Herself.* 1861. Ed. Jean Fagan Yellin. Cambridge: Harvard University Press, 1987.

Keckley, Elizabeth. *Behind the Scenes; or, Thirty Years a Slave and Four Years in the White House.* 1868. New York: Oxford University Press, 1988.

Kerber, Linda K. "Separate Spheres, Female Worlds, Women's Place: The Rhetoric of Women's History." *Toward an Intellectual History of Women.* Chapel Hill: University of North Carolina Press, 1997. 159–99.

"Mrs. Lincoln's Wardrobe." *New York Times,* 26 Apr. 1868: 3.

Review of *Behind the Scenes; or, Thirty Years a Slave and Four Years in the White House,* by Elizabeth Keckley. *Cleveland Daily Plain Dealer,* 23 Apr. 1868: 1.

Review of *Behind the Scenes; or, Thirty Years a Slave and Four Years in the White House,* by Elizabeth Keckley. *Hours at Home,* June 1868: 192.

Review of *Behind the Scenes; or, Thirty Years a Slave and Four Years in the White House,* by Elizabeth Keckley. *New York Times,* 19 Apr. 1868: 10.

Review of *Behind the Scenes; or, Thirty Years a Slave and Four Years in the White House,* by Elizabeth Keckley. *Putnam's Magazine,* July 1868: 119.

Stowe, Harriet Beecher. *Uncle Tom's Cabin, or Life Among the Lowly.* 1852. New York: Penguin, 1981.

Tompkins, Jane P. "Sentimental Power: *Uncle Tom's Cabin* and the Politics of Literary History." *The New Feminist Criticism: Essays on Women, Literature and Theory.* Ed. Elaine Showalter. New York: Pantheon, 1985. 81–104.

Washington, John E. *They Knew Lincoln.* New York: Dutton, 1942.

White, Deborah Gray. *Ar'n't I a Woman?: Female Slaves in the Plantation South.* New York: W.W. Norton, 1985.

Zafar, Rafia. *We Wear the Mask: African Americans Write American Literature, 1760–1870.* New York: Columbia University Press, 1997.

CHAPTER THREE

KATHERINE ADAMS

Freedom and Ballgowns
Elizabeth Keckley and the Work of Domesticity

We were shown through the damp cold rooms into the drawing room. The nation's drawing room—where the mobocracy assemble by the light of beautiful chandeliers and circulating amidst rich furniture—great men and accomplished women fancy they live in a country of equality as well as liberty. Query: do they ever feel their inequality more than on such occasions?
—Catharine Maria Sedgwick, describing a visit to the White House

IN MARCH OF 1866, President Andrew Johnson found occasion to remind Congress that both law and propriety stood against the intermarriage of blacks with whites. Drawing upon the late New York supreme court judge, James Kent, whose essays on constitutional law had become a primer in conservative legal thought, Johnson explained,

> Kent says, speaking of the blacks, that "marriages between them and the whites are forbidden in some of the States where slavery does not exist, and they are prohibited in all the slave holding States; and when not absolutely contrary to law, they are revolting, and regarded as an offence against public decorum." (CRV 75)[1]

If the words were not Johnson's, the sentiments were, and had frequently been voiced before.[2] In this instance, however, their context was somewhat obscure. The speech concerned Johnson's veto of the Civil Rights bill, a piece of legislation engineered by the Radical Republicans to extend and protect the rights of newly emancipated blacks. Demonstrating his entrenched racism toward blacks and conciliatory approach to Southern states, the veto marked a turning point in the President's battles with Congress over the design of Reconstruction. Most specifically, it constituted a direct intervention into contemporary debates over how to define and distribute the condition of democratic freedom in the postbellum era. Since emancipation, the Radical Republicans had argued that freedom had no meaning for anyone if not shared equally by all. As one Republican journalist put it, the failure to legislate equal civil rights would not only subvert the aim of emancipation, but tender "all the principles of democracy and freedom upon which our creed of Republicanism rests . . . false" (qtd. in Cox 48). The president, meanwhile, opposed any such move toward racial equality. A former slave-owner who believed blacks an inferior race, Johnson asked, "can it reasonably be supposed that they possess the requisite qualifications to entitle them to all the privileges and immunities of citizens of the United States?" (75). In vetoing this bill, he aimed specifically to prevent the convergence of black and white freedoms and to formalize the differences between them.[3]

What, however, might that aim have to do with racial intermarriage—an issue not mentioned in the Civil Rights bill? The answer concerns changes in racialist discourse that occurred as white supremacy accommodated itself to the new social, political, legal, and economic contexts of Reconstruction. Racial mixing was a persisting theme and personal obsession with Johnson, but it was not his alone. Nor was he first to deploy it within an attempt to mediate access to political freedom. The term *miscegenation,* coined just four years before Johnson's speech, had already gained currency in segregationist vocabularies. It had proved convenient for invoking not only the imagined integrity of racial identity and difference but also, crucially, the sanctified image of white domesticity.

Johnson acknowledges that interracial marriage lies somewhat outside of his present concerns, but explains that he raises it

> as an instance of the State policy as to discrimination, and to inquire whether, if Congress can abrogate all State laws of discrimination between the two races in the matter of real estate, of suits, and of contracts generally, Congress may not also repeal the State laws as to the contract of marriage between the two races? Hitherto every subject embraced in the enumeration of rights contained in this bill has been considered as exclusively belonging to the States. They are matters which in each State

concern the domestic condition of its people, varying in each according to its own peculiar circumstances and the safety and well-being of its own citizens. (75)

Here, Johnson predicts a domino effect: Once federal law supersedes state law in one area it will soon overturn all state restrictions including those which prohibit intermarriage between blacks and whites. A staunch Jacksonian Democrat, Johnson had long argued that any increase of federal sovereignty directly threatened popular sovereignty and signaled the death of democratic liberty. However, in arguing this causal relation, Johnson at once suggests a metaphorical one, taking miscegenation as a surface over which to map the union of black and white freedoms. In the above passage, the intrusion of black bodies into the space of white, conjugal privacy lines up with the intrusion of federal authority into the "domestic" concerns of individual states. Just as white Southerners were being called to protect wives and daughters from the "revolting" invasion of black bodies, Johnson poses himself here as protector of the "safety and well-being" of state sovereignty. By thus conflating the threat of inter-racial marriage (rape always the implicit reference here) with the figure of an over-powerful central sovereignty, Johnson constructs miscegenation as "an offense" both generated by and synonymous with the merging of black and white political conditions.

That conflation teaches full realization as Johnson continues through his reasoning. Initially, he seems to be retracing his logic concerning how the bill would inevitably lead to the legalization of intermarriage. But at the point where his argument should arrive back at the original conclusion—back at racial intermarriage—he suddenly substitutes a new outcome: black enfranchisement.

> If it be granted that Congress can repeal all State laws discriminating between whites and blacks in the subjects covered by this bill, why, it may be asked, may not Congress repeal, in the same way, all State laws discriminating between the two races on the subjects of suffrage and office? (75)

What Johnson's argument "returns" to, in the space logically designated for miscegenation, is the black vote. Rhetorically, miscegenation and co-sovereignty come to occupy the *same* space, and Johnson again places newly freed blacks at the bedroom door of the white body politic, preparing to violate its bed.

Johnson's speech provides a telling example of how the trope of domesticity—

specifically, of besieged domesticity—operates in rhetoric against miscegenation, and of how the two function together in a variety of postbellum arguments to produce the fantasy of a discrete and untouchable white freedom. Postbellum anxiety over intermarriage referred to a belief in immutable racial identity. That is, even as the term *miscegenation* presented the very fact of racial mixing, it drew meaning and affective power from the supposition of fixed differences between absolute racial types. White supremacists like Johnson drew on this binary logic of incompatible minds, bodies and spaces in arguments against black civil rights. Miscegenation supplied an image—on one side the bestial sexuality of black men, on the other the iconic purity of the white female body in its sanctified space of middle-class domesticity—through which to reify distinct freedoms and criminalize their union. Thus domesticity, that which demands protection, became a kind of protection itself. Its iconic, sacrosanct value acted as a prophylactic against the movement of various others (most pointedly blacks, white women, and the working class) into the domains of white male freedom and power.

In what follows, I explore this iconic function of domesticity in Reconstruction discourse. In particular, I examine how representations of domesticity engage race and gender ideology to produce and mediate postbellum conceptions of freedom, specifically the mythos of free universal sovereignty. As Lora Romero argues, domestic iconography is best considered as a "[horizon] of representation on which struggles for authority played themselves out"; its political significance obtains in that struggle "rather than in some essential and ineluctable political tendency inhering within [it]" (6–7). With such arguments, recent scholarship on domesticity has outgrown the containment-subversion binary previously established by Ann Douglas and Jane Tompkins. Like Romero, Gillian Brown, and others, I approach domesticity as a public trope capable of producing a range of political meanings. At once—and without resurrecting arguments for its inherent conservatism—I am interested in what makes domestic iconography so suited to representation of and conflict about the political.[4] Part of the answer, I believe, is domesticity's mark of separation—its promise of what Romero calls "a space insulated from politics," a space that disavows contact with materiality, individuality, and individual interest (4). This conceit of transcendence allows that domesticity can stand as a corrective set of values in the way that Tompkins and Nina Baym have famously argued, but not necessarily as an opposition to—or, in Baym's words, "in competition with"—a public-political ethos (27). The gynocritical gender binarism that informed such arguments obscures the way domesticity also acts as an ideal self-reflection of the political, a site onto which Utopian meanings can be projected but, at once, deferred. Like religious iconography, domesticity marks both relation and disjuncture, hinging between the diachronic and the synchronic, the real and the ideal.[5] Thus, it represents an ideal horizon which informs the political sphere even while constantly receding from it. It provides an untouchable backdrop against which the political can figure itself and into which the political will never be absorbed.

My analysis of domestic iconography focuses on the 1868 autobiography of Elizabeth Keckley, *Behind the Scenes: Or, Thirty Years a Slave and Four Years in the White House,* and on the incident which prompted Keckley to write it—the "Old Clothes Scandal" concerning Mary Todd Lincoln. A successful entrepreneur, Keckley had risen from slavery to ownership of a thriving dressmaking business. Her friend and most famous client was Mary Todd Lincoln, and Keckley wrote her book in what she describes as an effort to save Lincoln's reputation after the ex–First Lady was discovered trying to sell her used finery. For its first sixty pages, *Behind the Scenes* reads like a conventional antebellum slave narrative, portraying physical abuse, rape, broken families and, finally, freedom. The remaining three hundred pages provide an "as-told-by" exposé of the private lives of political figures, briefly recounting Keckley's employment with Mrs. Jefferson Davis, then detailing her four years as personal seamstress to the Lincoln White House. Thus, the majority of the autobiography concerns not Keckley, but her privileged viewpoint of the most iconic of iconic domesticities: the First Lady and the first home.

Much of the criticism on *Behind the Scenes* approaches its lopsided structure as a problem, seeking to absolve Keckley of privileging Lincoln's affairs over her own, and "turning her back" on the racial divisions of Reconstruction.[6] Here I will argue that the narrative never ceases to examine what divides the black condition from the white, or to analyze how racialized divisions continue to contradict (and underwrite) democratic fantasy even after emancipation. For this, however, Keckley must adopt a new strategy in order to confront shifts in conceptions of freedom and unfreedom as these worked to promote and protect white supremacy. By turning to the White House, Keckley centers an iconic image central to the white identity of nation and national freedom—Executive domesticity—and foregrounds her own relation to it in a manner that resignifies its meaning.

As I will argue, Keckley takes domesticity, a sign for an identity and freedom that specifically exclude her, and reveals it as a symbol (in her terms, a "surface") whose meaning is always conditioned by its material production (or "origin") in herself. Her narrative thus exposes the contingency of white domesticity and of white freedom, specifying a dependence upon enslaved and free black labor that compromises their iconic function. In this way, she writes her own theory of freedom and of the intermarriage of white and black conditions that founds it. Ultimately, however, *Behind the Scenes* was Keckley's undoing. For, by explicating her relation to iconic domesticity, she offered herself up as the indispensable threat to the transcendent status which is its core value. The book was publicly denounced for "indecency" and its circulation suppressed by Robert Lincoln. Shortly thereafter, a satire appeared called *Behind the Seams: by a Nigger Woman, Who Took in Work from Mrs. Lincoln and Mrs. Davis.* Savagely racist and indignantly patriotic, the satire appropriates Keckley's revelation for a means by which to purge and rearticulate the image of white freedom. In this, her book functioned much like the specter of the black body in Johnson's speech, and illustrated the effect that is my central interest here: the manner in which domestic iconography produces political meanings specifically by disavowing its own material and historical contingency *and* the tendency of that disavowal to protect norms of racial and gendered political power.

I: "The Nation's Drawing Room"

In September of 1867, two and a half years following the assassination of her husband, Mary Todd Lincoln traveled incognito to New York City. There she attempted to sell the extensive wardrobe she had acquired (along with debt amounting to more than $70,000) during her time in the White House. She was aided by her seamstress and confidante, Elizabeth Keckley, the ex-slave who had produced much of the clothing now offered for sale. Disaster began for Lincoln when she took her ballgowns and jewels to the commission brokerage of Brady and Keyes. The brokers recognized their customer, both as the former First Lady and as a goldmine in free advertising. Following Lincoln back to her hotel, they persuaded her to have them manage the entire project. At their bidding, Lincoln wrote to various Republican politicians whom she had known during her days in the White House, asking them to buy the cast-off clothing on behalf of democracy's most beloved martyr. As Keckley would later remember: "[Brady and Keyes] argued that the Republican party would never permit it to be said that the wife of Abraham Lincoln was in want; that the leaders of the party would make heavy advances rather than have it published to the world that Mrs. Lincoln's poverty compelled her to sell her wardrobe" (290). The letter campaign failed, as did subsequent attempts to sell items at consignment shops. So Brady and Keyes followed up with two bold moves. They published Mrs. Lincoln's letters in the Democratically-inclined New York *World* (where her accusingly worded pleas would most incriminate their Republican addressees), and announced a public viewing and auction of her goods.[7]

The incident, which instantly became known as the "Old Clothes Scandal," failed to relieve Mts. Lincoln's financial straits. The crowds who thronged the showrooms came to look, not buy. Worse, the affair called intense public censure upon Lincoln. She became, in the words of one reporter, "That dreadful woman" who had "thrust" herself upon "the open market with her useless finery" (*Republican*). Or, as the Rochester *Democrat* put it,

> Her fling at the three Republicans is probably an ebullition of female spite. Her letters are coarse and vulgar. From their publication a refined woman would have shrunk with horror. . . . She says these things were the gifts of friends. We do not believe it. She has lavished the money given her by the nation on diamonds, furs, and lace.

The reporter from the *Democrat* makes a typical move in attributing Mary Todd Lincoln's transgression to gender ("female ebullition") and class ("coarse and vulgar"). He is also typical in interpreting the act in terms of embezzlement. In the opinion of the American public, "the nation" had prior claim to the "diamonds, furs, and lace" on view at Lincoln's auction. By trying to cash them in she had crossed a boundary between public and private properties. She had commandeered for personal profit that which rightfully belonged to the democratic all.

The Old Clothes Scandal was not Mary Lincoln's first difficulty over the property rights of First Ladyship. While in the White House she had been frequently accused of misappropriation and patronage, demonstrating from the outset her limited understanding of the presidential commodity. On one hand, Mary had always recognized her husband's office as a marketable asset. Even six years before the Old Clothes Scandal, she was trying to sell refuse from the White House stables at a price well over the going rate (J. Baker 190). Lincoln reasoned correctly that even "useless finery" and horse manure became value-added products once touched by the iconicity of state power. Yet she overlooked the fact that the value of the presidential commodity-icon lay specifically in its incapacity for conversion to personal property and profit.

The head of a democratic state is a commodification of national power belonging equally and fully to all citizens. By virtue of this status, the American presidency does not, *must* not, possess itself. For, in order that icons of democratic power will belong simultaneously to everyone, they must belong to no one. This mandate stems from a double-bind concerning power and democracy: on one hand, a prohibition against power taking a centralized location; on the other, a need for centralized representations that will allow democratic subjects to recognize their own sovereignty. Thus, unlike the head of state in a monarchy, in whom a body natural and body politic may co-exist, the democratic head of state must disavow its body natural.[8] As Claude Lefort argues,

> The democratic revolution . . . burst out when the body of the king was destroyed, when the body politic was decapitated. . . . [It] is best recognized in this mutation: there is no power linked to a body. Power appears as an empty place. (303)

This is the myth of democracy: that power resides with no *one* body, but with a *body politic* that understands itself as a unity, as one.

In its function of representing-and-not-possessing power the American presidency symbolizes also the ideal of democratic freedom. The balance of universal sovereignty is that ideal. Freedom is possible only so long as the amorphous entity of national power refuses to particularize or belong more with one person than another. Like any Utopian ideal, the principle of democratic political freedom requires constant acts of representation—narratives and images to make visible that "empty place" of power that is available equally to all, to none more than another. The institution of the presidency is one such "empty place"—the head of the headless state that permits democratic subjects to experience themselves as free.

These rules surrounding the presidential commodity applied very directly to Mary Todd Lincoln. Even by the time of the Old Clothes Scandal, more than two years after Abraham's death, she bore traces of the iconicity associated with the head of state: writes the Springfield *Republican,* "She will not let the people . . . only remember her as the widow of a beloved patriot but insists on thrusting her repugnant personality before the world to the great mortification of the nation." Two years out of the White House, Mary Lincoln was still coded with nationalist meanings, still barred from "personality" and individuation. For many reasons, the work of representing-without-possessing power is incumbent more upon the First Lady than the president himself. He, after all, must also act as head of government and wield power in very concrete ways. Being more remote from it, the First Lady is more eligible to stand as the "empty place" of democratic power. Then, too, she—along with her White House and her "diamonds, furs, and lace"—are the crucial, domesticizing accessories of the presidential spectacle. The First Lady, and the home life for which she metonymically stands, enable the president perfectly to resemble (without himself being of) the ordinary citizenry. In total, the domestic spectacle of the White House provides a topological referent of those Utopian values of freedom and equality invested in the head of state.

As the nation's most prominent domestic space, the White House acquired Utopian values as did other—albeit, more middle-class—homes with the spread of domestic ideology. By Mary Lincoln's time, the White House was a sort of nationalist creche scene in which the First Family performed their private lives in full view—both democratically visible and democratically accessible. Citizens walked freely in and out of its unguarded entrances, clipping souvenirs from Mary's new curtains and haunting passageways to shake Abe's hand. Soldiers and vagrants slept in the parlors. In the words of one historian, "the Lincolns promptly discovered that the Executive Mansion was as much a public building as it was a home" (Donald 55). The two functions, of course, are not incompatible but, rather, fully merged: The White House was insistently coded as a public space *because* it was a home—the home of the body politic. This was not necessarily a comfortable arrangement, and Lincoln remarked that he "sometimes felt like a hotel keeper" (54).[9] Nevertheless, it was regarded as a natural extension of democratic principles that "our elected president, living in a house that the citizens consider to be their gift and property, should be at ease with his people and give them easy access to his home" (Boorstin

8). Thus, when Mary Lincoln canceled public concerts on the White House lawn during the mourning period for Willie, public outcry against "The Illinois Reine" never ceased until the concerts resumed.[10] With such incidents, Lincoln's public reminded her of the distinction between democracy and monarchy and claimed the Executive Mansion as a living monument to equality of power, government by the people, and political freedom.

After the fact and exercise of public ownership, there was still another way that the White House signified freedom to mid-century Americans. As Daniel J. Boorstin puts it, the

> "special democratic aura" of the White House derives not just from accessibility but also "representativeness"... This distinctly American architectural metaphor... offers the nation a scene of a president and his family leading lives not dissimilar from our own. It is a prosaic prospect, but one that elevates us citizens by reminding us that our president leads a life essentially like ours. (12)

In literal terms, of course, Boorstin is mistaken. The president's life, in the 1860s and today, beats no likeness to the vast majority of American lives. The White House is nothing like most American homes. Nevertheless, in alluding to the determined banality of the First Family's image, Boorstin aptly characterizes the performance of sameness that permeates presidential domesticity. With its decades of camera-ready pets, children, and fireside poses, the Executive Mansion has never stinted on those images that dominant culture incessantly marks as universal and archetypal. Sameness, after all, is the surest guarantee of equality and thus its image is that of perfect freedom—freedom from difference, freedom from lack. It is not true that the First Family's domestic self-portrait actually resembles its constituency, any more than it is true that Americans are all, in fact, equal. Yet the White House signals the promise of equality through a set of images and meanings ideologically wired to provoke an illusion of self-recognition in a nation of consumer subjects. In that these "representative" images and meaning are highly particularized by whiteness and affluence, it begins to become apparent how the idealized commodification of political freedom serves to limit and protect that freedom.

The White House persona most responsible for dispensing iconic effects of sameness and accessibility was the nation's first domestic angel. No one else was (or is) expected to dish up quite so much banality. Nearly 150 years before Hillary Rodham Clinton's compulsory cookie bake-off with Barbara Bush, Sarah Polk was accused of alienating votes because the other candidate's wife made superior butter (Caroli 62). Like any other domestic icon, the spectacle of the First Lady did not represent or describe the actual lives of middle-class white women. Iconicity is not historicity, and the public image of domestic womanhood signified ideals—such as freedom from contact with the public world of economic intercourse—which actual lives could never realize. When Mary Lincoln displayed the First Lady's gowns at state dinners or sat at the First Lady's writing desk to sign her name on White House stationery, she, the costumes, the desk and the name stood alike as property of the Nation, a composite, commodified image of the power belonging to all democratic citizens, a representation of the free and equal—free because equal—body politic. When Lincoln tried to sell these same costumes and props for personal profit, she crossed into the market economy and exposed herself as a body natural, "repugnantly individual" in the words of the *Columbus Sun,* and a threat to democratic freedom (qtd. in J. Baker 277).[11] Mary Lincoln was slated as a commodity of the symbolic economy, not as a capitalist of the market economy. By auctioning off her public body to feed her private one, she conflated the nation's symbolic and capitalist economies, and paid heavily for it.[12]

Yet, if Lincoln wore her iconicity badly, it was perhaps already determined that she would. She was required to uphold a myth that is inherently, indispensably, precarious. As Lefort's decapitation metaphor suggests, democratic freedom is a chronically vulnerable condition of national being:

> as long as [power] presents itself as the power of no one, as long as it seems to move toward a *latent* focus—namely, the people—it runs the risk of having its symbolic function canceled out, of falling into collective representations at the level of the real, the contingent.... Similarly, those who exercise it or aspire to it are exposed to the threat of appearing as individuals or groups concerned solely to satisfy their desires. (305)

Here is the putative predicament of democracy—it must prevent power from centralizing, but in doing so it leaves power vulnerable to division and co-option. Put another way, to maintain its representational status the democratic state must incessantly produce the ideal of collective freedom as separate from and endangered by the practice of freedoms by self-interested individuals.

This democratic predicament—the instability of its symbolic economy—is not meant to be resolved. It is productive. Democracies must constantly reenact their own fragility, inventing and banishing new threats to liberty. In Lefort's words, it is essential for the body politic "to assure itself of its own identity by expelling its waste matter" (298). Finally, then, Mary Lincoln still played a central part in the production of democratic fantasies of freedom. If she failed in her role as nationalist domestic icon, another was already scripted for her as the "waste matter" that would allow the body politic to reinscribe its own freedom in fantasies of perfect homogeneity. Lincoln was easily coded as a cultural other. As one reporter put it, "She was neither a woman of great refinement nor of high intellectuality" (*Argus*). Elsewhere, she was called Abe's "kitchen cabinet"—or, by critics even less kind, "this mercenary prostitute" who "injured the name and fame of her country and husband" (J. Baker 277).[13] In her orthodox role, Lincoln would have supplied that iconic image of womanhood, working in conjunction with White House domesticity to signify white male freedom. Yet her heterodoxy provided an equally useful spectacle of class difference and feminized self-interest.

What Mary Lincoln's expulsion from iconicity demonstrates finally, is that this bod(il)y politic(al) function serves to maintain precisely that which it professes to expunge—interested power. It benefits ruling interests by coding new claims to political power as inimical to freedom. Hence the gendered and class-inflected rhetoric of Mary's expulsion. Hence, too, the public condemnation that would greet Elizabeth Keckley when she wrote her own account of the Old Clothes Scandal. Like Lincoln's auction, Keckley's autobiography could be readily deployed as an imagined menace to the icons of democratic freedom. In this sense, she both aggravated the original offense and extended its utility.

II: Elizabeth Keckley's Mulatta Body Politic

The juxtaposition of Lincoln's Old Clothes Scandal with the Johnsonian logic of apartheid freedom brings into relief two features of Reconstruction discourse that would condition Keckley's arguments in *Behind the Scenes*. As we have already seen, both the scandal and the veto speech reproduce the fantasy of political freedom by invoking an embodied threat to iconic domesticity—the feminized body natural and the hyper-embodiment of black stereotypes.

The second similarity consists in that both drew upon an ideological distinction between material and symbolic economies. Johnson knew his veto of the Civil Rights bill opposed strong majorities in both the Senate and the House (indeed, Congress later overturned the veto and passed the bill into law). In order to justify his move—and specify black freedom as distinct from white—he turned to the rhetoric of free labor and to the ideal of an autonomous market economy.

There are two classes of freedom, Johnson argues: one white, one black; one political, one nonpolitical. For blacks he defines a liberty that is wholly confined within the market economy.

> The white race and black race of the South have hitherto lived together under the relation of master and slave—capital-owning labor.... They stand now each master of itself. In this new relation, one being necessary to the other, there will be a new adjustment, which both are deeply interested in making harmonious. Each has equal power in settling the terms, and if left to the laws that regulate capital and labor, it is confidently believed that they will satisfactorily work out the problem. (CRV 78)

For blacks, Johnson stipulates, freedom is the possession of one's labor. It derives from the free dynamics of the market and the absence of government intervention such as called for by the Republican bills. Here, Johnson fights his opposition with their own rhetoric. Posed as the antithesis of slavery, free labor had been key to abolitionist arguments. Now it stood at the heart of Republican plans for economic and racial Reconstruction. Indeed, many Republicans *and* Democrats believed market capitalism would inevitably bring prosperity and equality to the nation and to the war-torn South in particular.

However, free labor discourse comprised many conflicting tendencies: It was by no means inherently egalitarian or synonymous with the cause of racial equality. It could also serve, as in Johnson's speech, to circumscribe black freedoms and civil rights. Thus, one strain of free labor discourse said blacks did not require supportive legislation: Once they possessed their own labor the market would do the rest. Another racialist free-labor argument resists even this logic—which at least assumed a telos of ascension from laborer to capitalist and the ideal of economic autonomy—by rationalizing permanent segregation of labor and capitalist.

Johnson draws on this latter thread when he asserts that the opportunity to negotiate as "equals" with white capitalists satisfies the full extent of blacks' needs and desires.[14] If he aligns white freedom with the full exercise of civil and political rights, his notion of black freedom begins and ends with ownership of labor. Indeed, in the passage, the term "laborer" replaces the term "freedman" completely, while the term "capitalist" substitutes for "white." As the speech continues, the two positions, labor and capitalist, resolve into a permanently racialized opposition and transform from functions into identities.[15] Back in his days of championing poor whites against plantation owners Johnson had once imagined democracy "as a ladder . . . up which all . . . may ascend" (FIA 177). Now, as blacks begin their climb he removes the middle rungs. He had help. Since emancipation, Southern legislatures had been busy passing special "Black Codes" designed to keep freed people in a condition that was the old slavery in everything but name.[16]

But, both in the Southern marketplace and on Capitol Hill, the distinction between capitalist and laborer was unstable at best. The promise of the free labor model had already come true for a small but influential class of black entrepreneurs, as they fought their way through the obstacles of the white economic infrastructure to acquire land and establish businesses. The market may have provided a conceptual structure for containing black freedom, but, within its practice, distinctions between labor and capital, black and white, proved fluid. Under slavery, black and white bodies had been clearly distinguished by laws that made one property of the other. Now, even despite the Black Codes, the new ambiguities of this relation were impossible to contain. With "self-right," or ownership of their own labor, blacks now threatened to move into white domains and even to gain control over white bodies—first as agents in the market economy, then as co-sovereigns in the symbolic economy.[17]

In response to the instability of postbellum, economic racial relations, racialist discourse turned back to the logics of natural and absolute racial difference to legitimate and secure political apartheid.[18] Blacks, Johnson asserts, lack the "capacity to exercise with safety the highest rights of the Anglo-Saxon" (qtd. in Trefousse 236). He places citizenship in a rarified climate unsuited to the African race: Just as fish lack wings to fly, black bodies lack the "capacity" for freedom and self-sovereignty. A Thomas Nast cartoon (figure 1) from the period echoes this claim, depicting the houses of Congress overrun with Sambo figures whose distorted bodies and faces look grotesquely out of place beside a group of distressed white politicians. Both texts deploy ethnographic and anthropological "knowledge" regarding the immutability of racial types and their hierarchical organization. Once an essential justification for slavery—as in such works as John Van Evrie's *Negroes and Negro Slavery: The First an Inferior Race: The Latter Its Normal Condition*—the "science" of embodied difference now served to legitimate and naturalize arbitrary limits, providing a much-needed buttress to the Johnsonian segregation of freedoms.

Anti-miscegenation discourse added a new and formidable twist to this line of reasoning. The "truth" of racial division could be made even more true, real, and desired through rhetoric that insistently pictured its violation in embodied terms. And that division appeared most absolute in the juxtaposition of black male and iconic white female bodies. In Nast's cartoon, the figure of Lady Liberty who brandishes her sword from the top right corner looks more like a statue than a part of this human gathering, and seems nearly as out of place as the Sambo legislators. Yet her difference places her above rather than below this place and provides the authority to bring "peace" by banishing the blacks. Likewise, the domestic angel protected white freedom through her utter difference from the hyper-embodiment of blacks. This is the tactic in Johnson's reference to intermarriage and in the question, put repeatedly to those calling for black suffrage, "would you have your daughter marry one?" In fact, the very term *miscegenation* originated with this strategy, in a pamphlet entitled *Miscegenation: The Theory of the Blending of the Races, Applied to the American White Man and Negro*. Written during the 1864 presidential campaign, the pamphlet advances a bogus argument for improving the American race through racial amalgamation. The two anti-abolitionists who anonymously wrote it intended to subvert the Republican party and emancipation agenda by pushing their logic to an "absurd" conclusion. Here again, the hyperbolic conjuncture of black and white bodies aims to present the two races as more disjunct.[19] For postbellum America, the images of miscegenation and the mulatto acted as signs for the nation's worst failures, recalling the depredations of slavery. By aligning these images with a potential future of co-sovereignty, white supremacists sent a powerful message.

In April 1868, two years after Johnson's Civil Rights Bill veto and in the wake of Mary Lincoln's Old Clothes Scandal, Elizabeth Keckley published *Behind the Scenes: Or, Thirty Years a Slave, and Four Years in the White House*. The autobiography takes as its focus those relationships that are at stake in John-

Figure 1: "Colored Rule in a Reconstructed (?) State." Harper's Weekly, 14 Mar. 1874.

son's veto and the Lincoln scandal—relationships between white and black freedoms, white middle-class domesticity and black labor, and symbolic and market economics. As I have tried to demonstrate, dominant political discourse constructed each of these relationships as an opposition between mutually exclusive terms. Keckley turns these oppositions inside out. She reveals that the white ideal of political freedom relies intimately—in both its material and symbolic effects—upon the enslaved and free labor of blacks. In Lefort's terms, Keckley insists on precisely that possibility which haunts democratic society: She exposes the proximity of private bodies to democratic power and insists upon the contingency of its Utopian aspect. In the terms of postbellum racialist discourse, Keckley asserts that white freedom is and has always been the offspring of some form of miscegenation. She performs her own ethnography of white supremacist America to expose it as a mulatta body politic.

As a black woman Elizabeth Keckley stood outside of dominant postbellum debates regarding the meaning and distribution of political freedom. She was black but not male, so the Radical Republicans overlooked her in their work for "universal" civil rights. She was female but not white, and so omitted from the campaign for "women's" suffrage.[20] Yet, as an ex-slave and member of the Great Emancipator's household, Keckley lived in close proximity to those spectacular events and images through which Americans imagined themselves as a nation dedicated to political freedom. As representations of domesticity, these images resisted her direct identification.[21] Yet, as Rafia Zafar notes, "the fact that Keckley ... and others like [her] were employees within an intimate female world gave them a peculiar entree into, and a kind of power over, white women's lives" (156). In Keckley's case, this power had not only material but also symbolic aspect. That is, the fact of her material relation became significant at the symbolic level. For, as seamstress to the First Lady, she was the origin of one of white America's foremost images of political freedom. By re-presenting the domestic icon in the material context of her own life and labor, Keckley reveals the contingencies of that icon's performance of non-contingency. She brings to light precisely that which the First Lady's icon image should suppress: the racialized conditions of its production.[22]

In her preface Keckley figures her relation to domesticity and freedom as a relation of origin to surface. She begins,

> through me and the enslaved millions of my race, one of the problems was solved that belongs to the great problem of human destiny. . . . A

solemn truth was thrown to the surface, and what is better still, it was recognized as a truth by those who give force to moral laws. (xii)

In Keckley's reckoning, it was suffering and *un*freedom like her own that finally rendered liberty "as a truth," lending identity and meaning to the concept nearly a century after the Declaration of Independence. Enslaved bodies, that is, stand as the origin of freedom's truth—a status that Keckley characterizes as a service on behalf of "human destiny." Opposed to, but supported by those bodies is the superficial "surface," a public veneer of white language, law and imagery.

Slavery is not the only context to which Keckley applies her origin surface binary. In the passage immediately following the first, she resurrects it in relation to very different circumstances. Here, the subject has changed abruptly from slavery to the Old Clothes Scandal and Keckley is explaining her reasons for writing the book:

> The people knew nothing of the secret history of [Mary Lincoln's] transactions, therefore they judged her by what was thrown to the surface.... The veil of mystery must be drawn aside; the origin of the fact must be brought to light with the naked fact itself. (xiii–xiv)

Practically speaking, this second application of the origin-surface conceit alludes to the premise that markets the autobiography: Keckley has exclusive possession of secret, authenticating information—truths that are the origin of "naked facts" regarding the First Lady and the Old Clothes Scandal.[23] At the same time, however, the second passage refers to the first. The word "surface" repeats less than a page from its first appearance—an unmistakable echo that establishes a connection between the two topics of the autobiography: slavery and the White House. Deepening this connection is Keckley's reference to the "drawn veil"—a common metaphor in slave narratives for the exposure of concealed truths.[24] Used in relation to the First Lady, the veil signals a correspondence between her "secret history" and the undisclosed crimes of slaveholders. Further, it implies a continuity between Keckley's two primary roles in the book: the enslaved body that gives meaning to the word "freedom," and the laborer who decodes the "naked facts" at the surface of the White House.

This logic of origin and surface provides the structure through which Keckley will define her position throughout the book. She is a site of origination, located somewhere "behind the scenes" and beneath a surface of meanings that stand as incomplete, vulnerable and incomprehensible without her. This claim to originality is not simply a device to establish the truth of her revelations, although certainly this is part of its effect.[25] More centrally, Keckley aims to reveal the means by which *truth* is produced, that is, the dialectic between material origin and symbolic surface which generates political truths like *freedom*. Foundationalist authority is vulnerable in this dialectical process, and her text is most revelatory and powerful where it abandons such constructions altogether.

The spectacle of the suffering black body is a common source of authority in slave narratives and, initially, Keckley draws upon it to construct her enslavement as the devastating physical reality from which white understandings of freedom originate. Chapter Two, "Girlhood and its Sorrows," portrays Keckley being summoned by a Mr. Bingham who orders her to strip naked and beats her without cause. When she resists, her assailant only becomes more determined to "curb her will." At the end of a third beating, however, he abruptly bursts into tears and vows never to beat a slave again, "declar[ing] it would be a sin." Keckley links this sudden change of heart directly to her body, explaining "as I stood bleeding before him . . . my suffering at last subdued his hard heart" (35). The following day, Keckley's master takes up where Bingham left off and beats her again. This time his wife begins to weep and begs him to desist. As he administers a fourth beating, the master himself is converted (33–38). At the center of this parable on liberty—in which arbitrary and cruel power attempts to "conquer" its victim's "rebellious" spirit—is Keckley's body. Repeatedly, freedom's negative image is enunciated by her physical state: the humiliation of standing naked before a man as "a fully developed girl of eighteen," the "anguish" of the whip upon her back, the carefully enumerated injuries that disable her for weeks to come. In each scene of injustice, Keckley's body is the vividly rendered picture of oppression. In each moment of conversion to the principles of freedom and justice, that body, "the sight of [Keckley's] bleeding form," is what teaches the truth (37).

Such scenes occur frequently in antebellum slave narratives where, like iconic images of domestic white womanhood, the enslaved black body could pose as a source of pre-political authenticity and national truth. Of course, the two modes of identification differ fundamentally. The white, feminine image of domesticity signals the promise of democratic freedom by encoding itself as disembedded from history and radically non-contingent. The rhetorical trope of the suffering black body produces a similar effect by encoding itself as *hyper*-embedded, *wholly* subject to contingency. So that, as the absolute of unfreedom, the black body presents an inverted signified of the political signifier, freedom. Keckley's origin-surface formulation of slavery—set out in her preface and illustrated in the conversions from chapter two—seems to participate in this tradition. However, she will soon leave this tradition behind.

As Mary Lincoln's case shows, the strategy of drawing authority from association with a transcendent condition of privatization came with constraints. Likewise, the trope of martyred embodiment had its limits for blacks. Houston Baker argues that the embodying conventions of the slave narrative could become a "linguistic prison" that reinscribed identification of blacks with enslavement and lack (256). This was particularly so for women, whose enslavement was made to speak for unfreedoms other than their own in the rhetoric of white female abolitionist- suffragists. As Karen Sánchez-Eppler shows, the figure of the slave woman provided the "perfect conduit for the largely unarticulated and unacknowledged failure of the free woman to own her own body in marriage" (23).[26] By 1868, many black writers already recognized these dangers. In *My Bondage and My Freedom,* Frederick Douglass de-emphasizes the physical suffering which features in his first autobiography—a process that Ben Slote describes as "revising toward disembodiment" (20). Always a shrewd manipulator of democratic codes, Douglass exchanges the rhetoric of privatized embodiment for that of public disembodiment. The iconicity of the privatized voice could be a deadend both for the white woman who identified as domestic angel and the black men and women who invoked corporeal authority.

By itself, then, Keckley's appointment of an embodied signified of freedom would seem an impotent or, worse, self-defeating maneuver. If Chapter Two concluded Keckley's theorization of the relationship between bodies and surface, *Behind the Scenes* would do little to revise pre-emancipation racial constructs or to disrupt the new strategies of postbellum racialist discourse. Keckley avoids both traps. Even as her preface sets out her initial interpretation of slavery and freedom—"a truth was thrown to the surface"—she adds to it this crucial observation:

> ...what is better still, it was recognized *as a truth* by those who give force to moral laws. An act may be wrong, but unless the ruling power recog-

nizes the wrong, it is useless to hope for a correction of it. Principles may be right, but they are not established within an hour . . . each principle, to acquire moral force, must come to us from the fire of the crucible . . . it purifies and renders stronger the principle, not in itself, but in the eyes of those who arrogate judgment to themselves. (xii)

This qualification is an early hint that Keckley's origin-surface device will work toward more than the appropriation of authority to her own person. Although she anchors the principle of freedom in embodied experience, she acknowledges too that meaning is always contingent, always subject to power. Meaning, she suggests, resides in neither the origin nor the surface, but in the historical contexts and power dynamics that mediate their relation.

Keckley illustrates this more dialectical view of the relations among meaning-making, black bodies, and "ruling powers" with a later episode. Now recounting her life with the Lincolns, Keckley describes watching a spelling lesson between Mary and Tad. Tad, whose "book knowledge was very limited," is relying on the pictures and cannot be convinced by his mother or Keckley that *a-p-e* does not spell "monkey." He defends his position at length.

"An Ape! 'taint an ape. Don't I know a monkey when I see it?"

"No, if you say that is a monkey."

"I do know a monkey. I've seen lots of them in the street with the organs. I know a monkey better than you do, 'cause I always go out into the street to see them when they come by, and you don't."

"But, Tad, listen to me. An ape is a species of the monkey. It looks like a monkey, but it is not a monkey."

"It shouldn't look like a monkey, then." (217–18)

Keckley's recollection offers a pointed satire of white "knowledge" as a kind of childish and tyrannical ignorance—specifying ethnography and anthropology, where the identities of both apes and Africans were objectified and, frequently, conflated. Yet Keckley also signals a deep appreciation of the power that white knowledge production wields—specifically, power over herself. At the conclusion of the scene she adds wryly, "Whenever I think of this incident I am tempted to laugh; and then it occurs to me that had Tad been a negro boy, not the son of a President . . . he would have been called thick-skulled, and would have been held up as an example of the inferiority of [the] race" (219).

Keckley's afterthought marks the graver implications of Tad's reading lesson. The surface of white signification may be arbitrary and even ludicrous. Yet that surface—as produced by Tad, Andrew Johnson, racialist "science," and the mob who spat the epithet "Black ape Republican" at Abraham Lincoln as he arrived in Washington in 1860—conditions the national identity of her racialized person, right down to the thickness of her skull and the character of her freedom.

The power of white signification will not be dispatched by parody, moral condemnation, or any easy opposition between black authenticity and white inauthenticity. The privatizing trope of originary martyrdom does not afford an identity that transcends its culture; nor does it remove black bodies from subjection to the surface. In this scene, where the domestic setting merges with the ethnographer's study, Tad's assertion of meaning-making prerogative resonates within the changing nationalist context of knowledge production, where racialized bodies provide a ground upon which white supremacy signifies itself with ever-increasing emphasis and violence. Whether by choice or not, Keckley must operate in this context. To do so most effectively, she leaves behind the originary status of her once-enslaved body for that of her labor.[27]

Like Frederick Douglass, Keckley switches genres at the point where the rhetorical display of the martyred black body reaches its political limit. She drops the narrative conventions of the slave narrative and launches into as-told-by exposé with the Lincolns as her focus. This switch enables Keckley to exchange one identity for another among those available to her on the surface of white meanings. She continues to invoke the origin-surface binary and to associate herself with its first term by way of the body. But, by revising her narrative tactic, she encodes that body with new meanings. The second part of *Behind the Scenes* constructs Keckley as what William Andrews calls a "superlaborer" ("Changing" 227). It details the growth of her business, lists V.I.P. customers, and quotes their praises. Always, it emphasizes her independence. Drawing on free labor ideology (choosing a different strain than that which underwrites Johnson's apartheid logic), Keckley makes a great point of having bought her own freedom according to the terms of white contract law and market principles, providing a long list of sacrifices, transactions, and sums. With compulsive adherence to white legal categories, she establishes self-possession and effects a transformation of her body's meaning from one set of white codes to another, from commodity to economic agent.[28] It is important to note that this move up the ladder of free labor remains within a relative frame of discourse that Keckley does not control. Like the category of *martyr*, the category of *agent* can be appropriated and redeployed. Indeed, in the parody, *Behind the Seams*, black economic agency becomes just another commodity whose exchange produces white supremacist meanings. Yet, within the context of Keckley's autobiography, the new status is integral to resignifying the dominant construction of freedom.

The chief advantage of Keckley's genre shift from martyred body to laboring body is that it underscores her relation to Mary Todd Lincoln. From this point on, the First Lady becomes the focus of Keckley's investigation into the phenomenology of white freedom. This focus puts Keckley at a double-remove from the antebellum slave narrative which always posits, in one form or another, a foundationalist concept of freedom. In the spiritual autobiographies that preceded abolitionist texts, freedom occurs with receiving "the word" of God.[29] Later, abolitionist lecturers like the Grimkés draw on evangelical rhetoric to claim a freedom that resides in the equivalency of souls. Still other writers appropriate a transcendent freedom from the Utopian principles of democracy. Always, freedom is rooted in some authority located outside the domain of white culture. When Harriet Jacobs and Frederick Douglass bitterly recount the failures of freedom in Northern society, they point to a place beyond it. For Jacobs this is the metaphorical and material horizon of *home*; for Douglass it is the Utopian potential of universal suffrage and Constitutional principles. Keckley's gaze falls somewhere short of *beyond*. It focuses squarely on that surface of democratic fantasy controlled by white culture, and finds the indeterminate and contingent identity of freedom at the very center of white political symbolics. In sweeping and elegiac terms, Keckley describes the disappointments of Reconstruction for all freedmen and freedwomen; and she locates their source in Washington, DC:

> They came with a great hope in their hearts, and with all their worldly goods on their backs. Fresh from the bonds of slavery, fresh from the benighted regions of the plantation, they came to the Capital looking for liberty, and many of them not knowing it when they found it. (111)

In this passage and others like it, Keckley marks freedom as an empty promise around which real lives take disappointing shapes. Increasingly this emptiness converges with the "empty place" represented by Mary Todd Lincoln and the whole of the presidential spectacle.[30]

A number of critics have pointed out that as Keckley settles her gaze on Lincoln and the White House she appears increasingly distanced from other blacks and increasingly complicit with white meanings (e.g., Domina 142). Indeed, she seems not to include herself in the "they" of the above passage. Yet this complicity is consistently and wonderfully double-voiced. For, precisely where Keckley appears to espouse the master's logic, she exposes its contradictions and evils. In one such instance she describes meeting an "old freedwoman" who was unsatisfied with the terms of emancipation:

> "Why, Missus Keckley," said she to me one day, "I is been here eight months, and Missus Lingom [Lincoln] an't even give me one shife. Bliss God, children, if I had ar know dat de Government, and Mister and Missus Government, was going to do dat ar way, I neber would'ave corned here in God's wurld. My old missus us't gib me two shifes eber year." (141)

The ostensible purpose of this anecdote is to point up the other woman's mistaken view of democratic liberty and distance herself from it. "I could not restrain a laugh at the grave manner in which this good old woman entered her protest," recalls Keckley. "Her idea of freedom was two or more old shifts every year." Her remark echoes eerily with contemporaneous critiques of the Freedman's Bureau Program—a network of offices set up to support and advocate on behalf of freedpeople in the South. Speaking against a bill that would expand the bureaus' powers and jurisdiction, Andrew Johnson argued thus: "Pending the way many refugees and freedmen received support from the Government, but it was never intended that they should henceforth be fed, clothed, educated, and sheltered by the United States" (FBV 70). Here, as always, Johnson's first concern is increased federal power, and the threat posed to the Utopian freedom of universal sovereignty by federal intervention into the widespread poverty and homelessness suffered by newly emancipated blacks. By holding up the woman's mistake as ludicrous (in part by rendering it in minstrel-style dialect), Keckley seems to affirm Johnson's condemnations of a Republican welfare state and reinscribe an impassable barrier between the old freedwoman's desires and the commodity of iconic white freedom.

Yet this juxtaposition of official and unofficial ideas on freedom produces certain additional effects. As Keckley recounts the old woman's theory, the identity of the presidency begins to waver:

> She thought, as many others thought, that Mr. and Mrs. Lincoln were the government, and that the President and his wife had nothing to do but to supply the extravagant wants of every one that applied to them. The old woman had been in the habit of receiving annually two shifts from her mistress, and she thought the wife of the President of the United States very mean for overlooking this established custom of the plantation. (141)

At one moment, the First Family is the Utopian symbol of universal power and freedom, disavowing private power, uncompromised by material relation to the welfare of individuals. At the next, resignified through the eyes of the old woman, the White House becomes the Big House, and the First Family negligent masters.

The scene recalls a similar moment in *Incidents*, where a "poor, ignorant woman" comes to Jacobs, begging for confirmation that the "queen of 'Merica" had forced the president to free the slaves. Jacobs explains:

> She said her husband told her that the black people had sent word to the queen of 'Merica that they were all slaves; that she didn't believe it, and went to Washington city to see the president about it. They quarreled; she drew her sword upon him, and swore that he should help her to make them all free. (45)

Lauren Berlant points out that such moments demonstrate "how the slaves misrecognized, in potentially and sometimes strategically radical ways, what constitutes the nation" (Queen 225). Like Jacobs, Keckley injects radical indeterminacy into the presidential icon by reading it through the gaze of black political unfreedom. She builds on this indeterminacy when she adds: "[the woman] thought, as many others thought, that Mr. and Mrs. Lincoln were the government." The comment raises some uneasy questions. For if Mr. and Mrs. Lincoln are not the government, what are they? There is one obvious answer to this question. The democratic ideal of political freedom requires that Mr. and Mrs. Lincoln are not, as private persons, the government, and that the nation should not operate as a plantation, profiting neither a Big House nor a White House. Such an arrangement, thus translated from the market to the symbolic economy, would constitute monarchy. Although the market economy is imagined as an idealized force of democratization within free labor ideology, it loses its Utopian value and becomes coded as antidemocratic upon contact with political transactions. The old woman's mistake forces this contact. It strips the Lincolns of what Berlant refers to as the "fantasy norms of democratic abstraction" and embodies them as private persons. As Berlant argues, Jacobs's president is embodied by a "cold tip of steel" against his throat that "educates him about his own body's boundaries" (226). Keckley's First Family acquires their embodiment by virtue of the "shifes" that she places in their hands to transport them back from the symbolic into the market economy.

Yet, for all the similarities it reveals, this comparison of Jacobs and Keckley points again to the basic difference in antebellum and postbellum strategies. By invoking the "queen of 'Merica," and later the "Queen of Justice," Jacobs points to an external source of freedom much like the Utopian aspect of home that represents freedom for her elsewhere. Her two queens constitute outside authorities to whom the president can be imagined as subordinate and who could force him to free the slaves. True, this imagined possibility is undermined in *Incidents*; as Berlant points out, Jacobs introduces the queens only to bracket and even ironize their potential power (226). Yet it is the transcendent authority *of* this possibility that informs the misrecognition of the presidency in her text. In contrast, Keckley exposes the presidency on its own terms. It is not so much misrecognized as recognized more fully, when the juxtaposition of white and black meaning-making reveals the interdependence of symbolic and market economies. Here is Keckley's strategy of "complicity." This instance, where presidential power is focused by the black gaze, emblematizes the function of her text, her authorship, her deployment of the white image. Even as she affirms that the Lincolns do not act as embodied private persons who dispense material commodities such as shifts or federal funds, Keckley proceeds to establish that, as symbolic persons who inhabit a surface of iconic meanings, they are national commodities that circulate in the symbolic marketing of freedom. And she is the labor that produces them.

In her role as laborer, Keckley can stage a return to the iconic authority of domesticity, portraying her central position as seamstress and servant in the nation's First Home. For iconic domesticity is precisely that commodity which her labor produces in the presidential spectacles of private life and white womanhood. Through Keckley's eyes, we learn about the celebrated

1862 state dinner—not from the formal public dining room, but from the parlor where husband and wife negotiate arrangements. We worry with the couple, again, at Willie's sickbed as ambassadors assemble downstairs. We review the various merits of cabinet members through the medium of household gossip. Most important, we come at every historical event through the focal point of what Mary wears: what fabrics make up the skirt, what types of trim are used, how many tucks go in the bodice, and so on. These scenes of "average" home life make up the nationalist spectacle signifying the "universal" freedoms of whites. Keckley makes them her privileged domain—a "surface" meaningful only when explained through her eyes. She is the marginal but indispensable figure, an interlocutor like Raphael's angel, pointing at them but looking out at us.

Significantly, Keckley installs herself just beneath this surface instead of within it, resisting identification with that domesticity, or with the freedom it represents. Mary Lincoln's identification with both afforded her little freedom or power in the market or symbolic economies. Hence, in *Behind the Scenes*, Keckley capitalizes on her relationship to Lincoln to exploit the value of iconic domesticity despite racial bars to her direct identification with it and protected from the disempowerment that such identification could mean.[31] More than she seeks to signify her own identity through relation to domesticity, she sets out to resignify the identity of domesticity by explicating its relation to her. By extension, she will reveal the racialist, material basis of white freedom and portend the full significance of black economic freedom.

It is her labor as a seamstress, after all, that places Keckley in the political households of Jefferson Davis and Lincoln. As she portrays that labor, it is a constant element in the politics—sums, hours, office space, clientele, and, of course, products all connect in some way to the political history of her time. Like a nineteenth-century Forrest Gump, Keckley pops up behind some of the most significant political scenes of her time—needle always in hand. She listens to Abraham Lincoln review war strategy as she sews in Mary's sitting room, and overhears him pondering state affairs as she passes an open door, arms full of silk. Predicting victory for the North, she leaves the Davis family employ when they go South to Richmond (71–73). When questioned anxiously on whether Lincoln will be re-elected, Keckley "look[s] up from her work" to assure Mary that he will (148–49). She foresees the assassination two days before it occurs (178). Persistently, she figures her own free labor as fully a part of political life, her material production as deeply engaged with the symbolic economy.

Most important, as seamstress to the Davis and Lincoln families, Keckley is more than a uniquely qualified witness and translator of political spectacle. She is its creator, and as such claims intimate relation to the images she interprets. A prominent focus of the public outcry against Mary Todd Lincoln was objects—the dresses she tried to sell, the sixty large crates which she packed and took from the White House, a night stand Abraham Lincoln had particularly liked and which was taken to Chicago for Tad's use. The public was obsessively interested in these goods, reading article after article for their descriptions and cost. These objects were the props of Mrs. Lincoln's iconic status. Hinging between her symbolic function and her private personhood, her iconic privatized body and her private self-interest, they became the natural focus of her guilt. At the heart of the public's obsession lay the question of possession: Did these goods, and the power they symbolized, belong to Mrs. Lincoln or to the people? How could they belong to both at once? To the reporter from the Rochester *Democrat* quoted earlier, the answer was clear: "She says these things were the gifts of friends. We do not believe it. She has lavished the money given her by the nation on diamonds, furs, and lace."

Keckley intervenes at exactly the crucial point, then, when she meticulously describes her role in creating and caring for the First Family's clothing and home.[32] As seamstress to the Davis and Lincoln households, she is quite literally the "origin" of the images "thrown to the surface" of America's political consciousness. She tells, for instance, of stitching a robe for Jefferson Davis as he plans to wage war for the Confederacy (67–69). "This very robe," she muses, "must have sometimes been on his back as he issued directions to the Confederate army" (67–69). It is an impressive fantasy. For, at least in her own imagination, Keckley is now not merely standing behind the scenes but costuming and staging that spectacular redemption of freedom—the Civil War. The full import of this reverie only comes to light, however, when we discover that it is more than personal. Visiting a charity fair in Chicago, Keckley comes upon a waxen diorama of Jefferson Davis's surrender. Adorning his figure is another of her productions—a chintz wrapper sewn for his wife. The story of "old Jeff's" capture in female disguise was, by then, a favorite national joke, widely reported in songs and cartoons like the one shown here (Fig. 2). Keckley re-creates that joke, along with its public audience, then adds herself.

Figure 2: Harper's Weekly, *27 May 1865. With familiar logic, Davis's presumption to political power (C.S. stands for "Confederate States") is discredited simultaneously by the distance between "her" image and his own, and by the absurdity of their forced conjunction.*

When it was announced that I recognized the dress as one that I had made for the wife of the late Confederate President there was great cheering and excitement, and I at once became an object of the deepest curiosity. Great crowds followed me, and in order to escape from the embarrassing situation I left the building. (75)

As the image of Davis's humiliation is supplanted by the dressmaker who produced it, certain "naked facts" are "brought to light" as Keckley's preface has promised they would be. In part, the scene reiterates the book's basic materialist lesson: The public searches for the iconic image of its own freedom—in the "empty place" of the presidency, or in the humiliation of slavery's defender—and discovers the origin of that surface in the laboring black woman. The story forces the reader's gaze to *recognize* a new truth in this spectacle of the miscegenist material relations that create power and freedom. More, the scene suggests that within these material relations, Keckley has climbed up another rung of the free labor ladder to gain the status of capitalist. Both as seamstress and authoress, she creates and circulates the commodities which make up the symbolic economy. In addition to generating material profits, her products generate and regulate imaginary democratic communities.

The effect gains momentum. Increasingly, the state is replaced by its metonymic representation, that is, by the spectacular images created and controlled by Keckley. This effect culminates in the seamstress's request that she be permitted to keep the glove worn by President Lincoln during his second inauguration. "I shall cherish it," she explains, "as a precious memento of... the man who has lifted [my race] out of bondage. I shall keep the glove, and hand it down to posterity" (154). Here the glove is identified as a signifier of the state and of the state's protection of freedoms in liberal democracy. Keckley says she takes the glove as memento of "the man" but, even as she speaks, the signifier "glove" floats free from its relation to the man. To the democratic subject, the state resides in the glove—the spectacle—not in the man. The glove, furthermore, will remain when the man is gone. And its continuing power to signify "freedom" will draw from relation to Keckley rather than Lincoln. The hand inside the glove, the hand of *manu*mission, extends not from the white man, but from the black woman whose laboring and once enslaved body radically conditions its claim to ideality.[33]

III. Coda

If Keckley embraces the white surface of semantics and law that threatens to disempower her, she does so in order to explicate its dependence upon herself. She reveals that even as her freedom is a function of white laws and letters, the iconic images of white freedom are equally functions of her labor. However, while Keckley's shift from slavery to the White House allows her to reveal more effectively the dialectical nature of white freedom, it does not remove her from that dialectical process. Within a year, her own narrative and narrative strategy were appropriated and used against her in an 1869 parody by D. Ottolengul, *Behind the Seams: by a Nigger Woman Who Took in Work from Mrs. Lincoln and Mrs. Davis*. Ottolengul's narrator ("Betsy Kickley, a Nigger") commences by pronouncing herself an imposter: "I made up my mind that if I could find a publisher who would engineer my book, I'd try the thing on as I used to do with Mrs. Lincoln's dresses" (5). The declaration discredits Keckley as a narrator and interpreter of the political events described in her autobiography. Her assumption of authorship, Ottolengul implies, was a presumption of power and identity not her own. At the same time, "Kickley's" statement explicates and literalizes the way in which Keckley's text does reveal her presence within the presidential dress. In this version, however, Keckley's structural relation to that surface is rewritten as invasion and theft.

As the parody proceeds, Keckley herself becomes the surface and Ottolengul her origination as he "tries on" her voice in a kind of black face performance. Often the point is to ridicule, as when Ottolengul rescripts her life for Vaudeville—"Mr. Bangley's" assault, for instance, is referred to as a "matinee performance" followed by the next man's "debut . . . with a broom handle" (8). Yet a surprising amount of the parody simply summarizes the source with few changes, as though Ottolengul's chief aim is simply to occupy Keckley's voice, reversing her self-portrayal as the agent who directs the spectacle of white power. Even where Ottolengul merely retells, there is a crucial glimpse of him converting her black agency into a commodity controlled and circulated in his text.[34] A crucial gap opens between the white and black bodies, the integrity and autonomy of the former reconfirmed as the latter is distorted, distanced, and, finally, expelled.

Eric Lott suggests that the antebellum minstrel show promoted a sense of equality and socio-political alliance among whites of different classes. By providing a common enemy-other, the minstrel created a "white egalitarianism that, for all its real instabilities, buried class tensions and permitted class alliances along rigidifying racial lines, a vital need in this period of seeming disintegration" (138). Thirty years later, Ottolengul's Reconstruction minstrelsy performs the same function through "Kickley." "Mr. Lincoln was truly, a great and good man," she/he confesses, "and I almost feel ashamed of myself when I think of what I have still before me to write in this book, in relation to his widow" (14). Like the "domestic affairs" of state governments which require Johnson's protection, the domestic icon of "Lincoln's widow" is restored and cleansed by the presentation of Keckley's invading authorship. Indeed, Mary's own misappropriation of the domestic iconicity gets displaced onto "Kickley's" useful image when she confesses: "when Mrs. Lincoln left the White House, a great deal of furniture was missing—she did not take it, however—it was stolen by the niggers" (16). In her own text, Keckley had portrayed the dialectical production of truths, portraying the way in which "recognition" by "those in power" conditions all meanings. Now that reflection seems a kind of prescience, as those very words are resignified within the white-controlled public sphere. The dialectic between origin and surface takes its next turn, and Ottolengul reasserts the sanctity of domesticity and freedom on the white surface of meanings.

What, then, came of Keckley's involvement in these two economies—

market and symbolic? The material surplus of her labor disappeared when the scandal drove away her clientele. She died, tragically, in the Home for Destitute Colored Women and Children that she herself had helped to found. What does remain, however, is the text's deep reading of iconic domesticity: Keckley's exposure of how the intercourse of black and white identities engenders a mulatta body politic. The surplus effects of this image become apparent when Keckley literalizes her metaphor in the figure of her own mixed-race son. Musing upon the uncanniness of enslavement when viewed through the lens of George's mulatto racial identity, she writes,

> The Anglo-Saxon blood as well as the African flowed in his veins; the two currents commingled—one singing of freedom, the other silent and sullen with generations of despair. Why should not the Anglo-Saxon triumph—why should it be weighed down with the rich blood typical of the tropics? Must the life-current of one race bind the other race in chains as strong and enduring as if there had been no Anglo-Saxon taint? (47)

Keckley here echoes the Johnsonian fear of miscegenation—that "revolting... offense against public decorum"—and his fear that the political equality of blacks will imprison whites (CRV 75). Initially, her blood analysis appears to confirm a Johnsonian view of race relations wherein the Anglo-Saxon body is "weighed down" by its African blood.[35] Yet Keckley's comments send a sharply ironic response to such racialist logic. For here the fear of the enthralled (non)white body is projected, *not* onto the offspring of intermarriage, but onto a child produced and enslaved by the sexual, economic, and political violence of whites. This is a body imprisoned by Anglo-Saxon volition, by the rape of black women rather than the violation of white domesticity. Keckley thus mocks anti-miscegenation fears by articulating them in the context of her son's body. More, with her concluding images of a "race in chains" and an Anglo-Saxon "taint," Keckley displaces the putative decline of white racial purity with the history of black enslavement and re-assigns racialist terminology to white blood. Before our eyes, the Anglo-Saxon trades places with the African, the voice singing of freedom changes from white to black, and the identity of the racial prisoner becomes radically indeterminate. The consequence is another instance of misrecognition, recalling the old freedwoman who (mis)recognized the Lincolns for a plantation master and mistress. Now, however, it is the reader's gaze that misrecognizes, and the white supremacist theory of a freedom founded on the unfreedom of blacks that proves false.

NOTES

I would like to thank Bruce Burgett, Carole Chabries, Nellie McKay, and Cristine Varholy for their generous and invaluable input on earlier drafts of this essay.

1. See Horton 264–306 for analysis of Kent's *Commentaries on American Law* and its impact on midcentury political and legal thought, especially regarding race relations.

2. Trefousse describes Johnson's rage upon learning, while in Washington, that black troops have been lodged in his Nashville home. Immediately sexualizing this contact between white domesticity and black bodies, Johnson assumed his home was being run as a brothel (225). See Foner (*Short History* 84) and Cox (109) for more on Johnson's particular horror of miscegenation.

3. For full accounts and analyses of Johnson's differences with Congress over Reconstruction see Trefousse, Du Bois and Foner, *Short History*. On the effect of the Civil Rights bill veto upon these differences see Cox. For more on debates about the meaning of freedom in the period between the Thirteenth and Fourteenth Amendments, see Du Bois, Foner, McGlynn and Drescher, and Saville.

4. Wexler points out that the Tompkins-Baym/Douglas debate itself represents and replicates the way domesticity actually functioned in nineteenth-century discourse as a place to work out larger political stances. See Wexler and Romero for excellent reviews of the changing critical discourse on domesticity. For arguments concerning the political iconicity of nineteenth-century domesticity, see Barnes, Brown, Carby, DuCille, Romero, Smith, and Wexler.

5. A particularly good discussion of this point can be found in Berlant's treatment of the Statue of Liberty in *The Anatomy of National Fantasy* (19–34).

6. Foster and Andrews ("Changing") both describe Keckley as typical of postbellum black writers who de-emphasize slavery and postbellum racial injustice in order to appeal to a white audience weary of conflict. Elsewhere, Keckley's focus on Mary Lincoln has been interpreted as a strategy of "veiled" criticism or "black narrative undertell" (Zafar 175), a "false civility" (Young 139), a displaced mourning for the traumas and losses of slavery (Fleischner), and an attempt to unmark herself so as to pose as a neutral, disembodied subject eligible to dissolve into the body politic (Domina). Also concerning the surprising lack of self in this self-narrative, Olney has questioned its designation as autobiography, arguing it must be considered memoir since it does not sustain focus on its speaker's development (xxxiii).

7. For more detailed accounts of the scandal see J. Baker, Morrow, and Randall.

8. See Kantorowicz.

9. Other presidents shared Lincoln's sentiment. Andrew Jackson was compelled to

escape his presidential home by way of a window to escape being crushed during his inauguration celebration. Harry Truman looked back on his term in office saying, "It seems like there was always somebody for supper" (Boorstin 10).

10. Lincoln was often accused of modeling herself after Empress Eugénie Napoleon—the very image of feminized usurpation of power (see "The Truth"). This was not always a pejorative comparison, however, and Lincoln could also be praised for "giving life and character to the White House, as the 'rosy Empress' who won all hearts by her queenly manners" (*The Statesman*).

11. Strangely enough, the Lincolns and their property recently appeared again at the center of this problem of self-interest and political iconography. In "renting out" the Lincoln Bedroom to potential campaign contributors in 1996, President Clinton was perceived to use the nation's property as capital for his own political investments.

12. Mary Lincoln remained in the news for years as an object of ridicule and censure. The publicity probably influenced Congress's failure to authorize an adequate pension for her. She lived on very little money and grew increasingly preoccupied with her own financial debts and with the nation's symbolic debt to her. Neat the end of Lincoln's life she was subjected by her son Robert to an insanity trial and briefly committed to an asylum.

13. Patronage—the use of political appointments as personal and political favors—was openly practiced during both Lincoln's and Johnson's administrations when first the war and then Reconstruction left open a plethora of political offices and drew an "unprecedented" number of patronage seekers (Searle 364). When the president openly practiced patronage and indulged a constant stream of supplicants, he was praised for democratic accessibility. Meanwhile, the same newspapers repeatedly accused Mary of asking and bestowing political favors to promote her own interests. Thus, the anti-democratic aspects of patronage took form in her "womanly desires" and "powers of persuasion." During Johnson's administration similar criticisms of Mary Lincoln focused on the Old Clothes Scandal and the incriminating series of letters to the Republican politicians which asked for favors and hinted at past political debts to herself.

14. Throughout the Civil Rights and Freedman's Bureau vetoes, Johnson repeatedly reminds Congress of the great need for labor on Southern plantations, assuring, "there is no danger that the exceedingly great demand for labor will not operate in favor of the laborer" (FBV 71).

15. Foner argues that economic autonomy was still the prevailing ideal of democratic identity, so that, well into the period when free labor rhetoric was widespread, free labor was still often opposed to autonomy and land ownership as a form of dependency and servility. The two reconcile to some extent with the notion that free labor is not a permanent status but a means of climbing *to* economic independence (*Free Soil*).

16. For instance, it was generally true, as Johnson points out, that the ex-slave possessed "a perfect right to change his place of abode ... if ... he [did] not find in one community or State a mode of life suited to his desires, or proper remuneration for his labor." However, this right was all but negated by the common practice of paying workers only once a year. In this situation, a worker could not simply "move to ... where [their] labor [was] more esteemed and better rewarded" as Johnson suggests (Johnson 70–71). In fact, some states required freedmen to accept work from previous owners before accepting another offer. In a nation that defined freedom as contractual obligation by will rather than subjection, many blacks found themselves, working for the very whites they had previously addressed as master (and were often beaten for refusing to continue this form of address) (Stanley 5). For more on the white supremacist agenda in free labor discourse, see Foner (*Free Soil*) and Stanley. See Du Bois, Foner (*Short History*), and Genovese for more on the Black Codes.

17. Indeed, Johnson foresaw the need to prevent blacks from evolving to match his status: "while we ought to do our best to bring them ... up to our present level ... in doing so, we should, at the same time raise our own intellectual status so that the relative position of the two races would be the same" (qtd. in Trefousse 236).

18. For more on ethnographic theories of race see Frederickson, Jacobson, and Wiegman. See Keetley for a discussion of their impact upon slave narratives.

19. See Kaplan for a full summary of the pamphlet and discussion of reactions. See Bardaglio and Pascoe for accounts of how the postbellum embodiment of racial politics took form in new and newly enforced laws against interracial marriage. See Hodes for analysis of anti-miscegenist rhetoric in protests against black suffrage.

20. The Radical Republicans dumped women's political rights from their platform as they turned their efforts from abolition to black male suffrage. As for the rights of black women in specific, speakers like William Lloyd Garrison listed "mastery over a wife" among the rights owed to black men. Following their abandonment by the Republicans, the white organizers of the female suffragist movement debated whether to include black women in their interest group. Elizabeth Cady Stanton, among others, offered increasingly racist rationales for a white-only women's movement. For more on the racial politics of the women's suffrage movement, see Du Bois, Ginzberg, Sánchez-Eppler, and Stanley. For general analyses of the "neither one nor the other" status of black women in representational politics, see Hull, Scott, and Smith; and Collins. For an alternate analysis of its relevance to Keckley, see Young 109–11.

21. In the South, black women who left the fields to care for children and home after emancipation were criticized for "acting the lady" (Foner, *Short History* 38). Here again, domesticity marked the difference between freedom and slavery and, in conjunction with what Wexler calls "the imperial project of sentimentalism," organized working class and black subjects within white supremacist consciousness as an economic complement and ideological foil (75). Sánchez-Eppler points out that even a text like *Uncle Tom's Cabin*, which claims domesticity as a site for Utopian politics

and freedom, still constructs that domesticity and that freedom as "predicated upon the absence of black bodies: Tom's 'victory' wins him the freedom of heaven; George, Eliza, and the rest find their only in Liberia" (48). For one of the earliest and best discussions of how portrayals of black women in domestic fiction serve to reinforce image of white domestic virtues, see Carby.

22. Sánchez-Eppler makes an argument along similar lines concerning the relation between black bodies and domesticity in Harriet Jacobs's *Incidents in the Life of a Slave Girl*. She writes, "[Jacobs] locates freedom in feminized spaces; but while she haunts these houses, she cannot occupy them. In her effort to escape, her body literally lines the floors and ceilings of houses, just as in servitude her body and its labor sustains the Southern home.... Slavery can create the private, domestic realm precisely because the slave has no privacy and no claim on domestic space or domestic utterance" (87–88).

23. The book was also published under the alternative titles White House Revelations or Behind the Scenes and Behind the Scenes, the Great Sensational Disclosures, by Mrs. Keckley (Washington 231–34).

24. For more on the veil image in slave narratives, see Taylor, Stepto, and Zafar. For more on the significance of the veil image in Keckley, see Young and Zafar.

25. See Foster and Young for arguments that emphasize this strategy of self-authorization.

26. See Stanley for more on representations of enslaved black women in abolitionist rhetoric (25–28). For more on the "imprisoning" rhetoric of embodiment, see Moses and Sundquist.

27. Berthold points out that the disappearance of Keckley's body can also be taken as a "form of protection" in that it removes her from narratives portraying the excessive or contaminated sexuality of black women (112). For more on the constraints of embodiment in the slave narrative genre, see H. Baker, Moses, and Keetley.

28. This adherence seems at times to reach the point of excess. For instance, when instructed by her "master" to escape across the river, Keckley delivers what Andrews describes as a pledge of "her unswerving fealty to the ethics of the marketplace" ("Changing" 233): "'No, master, I do not wish to be free in such a manner.... I can cross the river any day, as you well know, and have frequently done so, but will never leave you in such a manner. By the laws of the land I am your slave—you are my master, and I will only be free by such means as the laws of the country provide'" (48–49).

This seems strangely pious endorsement of the legal contracts by which whites defined black freedom. It could not differ more from the sentiments expressed on the same issue in Harriet Jacobs's *Incidents in the Life of a Slave Girl,* where Linda Brent declares "the more my mind had become enlightened, the more difficult it was for me to consider myself an article of property; and to pay money to those who had so grievously oppressed me seemed like taking from my sufferings the glory of triumph" (511). For Keckley, writing in the postbellum context, the aim is not to preserve her suffering in a transcendent state of glory and triumph, but to parlay it into a more advantageous positionality within the contingencies of market capitalism.

I should add that, elsewhere in the autobiography, Jacobs is more equivocal about the ethics and legalities of the market. For instance, she echoes free labor ideologues like Frederick Douglass when she tells the story of the white slaveholder who stole three hundred dollars from her grandmother. Remarking bitterly, "a slave, *being* property can *hold* no property," Jacobs here deplores the fact that slaves lack agency in the market economy more than she condemns the general principles of that market (6).

29. See Andrews Introduction.

30. This theme bears out in personal contexts as well, such as her marriage to "Mr. Keckley," where her disappointments and his dissipation are emblematized in the fact that he has claimed to be free but turns out to be enslaved (50).

31. Here again, comparison between *Behind the Scenes* and *Incidents* points to basic differences between antebellum and postbellum narrative strategies. Jacobs's narrative dwells heavily upon the notion of motherhood to foreground similarities (and thereby discrepancies) between her identity and the "true womanhood" of her white readers. In contrast, Keckley scarcely mentions the death of her son, George, although she provides a lengthy account of Willie Lincoln's death and Mary's grief over it. Her strategy is to control and exploit the value of domestic womanhood without partaking of it. Like the freedwomen who rejected their "new right" to enter marriage contracts, understanding it as another kind of bondage, she avoids the disempowerment of domestic literary identity (Stanley 48–50). For other discussions of Keckley's silence on personal matters, see Zafar (155–57) and Domina (145) who both argue convincingly that her forbearance is a means of acquiring privacy otherwise denied, both rhetorically and materially, to black women.

32. For alternative accounts of Keckley's rhetorical strategy concerning the clothing, see Young (126–33) and Zafar. Both arguments focus on Keckley's subversion of Lincoln's status and trace the ways in which the writer gives the First Lady a "dressing down" (Zafar) or presents her in literal and symbolic modes of "undress" (Young).

33. Young and Domina argue similarly that Keckley's depiction of her presence in the White House is a means of intervening in nationalist icons. Young finds that Keckley "reshapes" or "redesigns" nationalist iconography, ultimately inverting its terms and transferring its authority unto herself. Domina argues that Keckley leaves the iconography intact, but she suggests that Keckley does so in order to place herself within it ("Keckley out-Lincolned Lincoln").

34. At some level, this is a literal interpretation of her, too, since it was generally believed that *Behind the Scenes* was written by James Redpath, a Republican journalist. In fact, it wasn't until the 1940s that attribution to Keckley was established. Ottolengul really believes Keckley's textual persona is already a white creation, and so his project should be understood less as revenge than as a continued manipulation of the black image.

35. In fact, it was not. An interesting subtext to Keckley's comments here is that George passed as white. We know this from his enlistment records with the Union army and his enrollment record at Wilberforce College. In both cases, Keckley's son registered as George Kirkland, taking the name of his white father after years of going by his mother's last name. His action later enabled Keckley to lie to the pension bureau, saying she had been married to the father in order to get a war pension (Washington 208–9).

WORKS CITED

Andrews, William L. "The Changing Moral Discourse of Nineteenth-Century African American Women's Autobiography: Harriet Jacobs and Elizabeth Keckley. *De/Colonizing the Subject: The Politics of Gender in Women's Autobiography.* Ed. Sidonie Smith. Minneapolis: University of Minnesota Press, 1992. 225–41.

———. Introduction. *Sisters of the Spirit: Three Black Women's Autobiographies of the Nineteenth Century.* Bloomington: Indiana University Press, 1986. 7–22.

The Argus [Albany], 11 July 1882.

Baker, Jean H. *Mary Todd Lincoln, A Biography.* New York: W.W. Norton, 1987.

Baker, Houston A., Jr. "Autobiographical Acts and the Voice of the Southern Slave." 1980. *The Slaves's Narrative.* Ed. Charles T. Davis and Henry Louis Gates Jr. New York: Oxford University Press, 1985. 242–61.

Bardaglio, Peter W. "'Shamefull Matches': The Regulation of Interracial Sex and Marriage in the South before 1900." Hodes 112–38.

Barnes, Elizabeth. *States of Sympathy: Seduction and Democracy in the American Novel.* New York: Columbia University Press, 1997.

Baym, Nina. *Woman's Fiction: A Guide to Novels by and about Women in America, 1820–70.* 2nd ed. Urbana: University of Illinois Press, 1993.

Berlant, Lauren. *The Anatomy of National Fantasy: Hawthorne, Utopia, and Everyday Life.* Chicago: University of Chicago Press, 1991.

———. *The Queen of America Goes to Washington City: Essays on Sex and Citizenship.* Durham: Duke University Press, 1997.

Berthold, Michael. "Not 'Altogether' the 'History of Myself': Autobiographical Impersonality in Elizabeth Keckley's *Behind the Scenes: Or, Thirty Years a Slave and Four Years in the White House.*" *American Transcendental Quarterly* 73.2 (1999): 105–79.

Boorstin, Daniel J. "Roles of the President's House." Freidel and Pencak 3–15.

Brown, Gillian. *Domestic Individualism: Imagining Self in Nineteenth-Century America.* Berkeley: University of California Press, 1990.

Carby, Hazel V. *Reconstructing Womanhood: The Emergence of the Afro-American Woman Novelist.* New York: Oxford University Press, 1987.

Caroli, Betty Boyd. *First Ladies.* Expanded edition. New York: Oxford University Press, 1995.

Collins, Patricia Hill. "Toward an Afrocentric Feminist Epistemology." *Black Feminist Thought: Knowledge Consciousness and the Politics of Empowerment.* Boston: Unwin Hyman, 1990. 201–20.

Cox, LaWanda. *Freedom, Racism, and Reconstruction: Collected Writings of LaWanda Cox.* Ed. Donald G. Nieman. Athens: University of Georgia Press, 1997.

The Democrat [Rochester], 5 October 1867.

Domina, Lynn. "'I Was Re-Elected President': Elizabeth Keckley as Quintessential Patriot in Behind the Scenes: Or, Thirty Years a Slave, and Four Years in the White House." *Women's Life-Writing: Finding Voice/Building Community.* Ed. Linda S. Coleman. Bowling Green: Bowling Green State University Popular Press, 1997. 139–52.

Donald, David Herbert. "'This Damned Old House': The Lincolns in the White House." Freidel and Pencak 53–74.

Douglas, Ann. *The Feminization of American Culture.* New York: Alfred A. Knopf, 1977.

Douglass, Frederick. *My Bondage and My Freedom.* 1855. Ed. William Andrews. Urbana: University of Illinois Press, 1987.

duBois, Ellen Carol. *Feminism and Suffrage: The Emergence of an Independent Women's Movement in America: 1848–1869.* Ithaca: Cornell University Press, 1980.

Du Bois, W.E.B. *Black Reconstruction in America: An Essay toward a History of the Part Which Black Folk Played in the Attempt to Reconstruct Democracy in America, 1860–1880.* New York: Meridian Books, 1964.

DuCille, Ann. *The Coupling Convention: Sex, Text, and Tradition in Black Women's Fiction.* New York: Oxford University Press, 1993.

Fleischner, Jennifer. *Mastering Slavery: Memory, Family, and Identity in Women's Slave Narratives.* New York: New York University Press, 1997.

Foner, Eric. *Free Soil, Free Labor, Free Men: The Ideology of the Republican Party before the Civil War.* New York: Oxford University Press, 1995.

———. *A Short History of Reconstruction, 1863–1877.* New York: Harper & Row, 1990.

Foster, Frances Smith. "Autobiography after Emancipation: The Example of Elizabeth Keckley." *Multicultural Autobiography: American Lives.* Ed. James Robert Payne. Knoxville: University of Tennessee Press, 1992. 32–63.

Fredrickson, George M. *The Black Image in the White Mind: The Debate on Afro-American Character and Destiny.* New York: Harper & Row, 1971.

Friedel, Frank, and William Pencak, eds. *The White House: The First Two Hundred Years.* Boston: Northeastern University Press, 1994.

Genovese, Eugene D. *Roll, Jordan, Roll: The World the Stoves Made.* New York: Vintage Books, 1976.

Ginzberg, Lori D. "'Moral Suasion Is Moral Balderdash': Women, Politics, and Social Activism in the 1850s." *The Journal of American History* 73 (1986): 601–22.

Hodes, Martha. "The Sexualization of Reconstruction Politics: White Women and Black Men in the South after the Civil War." *American Sexual Politics: Sex, Gender, and Race since the Civil War.* Ed. John C. Fout and Maura Shaw Tantillo. Chicago: University of Chicago Press, 1993. 59–74.

———, ed. *Sex, Love, Race: Crossing Boundaries in North American History.* New York: New York University Press, 1999.

Horton, John Theodore. *James Kent: A Study in Conservatism, 1763–1847.* New York: Da Capo Press, 1969.

Hull, Gloria T, Patricia Bell Scott, and Barbara Smith. *All the Women Are White, All the Blacks Are Men, But Some of Us Are Brave: Black Women's Studies.* Old Westbury, New York: Feminist Press, 1982.

Jacobs, Harriet. *Narrative of the Life of a Slave Girl: Written by Herself.* 1867. Ed. Jean Fagan Yellin. Cambridge: Harvard University Press, 1987.

Jacobson, Matthew Frye. *Whiteness of a Different Color: European Immigrants and the Alchemy of Race.* Cambridge: Harvard University Press, 1998.

Johnson, Andrew. "First Inaugural Address. October 11, 1853." *The Papers of Andrew Johnson,* Volume 2 (1852–57). Ed. LeRoy P. Graf and Ralph W Haskins. Knoxville: University of Tennessee Press, 1967. 172–84.

———. "Veto of the Civil Rights Bill, March 27, 1866: to the Senate of the United States" 74–78. "Veto of the Freedmen's Bureau Bill, February 19, 1866: to the Senate of the United States" 68–72. *Handbook of Politics for 1868.* Edward McPherson, clerk of the house of representatives of the United States. Washington City: Philp and Solomons, 1868.

Kantorowicz, Ernst H. *The King's Two Bodies: A Study in Mediaeval Political Theology.* Princeton: Princeton University Press, 1957.

Kaplan, Sidney. "The Miscegenation Issue in the Election of 1864." *Journal of Negro History* 34 (1949): 274–343.

Keckley, Elizabeth. *Behind the Scenes: Or, Thirty Years a Slave, and Four Years in the White House.* 1868. New York: Oxford University Press, 1988.

Keetley, Dawn. "Racial Conviction, Racial Confusion: Indeterminate Identities in Women's Slave Narratives and Southern Courts." *a/b: Auto/Biography Studies.* 10.2 (1995): 1–20.

Kent, James. *Commentaries on American Law.* 12th edition (1826–30). Ed. O.W. Holmes Jr. Boston: Little, Brown, 1873.

Kickley, Betsy [D. Ottolengul]. *Behind the Seams: by a Nigger Woman, Who Took in Work from Mrs. Lincoln and Mrs. Davis.* New York: The National News Company, 1868.

Lott, Eric. *Love & Theft: Blackface Minstrelsy and the American Working Class.* New York: Oxford University Press, 1993.

Lefort, Claude. "The Image of the Body in Totalitarianism." *Political Forms of Modern Society.* Ed. John B. Thompson. Cambridge: MIT Press, 1986. 292–306.

McGlynn, Frank, and Seymour Drescher, eds. *The Meaning of Freedom: Economies, Politics, and Culture after Slavery.* Pittsburgh: University of Pittsburgh Press, 1992.

Morrow, Honoré Willsie. *An Appreciation of the Wife of Abraham Lincoln.* New York: William Morrow, 1928.

Moses, Wilson J. "Writing Freely?; Frederick Douglass and the Constraints of Racialized Writing." *Frederick Douglass: New Literary and Historical Essays*. Ed. Eric J. Sundquist. New York: Cambridge University Press, 1990. 66–83.

Olney, James. "Introduction" to *Behind the Scenes*. Keckley xxvii–xxxvi.

Pascoe, Peggy. "Miscegenation Law, Court Cases, and Ideologies of 'Race.'" Hodes 464–90.

Randall, Ruth Painter. *Mary Lincoln: Biography of a Marriage*. Boston: Little, Brown, 1953.

The Republican [Springfield, MA], 3 October 1867.

Romero, Lora. *Home Fronts: Domesticity and Its Critics in the Antebellum United States*. Durham: Duke University Press, 1997.

Sánchez-Eppler, Karen. *Touching Liberty: Abolition, Feminism, and the Politics of the Body*. Berkeley: University of California Press, 1993.

Saville, Julie. *The Work of Reconstruction: From Slave to Wage Labor in South Carolina, 1860–1870*. New York: Cambridge University Press, 1994.

Searle, William. *The President's House: A History, Volume One*. Washington, DC: White House Historical Association, 1986.

Sedgwick, Catharine Maria. *Life and Letters of Catharine M. Sedgwick*. Ed. Mary E. Dewey. New York: Harper & Brothers, 1871.

Slote, Ben. "Revising Freely: Frederick Douglass and the Politics of Disembodiment." *a/b: Auto/Biography Studies* 11.1 (1996): 17–37.

Smith, Stephanie A. *Conceived by Liberty: Maternal Figures and Nineteenth-Century American Literature*. Ithaca: Cornell University Press, 1994.

Stanley, Amy Dru. *From Bondage to Contract: Wage Labor, Marriage, and the Market in the Age of Slave Emancipation*. Cambridge: Cambridge University Press, 1998.

The Statesman [OH], 8 October 1867.

Stepto, Robert B. *From Behind the Veil: A Study of Afro-American Narrative*. Urbana: University of Illinois Press, 1979.

Stowe, Harriet Beecher. *Uncle Tom's Cabin; or, Life among the Lowly*. 1852. Ed. Ann Douglas. New York: Penguin Books, 1986.

Sundquist, Eric. "Frederick Douglass: Literacy and Paternalism." *Critical Essays on Frederick Douglass*. Ed. William Andrews. Boston. G.K. Hall, 1991. 720–32.

Taylor, Gordon O. "Voices from the Veil: Black American Autobiography." *Georgia Review* 35 (1981): 341–61.

Tompkins, Jane. *Sensational Designs: The Cultural Work of American Fiction, 1790–1860*. New York: Oxford University Press, 1985.

Trefousse, Hans L. *Andrew Johnson: A Biography*. New York: W.W. Norton, 1989.

"The Truth about Mrs. Lincoln." *The Independent* 10 August 1882.

Van Evrie, John. *Negroes and Negro Slavery: The First an Inferior Race: The Latter Its Normal Condition*. New York: Van Evrie, Horton, 1863.

Washington, John E. *They Knew Lincoln*. New York: E.P. Dutton, 1942.

Wexler, Laura. "Tender Violence: Literary Eavesdropping, Domestic Fiction, and Educational Reform." *The Culture of Sentiment: Race, Gender, and Sentimentality in Nineteenth-Century America*. Ed. Shirley Samuels. New York: Oxford University Press, 1992. 9–38.

Wiegman, Robyn. *American Anatomies: Theorizing Race and Gender*. Durham: Duke University Press, 1995.

The World [New York], 3 October 1867.

Young, Elizabeth. *Disarming the Nation: Women's Writing and the American Civil War*. Chicago: University of Chicago Press, 1999.

Zafar, Rafia. *We Wear a Mask: African Americans Write American Literature, 1760–1870*. New York: Columbia University Press, 1997.

CHAPTER FOUR

XIOMARA SANTAMARINA

Behind the Scenes of Black Labor
Elizabeth Keckley and the Scandal of Publicity

WHEN ELIZABETH KECKLEY CONCLUDED her 1868 autobiography, *Behind the Scenes: Or, Thirty Years a Slave, and Four Years in the White House,* her parting words made clear to her readers what she had emphasized throughout: She defined success in the form of personal relationships rather than material wealth. Although the "labor of a lifetime had brought [her] nothing in a pecuniary way," she asserted, it had made her "rich in friendships, and," she added, "friends are a recompense for all the woes of the darkest pages of life."[1] The author was a popular dressmaker, and according to her, work was not simply about the material conditions of production but, more importantly, about the emotions of respect and attachment the production process entailed. Her interracial relationships with elite, white women clients, such as First Lady Mary Todd Lincoln, were a particular source of pride. Fastidiously interweaving her skilled dressmaking as a slave and a freedwoman with the meanings and affectivity this work generated, Keckley insisted on the potential for intimacy and loyalty between white and black women. On the basis of these work relations, moreover, Keckley claimed public legitimacy and authority for herself. In *Behind the Scenes,* labor is not only about exploitation and the accumulation of profits, it is, more importantly, about a specific black woman's production and circulation of social value.

Writing during the years immediately following the Civil War, Keckley depicted the social relations of dressmaking as a crucial site for mediating the nation's anxieties over the role ex-slaves and free blacks were to play in a changing economy and society. During this period of political upheaval, white Americans acrimoniously debated the terms for transforming the newly emancipated black population into a free labor force while ensuring their participation in the South's revitalization.[2] Although Southerners who sought to assert their authority over the former slaves promoted stereotypes of freedmen as "lazy" and unwilling to work, Keckley's *Behind the Scenes* testified to the productive possibilities of black workers. Born into slavery in 1824, Keckley worked industriously enough as a slave to buy her freedom at the age of thirty-one. After working as a freedwoman in St. Louis for a few years, Keckley moved to Washington, DC, shortly before the outbreak of war in 1861 and established herself as a reputable and popular dressmaker among the town's elite women. There, Keckley's clients—among them Varina Davis, wife of Senator Jefferson Davis (who would become the president of the Confederacy during the Civil War)—rewarded her with affection and respect for her exemplary work ethic. They helped her relocate permanently to the city and also recommended her to Mary Todd Lincoln, wife of the newly elected president, for whom she worked as dressmaker throughout the war. In this way, Keckley's life-story dramatized the possibilities of racial reconciliation and national progress attainable through the successful social and economic integration of freed blacks.

Yet although *Behind the Scenes* invited readings of its protagonist as representing freedmen's capacity and inclination to work, the focus of the narrative was rather extraordinary. In tracing the upward mobility of the industrious Elizabeth Keckley—from "Thirty Years a Slave," to "Four Years in the White House"—*Behind the Scenes* culminated with a lengthy description of the former slave's long-term relationship with one of the most prominent women of her day, Mary Todd Lincoln. Having worked closely with the First Lady from 1861 through the president's assassination and his widow's subsequent relocation to Illinois, Keckley made her employment and her familiarity with the Lincolns the focus of *Behind the Scenes*. Keckley publicized her labor in the Lincoln White House in an effort to intervene in the enormous public outcry that erupted in the national media over the "Old Clothes Scandal." The scandal became public in October 1867 after the former First Lady tried to raise funds for herself through the sale of her celebrated wardrobe. Although Mary Lincoln had been the object of unprecedented media scrutiny throughout her husband's term in the White House, the furor generated by her misguided efforts to solicit funds from Republican politicians was particularly fierce. In response, Keckley, who had acted as Mrs. Lincoln's agent in New York during the events leading up to the scandal, felt compelled to publish her account in part to clear her own name but principally to defend her employer from what she viewed as gross misunderstandings about Mary Lincoln's motives.³

Keckley insisted from the start that the description of her role as Mrs. Lincoln's respected "modiste" and "friend" (according to the title page) was intended not to champion herself but, rather, her much-maligned former employer. As Keckley asserted in her preface: "I have been her confidante, and if evil charges are laid at her door, they also must be laid at mine, since I have been a party to all her movements. To defend myself, I must defend the lady I have served." *Behind the Scenes* invokes Keckley's loyal service as a justifiable corrective to the public's misperceptions of the First Lady, rather than as self-serving publicity. It is for this reason that Keckley admonished her readers: "For an act may be wrong judged purely by itself, but when the motive that prompted the act is understood, it is construed differently" (xiv, xiii).

But the story of this groundbreaking African American text—one that seeks to elucidate black female working potential in the post-Emancipation era—is a vexed one. Tragically, Keckley's deferential intervention on behalf of Mrs. Lincoln was interpreted as its opposite, as a betrayal.⁴ *Behind the Scenes* did generate sympathy for the family of the nation's "martyred president," but the public did not view the dressmaker's representation of White House family life as either just or fair. In shocked reviews, critics rejected Keckley's assurance that her intimate labor in the Lincoln White House authorized her to speak publicly about the family. So great was the controversy that a particularly virulent and quasi-pornographic parody entitled *Behind the Seams: By a Nigger Woman, who took in work from Mrs. Lincoln and Mrs. Davis* appeared, taking advantage of the forum Keckley's colored publicity provided to indulge in pernicious race-baiting.⁵

Why did the public turn on her? How could a book in which a former slave claimed that she preferred "eternal slavery, rather than be regarded with distrust" be seen as anything but deferential, or, as some 1970s' critics termed it, "accommodationist"? Perhaps most significantly, critics, then and now, have neglected to address why the author entirely failed to predict the reaction to her book. Although Lincoln historians read *Behind the Scenes* as a prototype for today's political "kiss and tell" and Frances Smith Foster argues for the racist motives of contemporary critics, the disparity between Keckley's solicitous and defensive representation of herself and the outrage she provoked remains largely unexplained.⁶

Part of the continuing interpretive problems regarding the reception of Keckley's text has to do with the anomalous relation between *Behind the Scenes* and the African American texts that preceded it. For example, Frances Smith Foster points to *Behind the Scenes* as a "prototype" for a later-nineteenth-century genre of which Booker T. Washington's *Up from Slavery* is the most noted example. In this postbellum genre, the "school of slavery" equips the slave to overcome the hardships of postEmancipation reality.[7] But it is unclear in this analysis how Keckley's self-representation relates to the antebellum autobiographical tradition of the slave narrative best exemplified by Frederick Douglass's *Narrative of the Life of Frederick Douglass, an American Slave, Written by Himself* (1845) and Harriet Jacobs's *Incidents in the Life of a Slave Girl* (1861).

Most often, modern readers of Douglass's compelling narrative focus on the former slave's descriptions of his subversive acquisition of literacy as a young boy and his courageous physical resistance to the slave "breaker," Mr. Covey. For Douglass, learning to read and write helped him to recognize and dispel what he saw as the intellectually stunting tendencies of slavery, declaring that "to make a contented slave, it is necessary to make a thoughtless one."[8] This linking of literacy to reason allowed Douglass to justify his fight with Covey and to highlight his dramatic transformation from "slave to man." It was largely on the basis of this depiction of the ex-slave's literate masculinity that Douglass established himself as the authoritative racial subject to which he aspired.

For Harriet Jacobs, the author of *Incidents in the Life of a Slave Girl*, the cultivation of rhetorical authority entailed the delicate task of mediating the exposure of slavery's workings and Jacobs's history of sexual coercion as a slave woman. Where Douglass appealed to his audience by writing his way to manhood, Jacobs manipulated norms of gender and sexual victimization to rewrite herself as an heroic slave *mother* committed to resisting her and her children's degradation. Because of her compelling treatment of these overtly gendered thematics of sexual abuse and resistance, Jacobs's now widely read autobiography is seen as the best exemplar of the black woman's slave narrative.

Behind the Scenes diverges rather dramatically from the concerns expressed in these "classic" narratives depicting literacy and the obstacles slavery mounted for black women. Although it is clear that Keckley shared many of Jacobs's experiences as a slave woman—sexual violation, fears for her slave child, and so forth—in her narrative, she subordinates these overtly gendered concerns to the details of her work history. Through the innovatively combined auspices of slave narrative and memoir, *Behind the Scenes* focuses mainly on demonstrating how a slave woman might recast the coercions of slave labor so as to produce herself as an agent rather than solely as a victim of bondage.

It is Keckley's dramatically different tack, in which she redeploys the conditions of her subordination into "the conditions of possibility" (in the words of Gayatri Spivak), more than the problem of a "lack" of antecedents, that is most responsible for the misunderstandings, past and present, associated with this text. That is, the dynamics of the reception of *Behind the Scenes* reveal how problematic a black female worker's self-representation in terms of labor was and continues to be. Notwithstanding many fine investigations into the contributions of African American women workers, persistent misunderstandings about *Behind the Scenes* suggest that the complexity of the historical and textual scenes of Keckley's labor remains unread.[9]

Keckley's literary reformulation of black female agency along the lines of labor emphasizes, above all, the dignity of work in *all* its aspects: slave, free, interracial, and profoundly gendered. She testifies to the often-disparaged value produced by subordinated blacks and, in particular, black working women. Thus, even as historians have amply documented the varieties of work that African American women, slave and free, performed in white and black communities, this evidence exists in uneasy tension with claims about the oppositional relationship of black "identity" to work, and the black community's particular resistance to the degenering often associated with black women's labor in the marketplace. This was evident in the postbellum era, when black reformers who promoted racial uplift often exhorted black women to adopt bourgeois "domestic" embodiments as wives or as reformers in lieu of market participation as workers. But even today, many scholars agree with influential critic Paul Gilroy that "for the descendants of slaves, work signifies only servitude, misery, and subordination."[10] One assessment of black working women—"When Your Work Is Not Who You Are"—makes a similar argument. In this vein, the low status of black women's labor is often invoked, tautologically, as evidence of its irrelevance to black women's self-production and self-representation. As a result, for modern readers, the most compelling formulations of black female subjectivity have been those perceived as openly resisting forms of subordinated labor.[11]

Within these ambivalent rhetorical contexts, Keckley's effort to "speak" her labor proves a contested and easily misinterpreted practice. This suggests we still have few interpretive tools with which to account for this black woman's positive valuation of the interracial intersubjectivity embedded in her entrepreneurial work for white bourgeois women. Black male narrators can more readily appeal to American and African American culture's historical association of self-supporting labor with masculinity. But a compelling account has yet to emerge of independent black, female labor as the acme of respectability and loyalty, rather than the degendered "flesh" or "hypercorporealized" female body enslaved to production and reproduction.[12] Keckley's attempt to deploy race, gender, and class to just this end generated devastating critiques from whites and was perceived as a cautionary tale by African Americans.[13]

For Keckley, dressmaking represented an opportunity to link herself to a domain of labor that was perceived as skilled and commercially valued. The status and gender-inflected patterns of consumption associated with an expanding, capitalist economy afforded antebellum women of all races the possibility of lucrative careers as milliners and dressmakers.[14] But more importantly, as a skilled dressmaker, Keckley could participate in fashioning her clients' aspirations to elite femininity, thus establishing the social relations of this work as a way of inserting herself into a network of femininity and class taste that refuted conventional understandings of the "degraded" slave woman. In large part, then, the scandal that greeted Keckley's text arose from her reviewers' refusal to grant her the status associated with being a "modiste" and their concomitant reinscription of Keckley as "an angry negro servant,"[15] the most generic and commonly invoked type of black menial female worker.

As one recent analysis of the differences between the narratives of Harriet Jacobs and Elizabeth Keckley demonstrates, however, Keckley's emphasis on labor continues to create misunderstandings. Although critic William Andrews insightfully foregrounds the primary role that Keckley's labor plays in her narrative, his reading of her drive for recognition suggests a certain cynicism and even ambivalence. His analysis of Keckley's postbellum "materialism" highlights the difference between this discourse and Jacobs's appeal to an earlier "idealist" vision of "moral absolutism." But what appears in Andrews as a historicizing of discursive difference effectively flattens out or elides the significant interpersonal and gendered dynamics of Keckley's work relations. Framed within a "materialist" context, Keckley's single-minded concern with what Andrews terms her "career" makes her appear somewhat selfish to modern readers. As he describes it: "No one, least of all Keckley herself, is concerned about this slave woman's sexual respectability; at issue is something much more important—her financial reputation.... We may be sure that she wanted her postbellum audience to know of her unswerving fealty to the ethics of the marketplace.... Thus she links her sense of pride and respectability to an external standard—that of the marketplace—rather than an internal principle—what Jacobs would have called her 'virtue.'"[16]

Despite the fact that as a well-regarded dressmaker to elite women Keckley must have been perceived by her clients as subscribing to accepted norms of womanhood, Andrews reads Keckley's concern with work as almost antithetical to a concern with "sexual respectability." Not surprisingly, in an interpretation emptied of all gendered connotations, the dressmaker's emphasis on her "reputation" becomes telescoped into a concern with money and an "external," or superficial, standard for behavior indexed to the "marketplace." Consequently, when Andrews describes *Behind the Scenes* as an "unabashed and often plainly self-congratulatory success story," he inadvertently echoes assumptions that others, most notably Lincoln scholars, have formed regarding what they see as the self-serving and pecuniary motives behind Keckley's "kiss and tell" publicity.[17]

Although one might obviously question whether an ex-slave *would* necessarily see the marketplace as something "external" to herself/himself, the point to remember here, as Keckley goes to such lengths to show, is that the primary importance of her work is its interpersonal and/or sentimental dimension. That is, to reiterate from above, what the "labor of a lifetime" brings her is "nothing in a *pecuniary* way," yet it makes her "rich in friendships" (emphasis added). In *Behind the Scenes,* Keckley represents the interracial social relations cultivated through her work with white, bourgeois women as providing a forum of her own making, literally from which she may represent herself as supporting and buttressing her clients' femininity. That is, through her creation and support of her clients' elite female status, Keckley infers her own production of social, rather than simply monetary, value, and credibility.

In this sense, it is ironic that many modern readers have resisted the connection Keckley goes to such lengths to establish between the social relations of her work and her "virtue." In doing so, they rehearse some of the same problematic assumptions about publicity and "servants" echoed by reviewers in 1868 who saw Keckley as committing "an offense of the same grade as the opening of people's letters, [and] the listening at keyholes." That is, modern readers' filtering of *Behind the Scenes* through the lens of the "success" story obscures Keckley's effort to rewrite herself as a market agent who helps to produce social value by creating her gender identity through white female bodies and discourses of bourgeois femininity. It is this intimate relation between black and white female bodies, laboring and elite, "public" and "private," that makes Elizabeth Keckley's contribution to national debates on postbellum race relations so remarkable and potentially explosive.

Rather than viewing Keckley's deferential rhetoric as disingenuous or hypocritical, as do critics partial to Mary Lincoln, we might see the gap between *Behind the Scenes*'s avowed intentions and its reception as testifying to the conflict that exists between Keckley's represented labor and the symbolic, or cultural, weight of this representation. That is, Keckley's sentimental re-location of the "external" or "public" marketplace in which she is irrevocably embedded *within* the work relations of "private" white womanhood, intimacy, and loyalty produces rhetorical incompatibilities that destabilize postbellum discourses for labor, race, and femininity. Specifically, the norms for black female labor that operate throughout *Behind the Scenes* conflict with commonsense assumptions about privacy and the invisibility of the labor that produces the racial and class privilege at the core of white, sentimental subjectivity. In this way text and reception show how symbolic conflict erupts when dominated, "domestic," and even "loyal" black labor is literally and figuratively emancipated, moving out of its subordinate role "behind the scenes" to take the nation's center stage.

"Thirty Years a Slave . . ."

Behind the Scenes is divided into two sections that frame Keckley's life. A short slave narrative, that is less frequently analyzed (in particular, by Lincoln historians), is followed by the longer, infamous memoir describing her experiences as emancipated dressmaker to elite white women in the nation's capital. Although Keckley's three chapters on her life as a slave constitute only a small portion of *Behind the Scenes*'s fifteen chapters, their rhetorical configuration of bondage, work, and freedom are clearly central to the text's laboring logic. In these chapters, Keckley portrays the inhumanity of slavery, particularly its severing of family ties and the injustice of its racialized division of labor. Along with her description of the sale of her father away from her family, the "loan" of her person to a poor relative, and her sexual vulnerability, Keckley tersely narrates the injustices of what she terms the "dark side" of slavery.

But what makes Keckley's slave narrative so distinctive is her explicit refusal to represent slave life as unremittingly dark. As Keckley states in her preface, "[I]f I have portrayed the dark side of slavery, I also have painted the bright side. The good that I have said of human servitude should be thrown into the scales with the evil that I have said of it. I have kind, true-hearted friends in the South as well as in the North, and I would not wound those Southern friends by sweeping condemnation, simply because I was once a slave" (xi–xii). Here, Keckley's claims to balanced reporting are underwritten by the "good" she reveals "of human servitude." Before we marvel at such a statement, we might observe how this imperative for fair representation is expressed as an obligation of friendship. For Keckley, the preservation of her "kind, true-hearted friends" supersedes her slave status—"simply because I was once a slave"—a fact which motivates her deliberate writing against the grain of those earlier slave narratives that express only "sweeping condemnation."[18]

But what exactly constitutes the "bright" side that Keckley claims to represent? As the slave narrative proceeds, it would appear to us that Keckley's friends are few and far between. What we find instead is the narration of various scenes of labor which themselves represent the lessons that slavery, that "hardy school" in Keckley's words, teaches her. That is, Keckley's descriptions of her labor invoke slavery's paternalistic ideology in order to trade on the pedagogical potential that supposedly inhered in these social relations, thereby producing the "bright" side which bondage offered without eclipsing its "dark" side. Recalling the performance of her "first duty"—attending to her mistress's baby—Keckley describes this child as her "earliest and fondest pet," remarking on the fact that as a four-year-old, she herself was hardly old enough to assume such a responsibility. In this regard, she insists: "True, I was but a child myself—only four years old—but then I had been raised in a hardy school—had been taught to rely upon myself, and to prepare myself to render assistance to others . . . Notwithstanding all the wrongs that slavery heaped upon me, I can bless it for one thing—youth's important lesson of self-reliance."

Describing her labor as a child, caring for other children and performing other kinds of work, Keckley presents readers with a picture of the self-reliant slave girl who displays "character" (19). And it is here that Keckley's pedagogic claims evince an irony pertaining to their roots in slavery's paternalism. Although it could be argued that "self-reliance" on the part of a slave constitutes an accession to slavery's subordination, what *Behind the Scenes* illustrates is the way in which the slave's "principles of character" (19) can, in fact, shed light on her otherwise obscured productivity. Keckley's description of her early work suggests that one of slavery's crucial "lessons" was that the slave's work was necessary, and therefore valuable, notwithstanding slaveholders' protestations to the contrary.

This subversive self-knowledge is manifest in Keckley's repeated resistance to the devaluation of her labor. As she complains, "I grew strong and healthy, and, notwithstanding I knit socks and attended to various kinds of work, I was repeatedly told, when even fourteen years old that I would never be worth my salt" (21). In another instance, Keckley emphasizes the particular importance of her labor to the family: "With my needle I kept bread in the mouths of seventeen persons for two years and five months. While I was working so hard that others might live in comparative comfort, and move in those circles of society to which their birth gave them entrance, the thought often occurred to me whether I was really worth my salt or not; and then perhaps the lips curled in a bitter sneer. It may seem strange that I should place so much emphasis upon words thoughtlessly, idly spoken; but then we do many strange things in life, and cannot always explain the motives that actuate us" (45–46).

Keckley's investment in countering her master's assessment is evident in her pointed marshaling of contrasts: the lone needle providing many loaves for many mouths over many months. Furthermore, Keckley's confession about not understanding *why* she responds as she does suggests that she resents the taunt as an insult because it mystifies the *social*, not simply economic, value of her labor. That is, not only is the denial of her "worth" a mystification of the economic payoff her labor provides, it also obscures how her work is instrumental to the family's participation in the pleasures of its social, class position. Keckley resents the dismissal of her contribution to the master's position in slaveholding's class structure, as much, if not more than, the literal, material underestimation of her work. With this anecdote, Keckley does not simply link slavery's traffic in laboring bodies to its traffic in esteem and social status. Rather, she demonstrates how her role in the creation of status justifies her view of herself as a member-participant in the paternalistic slaveholding "family." As she wrote in a letter to her mother while working temporarily in another household in 1838: "[G]ive my love to all the family, both white and black" (41).[19]

In this manner, Keckley's dramatic, synecdochal representation of her work through the image of the lone needle and its production of economic and social values invokes another irony related to the necessity of her labor within a paternalistic framework. The depiction of her sewing does not merely dramatize the utility of the slave's labor for the market, but also *that of the slave woman's*. That is, by foregrounding the contribution her needle makes toward the family's social status, Keckley sheds light on the way in which the slave woman's simultaneous embeddedness in the "family" and her displacement therefrom renders typically obscured domestic labor, and the social value, or status, it generates, visible. Through the auspices of her labor's necessity and its marketability, Keckley perceives her female productivity as a means for generating this social value, not simply profits and/or slave children. As a result, she is able to make her extra/domestic labor discursively visible and evade being cast as the "unproductive" female worker or the slave woman exploited for her reproductive labor. Through this paradoxical appeal to slavery's paternalistic ideology of reciprocal obligations, Keckley is able to represent her own self-understanding and worth as a social agent, and a female one at that, in its system.[20]

Through this formulation, Keckley expresses the contradictory logic which she espouses for surviving her oppression: A woman can resist the dehumanization embedded in slavery's codes of coercion and devaluation by producing social value as a form of alternative "surplus value" which she might be said to accumulate. Even while Keckley recognizes her enslaved work as a primary site for social control, she foregrounds what is not given—the way in which a coerced labor performance could provide a form of self-production that countered mechanisms of racial and gendered inferiority and "dependence." After all, those "principles of character," such as self-reliance, to which she lays claim are not the primary "goal" of slavery's social relations, *even if slaveholders benefit from them*. Understandably, the principled character of conscientious slaves appears as a compromised form of resistance, because it translates into profits for slaveholders and the perpetuation of slavery's coercions. But in Keckley's schema of value, this is of less importance than acting in accordance with one's conscience, or more precisely, what appears as the same—acting in accordance with the value one produces. Through this willful reinterpretation of paternalism, Keckley claims credit, and hence considers herself valuable, on the basis of the social privilege her work as a slave woman affords others.

The centrality of this dynamic of reciprocating status, wherein Keckley sees herself as bestowing and thus in some measure participating in her master's social status, is amplified in the last part of the slave narrative which details her success as hired-out labor. If her work in the past supported a family of seventeen by providing them with the leisure and money necessary for maintaining their social position, Keckley's hiredout work, specifically as a dressmaker, involves her even more directly in maintaining the system of social status in the entire community and in particular, among elite, white women. As dressmaker, or *modiste,* to Southern, and later to Northern, bourgeois women, Keckley relies for her success on her adept interpretation of those dress codes that inscribe her clients' social status. As a result, Keckley's labor for and intricate class relations with these women make her investment in their elite femininity and their investment in the circulation of status synonymous.

Keckley's value as a dressmaker increases with her ability to make clothing that mediates her clients' class values, including those of feminine propriety, economic standing, and racial privilege. Keckley eagerly testifies to this competence and to the proper alignment of her identifications when she asserts that "in a short time I had acquired something of a reputation as a seamstress and dressmaker. The best ladies . . . were my patrons, and when my reputation was once established I never lacked for orders" (45). As this statement and the ensuing account of her clients' financing of her bid for freedom illustrate, the specificity of Keckley's lucrative occupation was fundamental to her identification with the class and gender stratification articulated by Southern whites.[21]

Keckley's identifications with white, elite femininity bear significant weight in the last portion of the slave narrative which describes how she exploited the widened network of sociality and esteem she inhabited to obtain her freedom. As she makes clear, the possibility of buying her freedom is made available to her precisely through the social credit she has earned while working as a hired-out slave. It is here that we see clearly how, for Keckley, "friends" and clients are one and the same.

The story of Keckley's bid for freedom speaks to her status in the community at large and especially among her female clients. Unable to accumulate the $1,200 necessary to purchase herself and her son because her owners' family "claimed so much of [her] attention," Keckley planned a fundraising trip to the North. Prior to her departure, she had no problems collecting the signatures of a number of gentlemen as "collateral" (against her return) until, that is, one of these men went so far as to offer to subsidize her escape in the form of an IOU to her mistress. Rather than taking advantage of this remarkable offer, Keckley was aghast. As she tells her readers: "I was . . . sick at heart, for I could not accept the signature of this man when he had no faith in my pledges. No; slavery, eternal slavery rather than be regarded with distrust by those whose respect I esteemed" (52–53). With this dramatic statement Keckley made the stakes clear. To acknowledge this white man's well-intentioned expression of personal regard implied its precise opposite and, indeed, meant jeopardizing all she had worked so hard to earn: the esteem and appreciation of her clients, the good intentions of her mistress, and, above all, the self-respect that her labor had produced. In this context, freedom had no meaning.

In the midst of this quandary, the "credit" that Keckley had established with her clients came to operate in a powerful way. Even as she was despairing over her situation, the aptly named "Mrs. LeBourgois" burst in on the seamstress and told her that she would not permit Keckley to go North "to beg for what we should give you." Instead, she emphasized: "[Y]ou have many friends in St. Louis, and I am going to raise the twelve hundred dollars required among them" (54). What follows in the few remaining pages of the slave narrative is the story of Mrs. LeBourgois's collection of funds from those "friends" whom

Keckley denotes as her "lady patrons of St. Louis" (63). This relation, in turn, is placed alongside the legal documents pertinent to Keckley's manumission. Despite Mrs. LeBourgois's intent to "give" her the money, Keckley "consents" to accept the money "only as a loan," in this way quite literally externalizing her social credit via a formal instrument of credit in anticipation of eventually purchasing herself with her own earnings. Through this materialization of her clients' trust and respect, Keckley was able to renounce her slave status while capitalizing on, instead of jeopardizing, the social "credit history" she compiled as a slave. Keckley thus concludes the first part of her narrative with a story of freedom intimately linked to a tale of interracial trust and confidence fashioned out of, and stitched together by, the labor of her own two hands.

". . . and Four Years in the White House"

Although almost all the scandalized critics of Keckley's text ignored the slave narrative that precedes the longer memoir, ironically, the lessons contained in these three chapters are the ones that set Keckley up for trouble with her Northern readers in 1868. For it is on the basis of these lessons that Keckley framed the memoir as the story of the physical and social intimacies that characterized her work for the nation's Southern and Northern "First Families," the families of Jefferson Davis and Abraham Lincoln. When she narrates the various scenes which she is behind, Keckley describes her position as a privileged witness derived entirely from her competent, deferential, and trust-inspiring performance of labor. It is as such an authorized working spectator, one might say, that Keckley emphasizes the "inside" knowledge she has of these families, as opposed to the "eavesdropper" or "listening at keyholes" forms of illicit access commonly associated with the public speech of servants.[22]

For Keckley, the spatial proximity and social intimacy she shared with her elite clients in the nation's capital emerge quite literally out of her enslaved work history. In this regard, Keckley was able to reside in Washington, DC, without paying the requisite fee charged free blacks after requesting the intervention of a client. She was initially employed by Varina Davis "on the recommendation of one of my patrons and her intimate friend" (65–66). Later Mrs. Lincoln remarked to another friend that Keckley's name (prior to meeting her) "is familiar to me. She used to work for some of my lady friends in St. Louis, and they spoke well of her" (80). Thus, when Keckley and Mary Lincoln met to discuss the dressmaker's employment they not only met as employer/employee but also as two women with "friends" in common. In this way, Keckley perceives her employment, from the start, as both economic and social.

This simultaneously social and economic relation to her elite clients means that Keckley enjoys physical and rhetorical access to the quotidian knowledges that circulate among her clients' bodies. That is, this intimacy not only marks the dressmaker as an "insider" to her readers but also, more importantly, provides Keckley with the rhetorical space for making her work visible to her readers and for symbolizing the moral, social value that she claims to generate through her work for these women. This social and physical intimacy creates a forum—in the etymological sense of a public marketplace where exchange takes place—in which the formerly trafficked slave derives status from her own working "traffic," qua intimacy, with the bodies of political elites.[23] Consequently, the physical access she obtains to her employers' politically renowned bodies—the spaces they inhabit, as well as the social interactions taking place in those spaces—not only characterizes the conditions of production for Keckley as dressmaker but the rewards of that production as well.

In the accounts of her labor for the First Family, Keckley constantly staged the links between her labor and her special relationship with the Lincolns through the intense and repeated use of work verbs and working scenes. While "fitting," "basting," "arranging" Mrs. Lincoln's dresses, or "combing her hair," Keckley witnesses the mischief of the Lincoln boys, the loving relationship of Mary and Abraham, and the stresses that political life imposed on the family during its tenure in the White House. Furthermore, in response to Mary Lincoln's solicitations, Keckley offers advice on various fronts, from the propriety of transforming state dinners into state receptions to the significance of Mr. Lincoln's proceeding into dinner accompanied by other women. She also proffered her opinion on the chances of Lincoln's re-election in 1864 and claimed responsibility for laying out the body of Willie Lincoln after the boy's death (95–97, 144–45, 147–51).

The manner in which Keckley's work role as skilled dressmaker translated into a "diversified" source of miscellaneous labor for the whole Lincoln family attests in part to the lack of specificity, or boundaries, that mark the deeply racial and gendered aspects of her labor. In this regard, historians have noted white workers' resistance to the (overly) familial tendencies inhering in paid domestic labor and their workers' dislike of "service" occupations, that of "servant" in particular.[24] Subverting this equation of familial service with low status, Keckley exploits Mary Lincoln's exploitation of her racial and gendered economic susceptibility. Whereas a skilled white "modiste" might perceive efforts to extract so-called unskilled, familiar labor as undermining her status, Keckley viewed such efforts as enhancing it. Rather than interpreting the Lincoln family's ready access to the various forms of her labor power as a sign of her social inferiority, Keckley represents it as marker of social affinity, a move that again displays the former slave's investment in a paternalistic model of work relations. In this manner, Keckley's racial deference to the family—in the sense of being ever at their disposal—bridges the gap between social inferiority and interdependence by assuming the sentimental position of the "loyal" and "devoted" personal (black) servant. Within this raced and gendered dynamic of "loyal" subordination, Keckley's work itself operates as a *social* site in which nonkin employer and employee can bond through affect.

This conjunction of intimately gendered labor and sentiment in *Behind the Scenes* culminates in Keckley's status as sole witness to Mary Lincoln's grief in the wake of her husband's assassination. To this end, Keckley pointedly relates the various efforts the First Lady's staff made to locate her immediately following the assassination for the purpose of consoling the distressed widow. In so doing, she stressed her unique role as Mary Lincoln's only working contact in the days that followed: "[Mrs. Lincoln] denied admittance to almost every one, and I was her only companion, except her children, in the days of her great sorrow" (193). The significance of this sole witnessing should not be underestimated, because Keckley clearly experienced it as a privileged token of trust and value. As that sole companion, Keckley insisted on her own status as a privileged member of the nation. Witnessing Mrs. Lincoln's grief provided Keckley with a singular form of knowledge in the sense that her grief was conceivably the most authentic expression, or the most intimate way of knowing the personal, emotional effects of Lincoln's assassination.

When Keckley described this episode of intimate labor she recast the idea of emotional labor not as the exploitation of black women but almost as its opposite, as a form of recognized participation in political affect. If part of the critique about extracting emotional labor from domestic workers has centered on the instrumentality involved in being seen as "one of the family," Keckley instead foregrounds her privilege in the structure of fictive kinship that the whole nation bears in relation to the country's First Family.[25] To have been Mary Lincoln's only trusted, if paid, companion during this highly charged moment is proof that Keckley—revisiting the central claim of her slave narrative—is more than "worth her salt" to her employer. It works to flag the unique, multifaceted role she played as dressmaker, confidante, and valued companion. Furthermore, in Keckley's opinion, it was on the basis of these many competences, rather than on the Lincolns' opportunistic deployment of her labor power, that she became involved in assisting the misguided widow with the business transactions that became known as the "Old Clothes Scandal."

Ostensibly, it was Keckley's narration of the secret history pertaining to this scandal that was largely responsible for her book's controversial reception in April 1868. The scandal erupted in October 1867 after the impoverished Mary Lincoln tried to extort funds from Republican politicians, and, when this failed, clumsily attempted to sell her extravagant wardrobe. (The phrase *Old Clothes* suggests how such a gesture was perceived.) When Mary Lincoln tried to call in political chits by publishing her requests for funds to Republicans in the Democratic paper, the *New York World,* she precipitated a humiliating resurrection of past political animosities. In short order, Mary Lincoln was made the subject of vicious attacks by way of the same publicity machine she herself was attempting to manipulate.[26]

Despite the forthright disavowals of impropriety that appeared in *Behind the Scenes*'s preface and throughout the text, Keckley was accused of promoting a crisis in bourgeois norms of privacy. After months of Mary Lincoln's name being dragged through the mud, hardly anyone involved in this episode was perceived as innocent, but the dressmaker was deemed by critics the most guilty. As one review admonished:

> We in no wise attempt to apologize for anything that Mrs. Lincoln may have said or done, but we do protest against this atrocious invasion of her privacy, and we hope the press will speak in earnest condemnation of this indecent attempt to entrap the reading public into

listening to the vile slanders of an angry negro servant. The violation of privacy is the besetting sin of a portion of the American press, but no newspaper of a higher grade than the *Police Gazette* has ever been guilty of anything so outrageous as the gossip of this woman Keckley.

The remarkable stream of invective hurled by the *New York Citizen* reviewer fashioned a rhetorical alliance between the sinning "American press," the "reading public," a Democratic paper, and a Republican widow held in low esteem, for the sole purpose of repelling an attack mounted single-handedly by "an angry negro servant." The review invoked the vindictive discourse of the fired, disgruntled employee, misrepresenting the facts of the case, repudiating the links Keckley established between her labor and the knowledge it imparted, and stripping her of her professional identity. Completely disavowing the dressmaker's legitimate physical proximity to these families, the reviewer perceived Keckley's publicity as derived solely through illicit forms of access. It constituted, as it claimed, "an offence of the same grade as opening other people's letters, the listening at keyholes, or the mean system of espionage which unearths family secrets with a view to black mailing the unfortunate victims... [N]othing is sacred to this traitorous eavesdropper."[27] Although Keckley emphasized the social value of her working publicity, the work she went to such pains to publicize was perceived as entirely peripheral and, indeed, invisible, in the light of the potential "entrapment" and public danger that this "negro waiting-maid's" publicity posed. To thus render Keckley's knowledge illicit, the labor in relation to which it was produced had to be "disappeared."

Yet, the self-justification in Keckley's preface and elsewhere in the text where she describes her efforts to defend the First Lady from unflattering publicity prove that the dressmaker was well aware of the risk of impropriety entailed in discussing White House life. In comparison to the "exaggerations," the "evil report," and the "curiosity" that characterized the media's hostile stance to the Lincoln family, Keckley explicitly invoked her work relations as enabling her to judge the propriety and necessity of relating the "secrets of the domestic circle." If Keckley can be accused of being indiscreet, her position was that she was less so than others and that her indiscretion was intended to contain, or compensate for, the malicious publicity surrounding the disgraced former First Lady. As she discloses in her preface, "The veil of mystery must be drawn aside; the origin of a fact must be brought to light with the naked fact itself. If I have betrayed confidence in anything I have published, it has been to place Mrs. Lincoln in a better light before the world."

Keckley's use of metaphorical unveiling in the name of improving Mrs. Lincoln's public image is revealing in more ways than one. Her expressed desire to place Mrs. Lincoln in a "better light before the world" reveals Keckley's assumption of public authority and credibility, while also suggesting the grounds for the reviewers' accusation of trespassing on Mary Lincoln's status as private, domestic subject. As becomes evident, Keckley's insistence on publicly figuring her work and the products of her labor—among them, Mrs. Lincoln—as generating social value, renders the privacy of the people for whom she works, and the spaces in which she works, untenable.

Servants, as adjuncts to domestic femininity, were commonly understood to inhabit a realm of ideological invisibility.[28] In this context, Keckley's notion of her work as socially tangible and as authorizing the publicity of her worth belies the scopic norms that structured the meanings and values of subordinate, domestic labor.[29] That is, the effects of Keckley's drive to render her work rhetorically visible unintentionally exposed Mary Lincoln to public scrutiny, divested of the veil of privileged propriety that the social relations of domestic labor were called on to produce. This "exposure" of the elite, female body, then, was not simply the result of a malevolent motive on Keckley's part but an effect that testified to the conflicting imperatives underwriting working visibility and domestic privacy or invisibility. In other words, this was predominantly a structural, not a "personal" problem.

The fact that Keckley "outs" Mrs. Lincoln in an unbecoming way sheds light on the incommensurability of Keckley's goals and her methods, and signals a series of conflicts that points to the limits associated with any rhetorical drive toward working visibility. In particular, Keckley's invocation of her employer's trust and her own work-related credibility exhibits a structural problem concerning her own relation to the representation of her labor. The scenes of work, intimacy, trust, and rhetorical authority that Keckley went to such lengths to describe in her text show that she mistakenly assumed that because all her employers vouched for her, she could "vouch" for herself. Ironically, it is on the basis of this assumption that modern readers are justified in denoting *Behind the Scenes* as autobiography, despite the many descriptions of Keckley's text as mere "gossip."

As I have argued, for Keckley, the bond between employer and employee represented a paternalistic reciprocity of status and obligations. In terms of publicity, this reciprocity worked so that Keckley's clients simultaneously publicized their class status, Keckley's skill, and her investment in these structures of status. But what appeared as relations of social reciprocity, especially as pertains to "publicity relations," masked relations of subordination: That is, the subordinate socioeconomic status of a worker-servant makes it impossible for workers, and especially "domestic" workers, to narrate the social, economic, and political value of their work themselves. To base her credibility on these working relations of multiple subordination—in relation to capital, class status, and publicity—leaves Keckley open to charges of insubordination and to marshaling her rhetoric against her employers, whatever her intentions might be.

These charges point to Keckley's failure to recognize how her subordinate status as "servant" meant that her work-related attributes could only be narrated by her employer, not by herself. The story of Keckley's quick and skilled production of a dress for the wife of Captain Robert E. Lee exemplifies how this particular dynamic of client patronage and promotion for the most part benefitted Keckley and helped her succeed in Washington, DC: "The dress was done in time, and it gave complete satisfaction. Mrs. Lee attracted great attention at the dinner-party, and her elegant dress proved a good card for me. I received numerous orders, and was relieved from all pecuniary embarrassments" (78). This example of sartorial publicity illuminates the basis of Keckley's success in the "great attention" her dress provides Mrs. Lee, but it also narrates the ambiguity inhering in Keckley's subordinate status and her potential misunderstanding of the public circulation of status. When she figuratively represents the "elegant dress" as a "good card" for herself—referring here to the social custom of presenting "cartes de visite"—Keckley interprets the dress as unequivocally speaking for itself and testifying to her skill. With this assumption Keckley overlooks the necessary mediation of Mrs. Lee, for whom the dress actually proves a "good card." That is, Keckley's skill is never unmediated and is only appreciated when it is "publicized" or worn by Mrs. Lee as she circulates herself, the dress, and Keckley's skill in the social context open to Mrs. Lee and the dress—but not to Keckley.[30] Although one might view *Behind the Scenes* as an autobiographical "good card" that succeeds in bypassing the mediation of Keckley's employers, the text's reception then and now suggests that Keckley's subordinate position vis à vis her clients provided her with more "credit" than was/is extended to her by her reading audience.

The vexed publicity relations concerning Keckley's skill foreground the contradictions inherent in the domestic worker's defense of her employer through publicity, as well as the infringement of the employer's mediation that occurs when Keckley vouches for herself. These contradictions signal the structural limits that inhere in workers' speech, even, paradoxically, speech that purports to highlight and trade on the status of the socially superior employer. For as soon as the worker's body appears "on stage," the illusion of status and racial privilege that she customarily produces "behind the scenes" is dispelled. We can see this dynamic in play, even as we see how Keckley tries hard to perform her intense, gendered, and class identifications with Mary Lincoln for the reading public. Unfortunately, Keckley's emphasis on Mary Lincoln's need for her labor succeeds too well, setting up the dressmaker in a unique, autonomous relation, not simply in regard to her labor but also in relation to the employer she represents. In the scenarios detailing Mary Lincoln's erratic machinations to obtain money, Keckley focuses on how Mrs. Lincoln engaged her to act as broker and mediator between herself and the designated clothes sellers. And here the problem this publicity produced became very apparent: The portrayal of Keckley's competence comes at the expense of Mary Lincoln's own.

In this regard, the dense textuality of the "secret history"—its palimpsestic layering of newspaper clippings; "press releases"; letters between Mary Lincoln, Keckley, the designated sellers, as well as Frederick Douglass, Henry Garnet, and others, interspersed with accounts of Keckley's meetings with prominent businessmen on behalf of Mrs. Lincoln (56–62)—testifies to Keckley's business acumen in a manner analogous to the slave narrative's display of the authenticating, credit—producing documents pertaining to Keckley's manumission. But the documents in this case suggest Keckley might have been deemed more credible if she had retained the slave narrative tradition of having others—specifically, white people with social authority—vouch for her character, in lieu of promoting herself. Instead, the multiple texts relating to the scandal only make sense in Keckley's autonomously framed narrative, based on the credibility she claims as Mary Lincoln's trustworthy "confidante." And in this light, despite Keckley's efforts to do otherwise, Mary Lincoln's poor judgment relating to her handling of her widowhood, her public image, and the attempt to sell her "old" clothes stands in sharp contrast to Keckley's own.[31] In other words, Keckley does not so much "upstage" as "show up" Mary Lincoln.

Keckley's expressions of devotion to her employer in *Behind the Scenes* and the text's exposure of Mary Lincoln thus dramatize the contradictions produced by women's work relationships that assume the propriety and the benefits of paternalistic, racialized personal attachments. Although Keckley understood the necessity of making her work visible as a precondition for publicizing her social and economic value to Mary Lincoln, her subordinate and instrumental relation to Lincoln meant that silence rather than speech—no matter how complementary—constituted the only valued, or even recognizable, form of loyalty.[32] Notwithstanding the framing of Keckley's speech as a product of racial and gender deference, the cultural terms and class prerogatives within which this deference was understood clashed incontrovertibly with the dressmaker's insistence on being viewed as "worth her salt." This suggests that the very concept of a domestic worker's autobiography is problematic in rhetorical contexts that disavow the social, public aspect of this "private" and invisible labor. Keckley's efforts to exploit cultural understandings of racial loyalty or "devotion" as a way of rendering her productivity visible consequently overstepped the boundaries erected through the obscured production of white racial and class privilege. In failing to attend to the structurally subordinating conditions of the black female worker's speech, Keckley's positive valuation of the interracial trust and confidence she enjoyed with her clients and/or "friends" is condemned to provoking only incredulity and denial, rather than the respect and esteem she envisions.[33]

When Keckley publicized her work as former slave and freedwoman to claim the value she produced, she depicted the difficult post-Civil War dilemma in which she and African Americans were bound. If there was any sense in which the process of Reconstruction offered the African American population an opportunity to speak for itself and to address anxieties over black contributions to the nation's well-being, Keckley's text dramatizes the problematic realities invoked by efforts to represent freedwomen/freedmen as productive, and hence, as deserving of social respect and, even, equality. In this way, *Behind the Scenes* illustrates how on the national stage, the terms invoked for racial progress could simultaneously be employed as tools for racial subordination, and why as the "prototype" of later black success stories, *Behind the Scenes* actually differs from its most famous variation, *Up from Slavery*.[34] Thus, Booker T.

Washington's later framing of black labor within the structurally subordinate terms for which he is so (in)famous does not appear merely as an opportunistic surrender to the nation's racial and class discourses but, rather, a response to the rhetorical difficulties of representing black productivity.

For black working women, in particular, the intimate relations between paid domestic work and bourgeois, white femininity may have offered the illusion of an entry into a domestic "marketplace" that would facilitate reciprocal exchanges of esteem, trust, and propriety between black and white women. But as outlined above, interracial working interdependence was premised on racial, class, and gender asymmetries that offered a tenuous basis on which to promote black working women's social legitimacy. And yet, we would be remiss in continuing to overlook what Elizabeth Keckley went to such great pains to describe, how that same working interdependence produced social bonds that she was loath to forego. As the record shows, her devotion to Mary Todd Lincoln did not end when the boom came down on her after the publication of *Behind the Scenes*. While employed in 1892–93 as a highly respected teacher of "Domestic Art" at Wilberforce University, Keckley was known for her past association with the famous First Lady. There, according to her biographer, Keckley possessed a "large trunk" that contained "pieces of goods that she had saved from the various dresses that she made for Mrs. Lincoln." These remnants bespeaking Keckley's loyalty and expertise were, in turn, "passed on" by Keckley "to her favorite pupils."[35] By circulating these swatches, Keckley kept alive the memory of her relationship with Mrs. Lincoln for herself and her students, thereby including a younger generation in her dissemination of the life-story of respect and value.

NOTES

1. Elizabeth Keckley, *Behind the Scenes: Or, Thirty Years a Slave, and Four Years in the White House* (1868; reprint, New York: Oxford University Press, 1988), 330. Many thanks to Kenneth Warren and Lauren Berlant for their illuminating responses to earlier versions of this article.

2. See Eric Foner, "Reconstruction and the Crisis of Free Labor," in his *Politics and Ideology in the Age of the Civil War* (New York: Oxford University Press, 1980), 97–128, for a discussion of the conflicts that erupted over freedmen's quest for autonomy and planters' need for labor during Reconstruction.

3. Critical publicity surrounded Mary Todd Lincoln (1818–82) throughout her tenure as First Lady: Kentucky-born, her loyalty to the Union was always being questioned; she was constantly being criticized for her extravagance. See Ruth Randall Painter, *Mary Lincoln: Biography of a Marriage* (Boston: Little, Brown, 1953), 412–15; Ishbel Ross, *The President's Wife: Mary Todd Lincoln* (New York: Putnam, 1977); and Jean Baker, *Mary Todd Lincoln: A Biography* (New York: W.W. Norton, 1987). Baker, in particular, describes Keckley's text as a form of "retaliation" (280), uncannily echoing the 1868 review of *Behind the Scenes* that appeared in the *New York Citizen*, 18 Apr. 1868, under the heading "Indecent Publications."

4. I derive my interpretation of deference from Stephanie Coontz's formulation of racialized patron-client working relations. See her *The Social Origins of Private Life: A History of American Families, 1600–1900* (London: Verso, 1988), 139.

5. The complete title of this obscure pamphlet, *Behind the Seams; By a Nigger Woman who took in work from Mrs. Lincoln and Mrs. Davis* (New York: National News Co., 1868), bespeaks the illicit connotations associated with the public speech of (black) personal servants.

6. William Andrews counters "accommodationist" interpretations of Keckley's narrative by referring to her postbellum political priorities in his article, "Reunion in the Postbellum Slave Narrative: Frederick Douglass and Elizabeth Keckley," *Black American Literature Forum* 23 (Spring 1989): 5–17. Justin G. Turner and Linda Levitt Turner, the editors of Mary Lincoln's letters, describe *Behind the Scenes* as "an early example of what has come to be a popular if questionable literary genre: a former employee's backstairs glimpse into the private lives of public figures." See their *Mary Todd Lincoln: Her Life and Letters* (New York: Knopf, 1972), 472. Frances Smith Foster corroborates most of Keckley's claims in her recent and extensive "Historical Introduction" to a special edition of *Behind the Scenes* (Chicago: Lakeside Press, 1998), xix–lxxvii. Of special interest is the fact Foster uncovers regarding the identity of Keckley's last owner, Hugh Garland. Garland, to whom Keckley appealed for permission to buy her freedom, was the attorney who argued against the citizenship claims of slaves Hugh and Harriet Scott, in the infamous Dred Scott case, *Scott v. Sanford* in 1857. ("Historical Introduction," xxxvi.) For the most complete description of the publishing scandal, see Foster's *Written by Herself: Literary Production by African American Women, 1746–1892* (Bloomington: Indiana University Press, 1993), 126–30. See also the review of *Behind the Scenes* in the *New York Citizen*.

7. Keckley is thus the first to invoke the metaphor of slavery as a "school."

8. Frederick Douglass, *Narrative of the Life of Frederick Douglass, an American Slave, Written by Himself* (1845; reprint, New York: Signet Classic, 1997), 102. See also Harriet Jacobs, *Incidents in the Life of a Slave Girl* (1861; reprint, Cambridge: Harvard University Press, 1987).

9. Deborah Gray White's *Ar'n't I a Woman: Female Slaves in the Plantation South* (New York: W.W. Norton, 1985) laid the groundwork for historical re-evaluations of

black women's labor in slavery. See also Jacqueline Jones's *Labor of Love and Labor of Sorrow: Black Women, Work, and the Family from Slavery to the Present* (New York: Random House, 1985); Angela Davis, "Reflections of the Black Woman's Role in the Community of Slaves," 1971, reprinted in *The Angela Y. Davis Reader,* ed. Joy James (London: Blackwell, 1998), 111–28. I borrow the concept of "rewriting ... conditions of impossibility as the conditions of ... possibility" from Gayatri Spivak, "Can the Subaltern Speak?" in *Marxism and the Interpretation of Culture,* ed. Cary Nelson and Lawrence Grossberg (Urbana: University of Illinois Press, 1988), 285.

10. Paul Gilroy, *The Black Atlantic: Modernity and Double Consciousness* (Cambridge: Harvard University Press, 1993), 40.

11. These arguments tend to forestall our recognition of how workers might have interpreted socially disparaging attitudes toward their labor as part of the cause, rather than simply an effect, of their structurally subordinated relation within the occupational hierarchy. For important interpretations that question the relation of work to black women's identity, see Sharon Harley, "When Your Work Is Not Who You Are: The Development of a Working-Class Consciousness among Afro-American Women," in *Gender, Class, Race, and Reform in the Progressive Era,* ed. Noralee Frankel and Nancy S. Dye (Lexington: University of Kentucky Press, 1991), 42–55, as well as Harley's recent anthology, *Sister Circle: Black Women and Work,* ed. Sharon Harley and the Black Women and Work Collective (New Brunswick, N.J.: Rutgers University Press, 2002); Bonnie Thornton Dill, "Making Your Job Good Yourself: Domestic Service and the Construction of Personal Dignity," in *Women and the Politics of Empowerment,* ed. Ann Bookman and Sandra Morgen (Philadelphia: Temple University Press, 1988), 33–52; and Mary Romero, Maid in the U.S.A. (New York: Routledge, 1992).

12. These terms are derived from Hortense Spillers's influential account of slavery's structural effects on gender in the black community. See "Mama's Baby, Papa's Maybe: An American Grammar Book," *Diacritics* 17 (Summer 1987): 65–81. Another black woman's text, Frances E.W. Harper's *Iola Leroy* (1892; reprint, New York: Oxford University Press, 1988), reveals the postbellum difficulties associated with representing the independent black working woman as respectable.

13. Foster, *Written by Herself,* 130.

14. See Suzanne Lebsock, *Free Women of Petersburg: Status and Culture in a Southern Town, 1784–1860* (New York: W.W. Norton, 1984), 180.

15. *Oxford English Dictionary* definition of "modiste" derived from the French word for fashion—*mode*—stipulates "one who makes, invents or deals in articles of fashion; especially a maker of ladies robes, millinery, etc." *Oxford English Dictionary* (compact edition, 1971), 577. This connection between fashion and labor thus reinforces the links between labor and status Keckley takes such pains to describe. "Angry negro servant" is the phrase the reviewer of the *New York Citizen* used to describe Keckley.

16. William Andrews, "The Changing Moral Discourse of Nineteenth-Century African

American Women's Autobiography: Harriet Jacobs and Elizabeth Keckley," in *De/Colonizing the Subject: The Politics of Gender in Women's Autobiography*, ed. Sidonie Smith and Julia Watson (Minneapolis: University of Minnesota Press, 1992), 229, 231, 233.

17. Ibid., 234.

18. As Foster suggests, the multiple texts allow Keckley to "authenticate her account without resorting to a posture of self-defense." See Frances Smith Foster, "Autobiography after Emancipation: The Example of Elizabeth Keckley," in *Multicultural Autobiography: American Lives*, ed. James Robert Payne (Knoxville: University of Tennessee Press, 1992), 57.

19. The date of this letter, 1838, is significant because it suggests that Keckley's identification with paternalism is not merely a pragmatic *a posteriori* response to postbellum political realities. By alluding to Keckley's identification with paternalism I mean to foreground the feelings of obligation, dependency, and interdependence that she associates with her own Southern history. See Elizabeth Fox-Genovese and Eugene Genovese, *Fruits of Merchant Capital: Slavery and Bourgeois Property in the Rise and Expansion of Capitalism* (New York: Oxford University Press, 1983), 117. As they observe, the "commitment" of slaves to a paternalist "dependency relationship" did not itself signify an endorsement of slavery (and Keckley's example proves his point that slaves "knew their white folks too well to see them as ten feet tall"). Rather, slaves appealed to these relations of interdependence as a form of protection.

20. This appeal is paradoxical, not only because a slave is "buying into" an ideology that mystifies slavery's power relations but also because it inverts the paternalistic dynamic itself.

21. Lebsock (180) describes dressmaking and millinery as the most artisan-based and lucrative careers for antebellum women.

22. Arjun Appadurai describes the privileging dynamics of this deferential model of publicity as "mark(ing) the speaker as someone who knows something special and who has the privilege of passing it on." See his essay, "Topographies of the Self: Praise and Emotion in Hindu India," in *Language and the Politics of Emotion*, ed. Catherine A. Lutz and Lila Abu-Lughod (Cambridge: Cambridge University Press, 1990), 98.

23. For a perspective on the little recognized, yet public, nature of intimacy, see Lauren Berlant, "Intimacy: A Special Issue," *Critical Inquiry* 24 (Winter 1998): 281–88.

24. See Coontz, 139; and David Roediger, *The Wages of Whiteness: Race and the Making of the American Working Class* (London: Verso, 1991), 47.

25. See Romero, 123–26. *Like One of the Family* (Brooklyn: Independence Publishers, 1956) is the ironic title of Alice Childress's 1956 novel about domestic workers and their employers.

26. For a summary of the scandal in the media, see Painter, 405–15.

27. *New York Citizen*, 4.

28. See Christine Stansell, *City of Women: Sex and Class in New York, 1789–1860* (Urbana: University of Illinois Press, 1987), 160.

29. The literature on the semiotic and social invisibility of domestic servants is wide ranging. See Faye Dudden, *Serving Women: Household Service in Nineteenth-Century America* (Middletown, Conn.: Wesleyan University Press, 1983); and Karen Halttunen, *Confidence Men and Painted Women: A Study of Middle-Class Culture in America, 1830–1870* (New Haven: Yale University Press, 1982), for accounts of the spatial divisions that helped obscure the presence of workers and their work in the bourgeois household.

30. Another striking instance of Keckley's misrecognition of the contexts in which her dresses circulate concerns a dress she made for Varina Davis. Keckley's description of her 1865 Chicago fair encounter with a wax figure of Jefferson Davis wearing a dress displays complete lack of awareness of the role of this dress in the North's efforts to ridicule Mr. Davis's manhood. Instead of referring to this context of insult, Keckley (75) describes the "pleasing discovery" that the dress was one she had made. See Nina Silber, "Intemperate Men, Spiteful Women, Jefferson Davis," in *Divided Houses: Gender and the Civil War*, ed. Nina Silber and Catherine Clinton (New York: Oxford University Press, 1992), 283–305.

31. Both Andrews and Foster elaborate at length on the historical and political circumstances that govern this change in perspective from the antebellum slave narrative. See Andrews, "Changing Moral Discourse," 237; and Foster, "Autobiography after Emancipation," 57.

32. Although Lincoln scholars inevitably attribute Keckley's at times unflattering depiction of Mary Lincoln to motives of revenge, others have stressed Keckley's unconscious hostility to the former First Lady. See Jennifer Fleischner, *Mastering Slavery: Memory, Family, and Identity in Women's Slave Narratives* (New York: New York University Press, 1996), 96–97. My analysis suggests that any consideration of this relationship must attend to the work-produced, or work-mediated, nature of this bond.

33. This understanding of the structural rhetorical asymmetries existing between worker and employer speech builds on, yet moves beyond, understandings of the aesthetic disadvantages commonly associated with "working-class" autobiography. That is, Keckley does not encounter a literary standard problem per se. What she does is deploy wildly incompatible modes of representation that conflict over the made-public labor involved in private subjectivity. See Regenia Gagnier, *Subjectivities: A History of SelfRepresentation in Britain, 1832–1920* (New York: Oxford University Press, 1991).

34. Perhaps if Keckley had placed more emphasis on her reform work as president of the Contraband Association, her text might have been more readily perceived as referring to the abolitionist tradition of racial elevation. Yet Keckley's rendering of some of the freed population that sought refuge in D.C. ("contrabands") during the war in comic dialect reinforced the idea of former slaves as degraded labor and underscored the difference between them and Keckley. See Lynn Domina, "I was Re-

Elected President: Elizabeth Keckley as Quintessential Patriot in *Behind the Scenes*," in *Women's Life-Writing: Finding Voice/Building Community*, ed. Linda Coleman (Bowling Green, Ohio: Bowling Green State University Popular Press, 1997), 139–51; and Fleischner, 93–132.

    35. John E. Washington, *They Knew Lincoln* (New York: Dutton, 1942), 213.

CHAPTER FIVE

SARAH BLACKWOOD

"Making Good Use of Our Eyes"
Nineteenth-Century African Americans Write Visual Culture

IN HIS 1854 SPEECH, "The Claims of the Negro Ethnologically Considered," Frederick Douglass critiques the use of illustrated portraits in scientific works of mid-nineteenth-century ethnology.[1] He describes how images of the "European face" are calculated to convey "beauty, dignity, and intellect," while "The Negro, on the other hand, appears with features distorted, lips exaggerated, forehead depressed—and the whole expression of the countenance made to harmonize with the popular idea of Negro imbecility and degradation" (510). Douglass provides a unique glimpse into his own experience of nineteenth-century visual culture when he concludes that while "[t]he importance of this criticism [of images of African Americans] may not be apparent to all;—to the *black* man it is very apparent. He sees the injustice, and writhes under its sting" (514).

Douglass's address engages directly with mid-nineteenth-century visual culture and its depictions of black life and selfhood. His commentary on the experience of viewing the images of blacks that appeared in newspapers and popular books at midcentury is part of a rich and complicated tradition of African American textual engagement with visual culture. Recent scholarship has begun to attend to the intersections between African American literature, material culture, print culture, and visual technologies, usefully troubling a set of artificial critical boundaries that often led text, image, and object to be considered in isolation from one another. Marcy J. Dinius, for example, has shown the necessity of approaching nineteenth-century visual culture through the textual, emphasizing what she calls the "cycle of mediation and influence between print and daguerreotypy" (5), or how a public came to know daguerreotypy, and later photography, in large part through what was *written* about these technologies. Specifically addressing the mutual influence of nineteenth-century visual culture and African American imaginative traditions, important recent volumes by Michael A.

Chaney and by Maurice O. Wallace and Shawn Michelle Smith articulate just how intertwined nineteenth-century visual culture and African American life were: Wallace and Smith note that "photography emerged not out of a social and material vacuum but out of the world slavery made," arguing that scholars must take into account both "the early history of photography in African American cultural and political life and the dialectical bearing of photographic vision on the wider logic of nineteenth-century racial thought" (3). This recent scholarship remains in useful tension with a still-suggestive critical narrative about the absence of black perspectives and participation in nineteenth- and twentieth-century visual culture. Michele Wallace's groundbreaking essay "'Why Are There No Great Black Artists?' The Problem of Visuality in African American Culture" addressed what she termed "the visual void in black discourse" (333). More recently, Stephen Best elegantly responded to an excellent collection of essays published in a 2011 special issue of *Representations* on "New World Slavery and the Matter of the Visual" by asserting that "slaves are not the subject of the visual imagination, they are its object" (151).

Thus, it seems the time is especially ripe to explore in detail how nineteenth-century African American writers engaged with the often-objectifying visual culture of that era. While it is true that we have comparatively little visual work produced by slaves, ex-slaves, or free people of color, we have a lot of writing through which we can piece together at least a partial sense of black visual subjectivity. In the pages that follow, I will consider what nineteenth-century visual culture looks like when viewed through texts written by African Americans. I offer as a case study a famous nineteenth-century image—a photograph of Abraham Lincoln and his son Tad taken in 1864—and the surprising and altogether changing impression that a work of African American literature has upon it. Elizabeth Keckley, a former slave and Mary Todd Lincoln's dressmaker, wrote a scandalous memoir titled *Behind the Scenes: Or, Thirty Years a Slave, and Four Years in the White House* (1868) that provides the reader-viewer a completely different vantage upon the image that became so representative of fatherly instruction and care. Keckley's memoir exemplifies the abundance of interpretive possibility that emerges from a reconsideration of nineteenth-century African American texts in conjunction with the maddening and vibrant visual culture within which they existed.[2] This essay offers a new reading of a famous and calcified image of dominant white history by emphasizing the extent to which that history is partial, or even untrue, when detached from the African American perspectives that were intimate to its scene of production. In offering this case study, this essay also aims to develop critical approaches to the study of the visual, exploring how narratives, histories, and theories of nineteenth-century visual culture are altered in relation to the perspectives articulated in texts written by African Americans of the era.

Writing the Visual

In order to piece together a narrative about how nineteenth-century black writers understood both their presence and absence (their simultaneous subjectivity and objectification) within the visual field of the era, one must have a nimble sense of what visual culture is and where one might find its traces in *texts*.[3] In addition to the objects and images that comprise what we traditionally think of as nineteenth-century visual culture—daguerreotypes, lithographs, illustrated periodicals, cartes-de-visite, greeting cards, decorative prints, theater posters, celebrity portraits, commemorative sculpture, oil paintings, advertisements, and so on—we must also necessarily include the texts through which these objects come to be understood. This exercise in inclusion is particularly important for our study of African American imaginative expression because the visual (especially in its high art manifestations) has a high cost of entry for participation and because blacks were so often subject to visual depiction by whites. If nineteenth-century African American visual culture refers to works of art produced by blacks, our archive is suggestive but slim, including daguerreotypist Augustus Washington, engraver Patrick Reason, painter Robert Scott Duncanson, quilter Harriet Powers, and sculptor Edmonia Lewis. If nineteenth-century African American visual culture refers to visual artifacts that *depict* blacks and slavery, our archive—including Josiah Wedgwood's medallion of the kneeling slave, illustrated fugitive notices, fine art depictions of the slave trade, Topsy dolls, and much more—is enormous, yet horrifically skewed. Best describes the problem of working with these materials as a "pursuit of degraded fragments in an impoverished archive" (159).

Visual culture, however, need not cohere only in material imagery, but rather can be explored as flowing from specific viewing practices and "ways of seeing."[4] The relatively small archive of visual culture objects produced by African Americans should not be mistaken for a lack of black participation in visual culture practices. I suggest in this article that some of the least "impoverished" evidence that we have of nineteenth-century black viewing practices is found in texts.[5] This essay, however, is about more than just expanding an already-robust archive of black texts about visuality; instead, this essay argues for altogether reconfiguring the archive and the narratives we construct about nineteenth-century visual culture. By gathering the insights African Americans had into visual culture, a series of counternarratives about visual technologies and cultures emerges. For example, where we might conclude that the invention of photography went hand in hand with new forms of objectivity and realism in representation, I would argue that African American writers employed photographic tropes in their texts to question the so-called objectivity that came to define the photographic worldview. Because scholars have for so long omitted the voices of African American writers from our accounts of nineteenth-century visual culture, we have missed the variety of narratives about this visual culture that might serve to complicate our sense of how visuality mediated people's experiences of materiality and truth.[6]

Attention paid to how African American writers understood, challenged, and sought to change notions of vision, sight, and the gaze in their texts shifts our attention from objects to actions, from stability to movement, from representation to practice. Manifesting a suggestive interest in the visual as negotiated practice, Keckley's memoir is in conversation with visual culture on a variety of levels. In its pages, she directly refers to multiple forms of specific image-based representation, including photography, sculpture, and woodcuts. As such, the memoir is of a piece with moments like the one with which I opened, where Douglass critiques how portraits of black individuals are skewed in the white-dominated visual marketplace. But even beyond such specific visual references, Keckley's memoir employs a complex rhetorical argument about visual literacy and epistemology, or how one comes to see the world, and, through that sight, understand it.

Taken together, the moments in which black writers specifically mention visual culture and the sophisticated metaphoric language they employ to explore the visual register—the way that the gaze works, what sorts of knowledge are produced through sight—rewrite received wisdom about the African American literary tradition as founded on textual literacy, and even nineteenth-century visual culture more generally (as fueled by an increasing hunger for the "real thing").[7] Historically, critical examinations of the racialized visions of nineteenth-century visual culture have been polarized, with scholars finding the visual either wholly foreclosing or potentially liberating for nineteenth-century African Americans. Such readings tend to understand the visual as a set of static images, rather than the active, negotiated process that we find in texts written by African Americans of the era. This essay suggests that nineteenth-century African Americans attempted to *write* visual culture neither to replace supposedly false representations with true ones nor to reveal the visual as either foreclosing or liberating, but rather to proliferate representation. As representations proliferate, the visual register's claims to truth weaken, and viewers are urged to question the images held most dear (including those of the "Great Emancipator"). Black writers' discourses of visuality indict the obstructing, diminishing, and indexing force of what I will call "white sight," a set of viewing practices that claim an interpretive and epistemological authority that is fused with racial identity.[8] These textual explorations of the visual remind readers and viewers that black people were watching, and through this sight producing their own forms of interpretation, epistemology, and authority. By restoring black writers' insights into visual culture to the larger context within which they occurred, an entirely different picture of the nineteenth century begins to come into view.

"So Difficult to Instruct": The Epistemology of White Sight

In 1864, Anthony Berger photographed Abraham Lincoln and his son Tad in the Mathew Brady studio (see Fig. 1). The image shows the President and his youngest son gazing down at a book together. The image was reproduced many times in engraving, oil, lithograph—in almost any medium one can think of—after it appeared on the cover of *Harper's Weekly* shortly after Lincoln's assassination in April 1865 (see Fig. 2). The image is often read as a sentimental vignette in which a father and son read a book together, emphasizing the importance of literacy and education in preparing and cultivating the country's next generation. Harold Holzer, addressing the appearance of the famous photograph in the background of a watercolor painting titled *Negro Boy Dancing* (1878) by famed realist painter Thomas Eakins, suggests that its inclusion there was meant as "an enduring touchstone representing freedom and opportunity" (118).[9] Such an interpretation, however, becomes murkier when we realize that the book Lincoln held in his lap while posing for the por-

Figure 1: Anthony Berger, "Abraham Lincoln, U.S. President, Looking at a Photo Album with His Son, Tad Lincoln, Feb. 9, 1864," photograph. Image courtesy: Library of Congress.

trait was not, in particular, an emblem of textual literacy's opportunity—the book was neither a Bible nor a scholarly tome, but rather a photograph album that happened to be lying around the studio.

The nature of the book, it turns out, was a matter of much concern to Lincoln as well as to the artisans and businessmen who marketed the image in its many forms after Lincoln's death. The image appeared in multiple variants, including reproductions that drop Mary Todd into the frame (see Fig. 3), as well as the many engraved and lithographic versions that place Lincoln and Tad, in the same pose, into another setting altogether (see Fig. 4). These images' diversions from "reality" were not much commented upon. But in many reproductions, the book is made to look like a Bible (see Fig. 5). By comparing two different versions of the image produced by H.B. Hall and Sons, we see how the representation of

Figure 2: "President Lincoln at Home.— [Photographed by Brady.]" Cover of Harper's Weekly *(1865). Image courtesy: American Antiquarian Society.*

the book itself changed from reproduction to reproduction (see Fig. 6). Lincoln himself commented on the possibility that the book could be made to look like a Bible: He is reported to have been concerned that such a depiction would be "a species of false pretence" (qtd. in Ostendorf and Hamilton 183).[10] Perhaps one reason that the nature of the book was so meaningful to both Lincoln, and ultimately the public, is that Tad Lincoln, the spoiled and indulged youngest son of the president, was effectively illiterate at the time of the portrait. In fact, Tad did not learn to read until after his father's assassination in 1865, when he was twelve years old. In his 1871 *New York Tribune* obituary of the boy (who died at eighteen), Lincoln's secretary John Hay described Tad as "unlettered," writing that Lincoln "was pleased to see [Tad] growing up in ignorance of books . . . 'Let him run,' the easy-going President would say; 'he has time enough left to learn his letters and get pokey.'"

Familiarity with this backstory certainly complicates our understanding of this image as a depiction of fatherly instruction, literacy, education, and agency. How did we come to view this image as such? Keckley seems to have understood how fictional narratives of white knowledge were constructed via an image such as the Berger photograph. The representation of Tad's illiteracy that Keckley offers in *Behind the Scenes* is a significant but understudied contribution to an archive of black viewing practices as they were explored in texts written by African Americans.[11] Keckley's memoir caused a stir when it

*Figure 3: Currier and Ives, "President Lincoln at Home,
Reading the Scriptures to His Wife and Son," 1865, lithograph.
From the Lincoln Financial Foundation Collection; courtesy of
Allen County Public Library and Indiana State Museum.*

came out as it dwelled on, among other things, embarrassing details related to Mary Todd Lincoln's financial troubles after her husband's assassination. It incited at least one racist parody, a twenty-three-page text titled *Behind the Seams; By a Nigger Woman Who Took in Work from Mrs. Lincoln and Mrs. Davis* (1868), which opens with a preface "signed" with an *x* meant to represent the "mark" of "Betsey Kickley." This virulent text attacks Keckley by reconfiguring her as illiterate, even as it puts distorted words on paper for her.

If the author of *Behind the Seams* (the text is copyrighted to someone named "Daniel Ottolengul") actually read Keckley's engaging memoir, he would have

Figure 4: Kelly and Sons, "Abraham Lincoln and His Family," 1865, hand-colored lithograph. From the Lincoln Financial Foundation Collection; courtesy of Allen County Public Library and Indiana State Museum.

encountered in it Keckley's own pointed exploration of the vagaries of literacy as she experienced them in a household full of boisterous and seemingly ill-educated white boys. On the surface, Keckley's memoir engages the trope of literacy and the presumption that literacy is inextricably linked to the power to liberate oneself. Further, the memoir poses the significance of literacy for African Americans against the trivializing and dismissive manner in which the president's son could treat the power of words.

But Keckley goes beyond this familiar trope of literacy. She does so by linking Tad Lincoln's *textual* illiteracy with a form of *visual* illiteracy, claiming that his inability to read has perhaps less to do with books and words and more to do with the world he does not see fully. Such visual illiteracy, what I refer to as *white sight*, is both a symptom and a cause of the racism that enabled practices like slavery. Keckley's scandalous representation of Tad's illiteracy illustrates the production of white forms of knowing, an epistemology encouraged by a white sight that shapes (or as Douglass would have it, "distort[s]") the world that it pretends to view coolly and objectively. Scholars have noted rightly

Figure 5: H.B. Hall and Sons, "Lincoln at Home," engraving. From the Lincoln Financial Foundation Collection; courtesy of Allen County Public Library and Indiana State Museum.

that the acquisition of textual literacy was typically a watershed moment for enslaved narrators. But textual literacy was not simply celebrated by the formerly enslaved, despite its close association with freedom. The most familiar scenes of "reading and writing" (broadly construed) in slave narratives often point out the places where textual literacy either fails to translate into a broader ability to read the world or limns a limited sense of the world. They also expand Euro-American and white notions of textual literacy to include the body and a recognition of the cross-pollination of white and black forms of literacy.[12]

Keckley's surprising account of Tad Lincoln's inability to read, which ap-

Figure 6: H.B. Hall and Sons, "Abraham Lincoln and His Son Thaddeus" [sic], hand-colored lithograph. From the Lincoln Financial Foundation Collection; courtesy of Allen County Public Library and Indiana State Museum.

pears in Chapter Twelve of *Behind the Scenes*, thus emerges as a focal point around which issues of literacy and epistemology—both textual and visual— coalesce. Forced to stay in and work on his lessons though he "jumped about the room, boisterously, boy-like" (95), Tad insists to his mother that "A-p-e" spells "monkey" (96). They argue about this for quite some time, and before getting into the symbolic richness of the animalistic language, I would like to begin where Keckley ends, with a radical argument about white illiteracy: "Whenever I think of this incident," she notes, "I am tempted to laugh; and then it occurs to me that had Tad been a negro boy, not the son of a President, and so difficult to instruct, he would have been called thick-skulled and would have been held up as an example of the inferiority of the race." She goes on to insist that she does not mean to "reflect upon the intellect of little Tad" but only "that some incidents are about as damaging to one side of the question as to the other. If a colored boy appears dull, so does a white boy sometimes; and if a whole race is judged by a single example of apparent dullness, another race should be judged by a similar example" (97).

As is true throughout *Behind the Scenes,* Keckley refuses fully to conceal her wicked wit behind middle-class domestic platitudes. While it remains plausible that, as Keckley claims, she does not wish to "reflect upon the intellect of little Tad," it seems to me far more likely that Keckley's real argument here is that "another race *should* be judged" (emphasis added) by this "single example of apparent dullness." After all, why not? The question of representativeness—who shall represent the race?—would become central for African Americans toward the end of the nineteenth century. Moreover, Keckley, positioned at the very heart of American representative democracy— in the president's home—suggests that we take seriously the case of the illiterate son of a president.

While others did not seem to think it was important that Tad know how to read or have "book learning," Keckley understood the boy's illiteracy as a deficiency that went beyond the ability (or lack thereof) to read words, to a more significant inability to read the world. Consider this exchange between Mary Todd and the son Keckley finds "deficient":

> "Well, what does A-p-e spell?"
>
> "Monkey," was the instant rejoinder. The word was illustrated by a small wood-cut of an ape, which looked to Tad's eyes very much like a monkey; and his pronunciation was guided by the picture, and not by the sounds of the different letters.
>
> "Nonsense!" exclaimed his mother. "A-p-e does not spell monkey."
>
> "Does spell monkey! Isn't that a monkey?" and Tad pointed triumphantly to the picture.
>
> "No, it is not a monkey."
>
> "Not a monkey! What is it, then?"
>
> "An ape."
>
> "An ape! 'taint an ape. Don't I know a monkey when I see it?"

"No, if you say that is a monkey."

"I do know a monkey. I've seen lots of them in the street with the organs. I know a monkey better than you do, 'cause I always go out into the street to see them when they come by, and you don't."

"But, Tad, listen to me. An ape is a species of the monkey. It looks like a monkey, but it is not a monkey."

"It shouldn't look like a monkey, then. Here, Yib"—he always called me Yib— "isn't this a monkey, and don't A-p-e spell monkey? Ma don't know anything about it"; and he thrust his book into my face in an earnest, excited manner.

I could no longer restrain myself, and burst out laughing. Tad looked very much offended, and I hastened to say: "I beg your pardon, Master Tad; I hope that you will excuse my want of politeness."

He bowed his head in a patronizing way, and returned to the original question: "Isn't this a monkey? Don't A-p-e spell monkey?"

"No, Tad; your mother is right. A-p-e spells ape."

"You don't know as much as Ma. Both of you don't know anything;" and Master Tad's eyes flashed with indignation.

Robert entered the room, and the question was referred to him. After many explanations, he succeeded in convincing Tad that A-p-e does not spell monkey, and the balance of the lesson was got over with less difficulty. (96–97)

Significantly, this anecdote about the acquisition of textual literacy is also a story about learning how to see. Children are commonly taught language through pictures, the idea being that the concrete, representational quality of an image will help them grasp the abstract and arbitrary quality of language. Tad insists that the visual sign should always correlate exactly to the abstract signified. But as his mother points out, some things (apes) look very much like other things (monkeys). The "small wood-cut of an ape, which looked to Tad's eyes very much like a monkey" prevents him from being able to read the actual word in front of him—the image trumps the word in this case. The passage links the inability to sight-read to an inability, on the part of whites, to "see" and thus "read" the substance of difference and categorization—the very issues at the heart of the culture's language of racism. In this passage, that is to say, Keckley critiques white sight.

Although this moment is casual, many of its aspects point toward the larger stakes of Tad's power to label. Keckley brings the reader out of the scene very briefly in the aside that follows Tad's reference to her as "Yib"—she mutters to us, "he always called me Yib"—to draw a connection between Tad's misnaming of the ape and his misnaming of her. Tad's naming, as well as his mother's response, is an example of the kind of taxonomic practice that rationalized racist systems such as slavery. Mary Todd Lincoln, employing the language of speciation, declares (incorrectly) that "an ape is a species of monkey. It looks like a monkey, but it is not a monkey." Apes are not species of monkey, though they are both primates. It is unlikely that Mary Todd Lincoln was familiar with nineteenth-century debates over taxonomical classifications of humans, apes, or monkeys, but it bears noting that Linnaeus had, in the 1730s, scandalously included humans in the primate order. In the mid-nineteenth century, however, American School ethnographers such as Samuel George Morton, Josiah Nott, and George Gliddon (writers whom Douglass critiques in "The Claims of the Negro") attempted scientifically to prove that blacks and whites were different species, and that sexual reproduction between the races would ultimately lead to sterility, physical weakness, and the end of humankind. Mary Todd Lincoln was most likely not parroting or even invoking such views, but Keckley stages the argument between Lincoln and her son about monkeys and apes to highlight the simple problematic that lay behind the gruesome intellectual contortions men such as Morton, Nott, and Gliddon undertook: If people of African descent look like humans, how can we treat them like animals?

Mary Todd Lincoln, attempting to instruct her youngest child, unknowingly explains the answer to such a question: "It looks like . . . but it is not." The scene of instruction that Keckley allows us the pleasure of peeping in on gives the reader a glimpse of how both white literacy and illiteracy work. Tad's illiteracy extends even to his inability to read *images* accurately; he is blinded by his own preconceptions and so things appear to him the way he has already decided they should appear. But Lincoln's literacy allows her no better clarity. She finds herself making weak claims that convince no one. Brought together with the significant critique Keckley offers in conclusion to this anecdote—that the white race *should* be judged by Tad's "apparent dullness"—the passage offers a devastating critique of not only white *illiteracy* but also white *literacy*.

As mother and son jostle here for epistemological authority, Keckley's relating of the scene asks readers to think about how literacy, illiteracy, and sight are put to use as knowledge-making systems. Tad's position as both empowered voice of white epistemological authority and disempowered voice of a child having to learn is exemplified by his speaking in negatives. When he asks, "Don't I know a monkey when I see it?" he simultaneously asserts his privileged position to name and also undercuts that assertion—he is acting the part of the empowered subject but has not fully learned how to inhabit it. Keckley has chosen this moment of instruction to dramatize how a person is initiated into a particular way of seeing. Tad repeatedly appeals to his own authority, which is based on what he sees and thus knows to be true. His authority is explicitly linked to his mobility as a male subject; he "go[es] out into the street to see them," whereas his mother does not. Dispensing with the ludicrous possibility of his mother's epistemological authority—"Ma don't know anything about it"—he appeals to Keckley, who he assumes will agree with him, as "Master Tad." But when this foray fails as well, he shuffles the epistemological hierarchy again. If his mother's knowledge is wanting, Keckley knows even less; both of them together "don't know anything." Ultimately Robert Lincoln, the fully formed white male subject, intervenes and "convinc[es] Tad that A-p-e does not spell monkey."

In Keckley's description, the question of literacy, both textual and visual, becomes inextricably linked with an ethical vision of the world. The existence of hordes of literate slaveholders has taught black writers that literacy is a tool without an inherent value system. A reader of Chapter Twelve of Keckley's memoir must confront fundamental questions about the failures of the sort of textual literacy we have come to think of as liberating, about the workings of visual literacy, and about the way both sorts of literacies must be understood within a rubric of educative justice. What is Tad taught here? Is he being taught how to read, or is he being taught how to see the world? The passage suggests that, in looking at this "wood-cut of an ape, which looked . . . very much like a monkey," Tad learns how to identify authority and how to toggle between seeing the world as you believe it to be and seeing the world as the subject position you hope to occupy sees it. Keckley emphatically, fascinatingly, refuses to depict herself in the position of learning anything during this scene of instruction. She also refuses to teach the white child any sort of homespun wisdom that a black caretaker might have been expected to provide. Instead, this memorable scene teaches the reader how to begin seeing the world as it *should* be ("another race should be judged"). As Tad tries with increasing excitement to redraw the picture that he sees into a picture that he recognizes, Keckley laughs at him, and then she *writes*.

"Making Good Use of Our Eyes"

The story that Keckley tells about Tad's lack of literacy helps readers understand how white epistemological authority takes shape through metaphors and experiences of sight in the mid-nineteenth century. But Keckley does more than dismantle the picture a reader-viewer holds in her mind of a young boy learning at the side of the "Great Emancipator." She also builds up a structure through which a reader-viewer can begin to understand black viewing practices. The memoir itself, a promised glimpse "behind the scenes," is structured on a specific discourse of black visuality. Jennifer Fleischner has considered the remarkably complex intimacy between Mary Todd Lincoln and Keckley, and I do not wish to downplay that intimacy here. The extent to which Keckley meant the memoir to be a sensational and revealing tell-all is debatable; Fleischner suggests that Keckley meant her book to be "serious, sentimental," but that its marketing as "A Literary Thunderbolt" (316) had a hand in shaping it into the betrayal Lincoln felt it was (318).[13] Rather than focus on biographical intention, affect, and aftermath, however, I would like to consider how Keckley's text, from its very first pages, manifests its visual register rhetorically.

Keckley's memoir employs, quite explicitly, the language of photography, cameras, truth, and illusion, forcing the reader to consider the powerful and destabilizing visual agency exercised by black and enslaved individuals. Though the memoir's first chapter links itself to the classic slave narrative tradition by opening with the oft-repeated statement "I was born a slave" (9), Chapter One does not, in fact, mark the absolute beginning of Keckley's narrative. Preceding the "I was born a slave" statement is a Preface that offers an account of a different sort of literacy, suggesting that there is another tradition in nineteenth-century African American writing waiting to be understood more fully.

Just as Nathaniel Hawthorne does in *The House of the Seven Gables* (1851), Keckley opens *Behind the Scenes* with a Preface that considers the relationships between "romance" and "fact" and "dark" and "bright" (3). Alan Trachtenberg has shown how Hawthorne's language in that Preface has everything to do with Hawthorne's attempt to analogize writing with the daguerreotype, embracing both the magical and mimetic qualities of that new mode of visual representation (460–61). Keckley goes a step further, analogizing herself as a slave with both the camera and the photograph: "God rules the Universe. I was a feeble instrument in his hands, and through me and the enslaved millions of my race, one of the problems was solved that belongs to the great problem of human destiny; and the solution was developed so gradually that there was no great convulsion of the harmonies of natural laws. A solemn truth was thrown to the surface" (3–4). Like a camera, Keckley is an instrument through which truth can be developed on a surface. As the Preface unfolds, Keckley continues to focus on this surface. She believes she has "aided in bringing a solemn truth to the surface *as a truth*," repetitive phrasing that is confusing until we read, in the next paragraph, her understanding that she believes Mrs. Lincoln to have been unfairly judged by people who "knew nothing of the secret history of her transactions, therefore they judged her by what was thrown to the surface" (2).

Keckley has faith in the capacity of the photographic surface to display solemn truths but also understands that often surfaces deceive or conceal secrets below. Importantly, the secrets Keckley promises to reveal are Mary Todd Lincoln's: "If the world are to judge her as I have judged her, they must be introduced to the secret history of her transactions. The veil of mystery must be drawn aside; the origin of a fact must be brought to light with the naked fact itself" (5). Here Keckley defends herself from a charge that was, indeed, forthcoming from contemporary critics: that she did not honor the servant's duty to keep sacred the secrets of her employer. The reader realizes that her emphatic representation of herself as a camera—that recording angel—is only the most thinly veiled of threats to a white world that mandated black textual illiteracy and presumed black visual illiteracy. In contrast to an assumption of black difference and, to use Keckley's word, "dullness," Keckley posits a powerful black visual acuity as an observant, interpretive, and recording force. We are (and have always been) here, she seems to say, remembering that your sons are illiterate, keeping track of the money you try to earn by selling your gowns, knowing which tea cups are cracked.

Keckley's text is not alone in its assertion of a critical black gaze. Hannah Crafts employs a similar discourse of visuality in *The Bondwoman's Narrative*

(c. 1853–61). The novel's engagement with the visual is complex. The first chapter famously contains a scene in which the slave's mind is awakened not via the acquisition of textual literacy but via an aesthetic experience in a portrait gallery. This expansive experience of the visual, however, is directly posed against the use of a portrait to foreclose and discipline, as when Mistress is revealed to be mulatto when the villain Mr. Trappe discovers a photographic portrait of her enslaved mother.[14] On balance, these two scenes seem to cancel one another out, the one embracing the visual as a realm of freedom and expressivity, the other identifying the visual as inventorying and entrapping. But the text teeters on this edge, I would argue, deliberately. One small moment from the beginning of the novel suggests why.

As the slaves and servants prepare the house for the arrival of the new mistress, Hannah describes how, previously, "all except certain apartments had been interdicted to us." Their bodily movement was restricted, even in the house that they kept running and abundant with unremunerated labor. But, Hannah notes, even within this system of restriction and abuse, "no one could prevent us making good use of our eyes" (14). In the novel, Hannah hides behind curtains and watches the dramas of the household. The reader sees Hannah "examine and inspect [Mistress's] appearance" noting that "I was studying her and making a mental inventory of her foibles" (27). This is an unruly world of gazes and countergazes, of eyes fettered in enslaved bodies but free in observation.

The novel's sophisticated use of portrait galleries, photography, and scenes of voyeurism and visual fantasy demands a critical framework that recognizes black writers' engagement with mid-nineteenth-century discourses about art, photography, mechanical reproduction, surveillance, spectacle, and visual pleasure.[15] Again, I want to contend that, for black writers, visual culture was not only a collection of material objects; it was also a process through which individuals came to understand the world and their place in it. Often a work of visual art spurred a black artist to think through that work's place in a matrix of competing visual discourses, as it did in Harriet A. Jacobs's account in her narrative of seeing a painted portrait of a black person for the first time. One of the first things that Jacobs's alter ego Linda Brent does after fleeing enslavement in North Carolina is visit "an artist's room." In the chapter titled "Incidents in Philadelphia," Jacobs narrates how Mrs. Durham, the wife of the minister who has taken Jacobs in, "took me to an artist's room, and showed me the portraits of some of her children. I had never seen any paintings of colored people before, and they seemed to me beautiful" (162). On one hand, this is the complicated moment of "facing": of an African American finding confirmation of her humanity in positive and nonrasist visual representations of the black self.[16] Jean Fagan Yellin speculates that in this scene Mrs. Durham and Jacobs visit the Philadelphia painter Robert M.J. Douglass Jr. (Jacobs, *Incidents* 303n6), an African American artist who had been trained by white portraitist Thomas Sully, suggesting that the slim archive of black artists that I discuss above is still in the process of expanding.

But most significant, I contend, is Jacobs's use of the verb *seemed*. With this single word, she places the reader on that edge between the visual as possibility and the visual as restraint. If Jacobs's experience in the portrait gallery is about finding in material imagery confirmation of her humanity, it is equally about the portrait *process,* about the cultural literacy that the production and reception of portraits requires or presumes, and about the possibilities for misrecognition, subterfuge, and evanescence (as opposed to the status, permanence, and visual authority that white portraiture often embraced) inherent in visual depictions of the contested self. The portraits, as Jacobs describes them, *seem* beautiful rather than *are* beautiful. The modesty of Jacobs's phrase is surprisingly suggestive, as what at first appears to be a deauthorized aesthetic judgment evolves into critical commentary. Never having seen a portrait of a "colored" person before, and so having no basis for comparison or evaluation, Jacobs cannot declare whether the image is beautiful. This is the sort of aesthetic disenfranchisement that has made coming to terms with antebellum African American ideas about, participation in, and reception of nineteenth-century popular visual culture so difficult. We might view Jacobs's account of the artist's room as evidence of an impoverished experience of the visual world, yet we should also consider how Jacobs's textual exploration of what portraits mean, and crucially how they come to mean, is of a piece with Keckley's explosive consideration of visual literacy. All of them together— Keckley, Crafts, and Jacobs—are making good use of their eyes.

To conclude, I want to suggest some directions that this brief overview of the appearance of visual culture in texts by nineteenth-century African Americans might take. We have only just begun to understand the variety of ways that black writers employed the visual in their texts. The examples of Douglass, Keckley, Crafts, and Jacobs suggest that we continue to mine both canonical and lesser-known works by black writers to deepen our understanding of their participation in a national conversation about the place of the visual in a modernizing culture. I am currently at work on a coedited collection of primary texts by black writers that exhibit interest in visual culture and discourses of visuality; I hope that this project will encourage more study by gathering together a large selection of primary texts that have often been passed over in nineteenth-century visual culture scholarship.

The texts that I have considered in this essay by no means exhaust the archive of materials related to black viewing practices in the nineteenth century. Tying together my examples here has been a particular interest in how the visual might offer alternative views of authority, of who gets to decide what is truth. In the speech with which I opened, Douglass goes even further than simply noting the different visual world experienced by "the black man." Just prior to his moving description of how he "writhes" under the "sting" of "distorted" portraiture, he writes:

> It is the province of prejudice to blind; and scientific writers, not less than others, write to please, as well as to instruct, and even unconsciously to themselves, (sometimes) sacrifice what is true to what is popular. Fashion is not confined to dress; but extends to philosophy as well—and it is fashionable now, in our land, to exaggerate the differences between the Negro and the European. If, for instance, a phrenologist, or naturalist undertakes to represent in portraits, the differences between the two races—the Negro and the European—he will invariably present the *highest* type of the European, and the *lowest* type of the Negro. ("Claims" 510)

For Douglass, racial differences and political equality are constantly being measured, evaluated, stratified, and contested via visual technologies, metaphors, and cultures. He points out the subjective nature of supposedly objective scientific authority, which employs the visual precisely because of the fiction of its capacity for representing truth. It is useful to read "Claims of the Negro" within the context of nineteenth-century visual culture not only because Douglass makes a series of remarks about the specific visual form of portraiture, but because he uses the visual (more broadly conceived) to articulate his central argument about science, objectivity, and authority. The speech's argument—like that of the other writers I discuss—is about how we come to see things as true: indications, signs, traces, seemings, clarity. Douglass deploys a vocabulary—about "resemblance," "appearance," "marks" (all words he uses multiple times in his speech)—that emphasizes the extent to which mid-nineteenth-century racial discourse is a deeply visual rhetoric. He focuses on portraiture as a specific visual form that gives the lie to scientific authority by identifying how race scientists distort their evidence as much as they distort black facial features in their illustrations.

Perhaps most fascinatingly, Douglass does not turn away from the visual after identifying its powers of distortion. Instead, he reflects, "I think I have never seen a single picture in an American work, designed to give an idea of the mental endowments of the negro" and then goes on to describe a wonderfully alternative portrait gallery. There are no George Washingtons adorning these walls; here Douglass paints for his listeners a gallery hung with likenesses of "A. Crummel, Henry H. Garnet, Sam'l R. Ward, Chas. Lenox Remond, W.J. Wilson, J.W. Pennington, J.I. Gaines, M.R. Delany, J.W. Loguin, J.M. Whitfield, J.C. Holly, and hundreds of others I could mention" ("Claims" 510–12). How does this imagined gallery fit into the archive of African American visual production? What does its abundance tell us about the bemoaned slimness of the African American visual archive? How do we understand this gallery in relation to the era's national visual culture? This alternative portrait gallery implores us to return to nineteenth-century African American writing about visual culture to explore how it dealt with the racism of that visual culture not by turning away but by reconstructing its museum.

In many ways these alternative portrait galleries remain invisible or rarely visited. The iconic and moving image of President Lincoln and his son continues to loom large in our cultural imaginary without concomitant interest in the sort of behind-the-scenes commentary someone like Keckley could add to a discussion of visual culture in the nineteenth century.[17] Keckley's written depiction of Tad Lincoln's literacy should open more eyes to the importance of this discussion, generating interest in how African Americans understood the increasingly visual world in which they lived (and within which they often found themselves as objects of visual study) and how black writers used the visual in their writings to explore different forms of literacy and epistemological power. As the example of Keckley's "rewriting" of the portrait of the president and his son attests, black writers' insights into American iconography often undo the assumptions that tie that iconography to sets of cultural values, even those values seemingly embraced by black writers as well (for example, the power of literacy). But even more, the robust discourse of visuality found in texts written by African Americans offers new perspectives on some of the most fundamental aspects of the visual nineteenth century: the relationship between technology and vision, the significance of the visual in the age of mechanical reproduction, the increasingly important role of visual representations of racial, sexual, and social difference, and the visual as interface between public and private. As such, we have only begun to understand the central role that nineteenth-century black writers and thinkers played in modernity's visual turn, or how the destabilization of vision as a vital form of knowing contributed to increasingly fractured understandings of the self and the world.

NOTES

I would like to acknowledge the many people who helped me refine the ideas in this essay, including the editors and reviewers of *MELUS,* Lauren Klein, Janet Neary, Kyla Schuller, and Karen Weingarten.

1. Frederick Douglass delivered this address to the prestigious literary societies of Western Reserve College during commencement week. See John W. Blassingame's brief introduction to it in *The Frederick Douglass Papers, Series One* for more details on what Douglass called an "enthusiastically received" speech (qtd. in Blassingame 498).

2. Elizabeth Keckley's memoir has rarely been considered in relation to visual culture. One exception is Lisa E. Farrington's *Creating Their Own Image,* which considers Keckley's participation in the visual culture of fashion as Mary Todd Lincoln's dressmaker (43–44).

3. Michael L. Wilson wonders whether visual culture is "a useful category of historical analysis," pointing out that "Scholars of *visual culture* seem unable to reach consensus on what, exactly, their object of inquiry might be and how it is to be studied" (27). As will become clear, I believe that an expansive definition of *visual culture* is necessary in studying African American imaginative traditions, for two opposing reasons. With some exceptions, most nineteenth-century black individuals lacked the resources (training and materials) to fully participate in the professional production of so-called fine art (such as painting) or vocational art (such as engraving). However, because textual literacy was also restricted, many black individuals honed their visual literacy skills and later wrote about this specific form of "reading" the world.

4. I take the phrase from John Berger's foundational text of the same name. Jonathan Crary has explored the recursive relationship between new visual technologies and new forms of selfhood in nineteenth-century (mostly European) modernity (1–25).

5. Grey Gundaker has explored how black viewing and literacy practices are also manifest in African American vernacular, oral, and folk art cultures (defined broadly, from grave-markers to yard work to healing practices to gang signs).

6. The debates about objectivity that accompanied the invention of photography and other technologies of modernity have been explored by many visual theorists. However, the contributions to this debate by black writers, artisans, artists, and thinkers have often gone unremarked. Objectivity was certainly not a stable epistemological framework in the nineteenth century; it makes sense to ask what significance the category of objectivity might have had to nineteenth-century African Americans, whose lived experience of objecthood made this epistemological question also ontological.

7. Miles Orvell's study explores the complex ways in which visual culture's relationship to reality shifted at the end of the nineteenth century.

8. This is not to say that dominant or white culture was confident in the objectivity of sight. A key aspect of the development of modernity throughout the nineteenth century was doubt about vision and its claims to truth-telling. In addition to Crary, see Marcy J. Dinius (12–85) on the clash between daguerreotypy's romanticism and its "mechanical objectivity" (4). However, this sort of epistemological doubt often disappeared when confronted with questions of racial identity and racialized authority. "White sight" is thus a fantastical and yet powerful fiction.

9. Alan C. Braddock has written of the ambiguous nature of the photograph's inclusion in this painting, suggesting that the image employs the iconic Lincoln photograph as an ironic commentary on the experience of so-called black freedom after the Civil War (135–37, 146–48). Harold Holzer, acknowledging that this interpretation is "perceptive," concludes that it is nonetheless "gloomy" (118).

10. The original Anthony Berger photograph was commissioned by the artist Francis Carpenter as a study for a painting that was never made. (Carpenter did go on to make the painting *Emancipation Proclamation* after living in the White House for six months.) Interestingly, no one seemed to realize the value (emotional or financial) of photographic images of Lincoln until after his death. The Berger photograph was not reproduced until almost a year after it was taken. Lincoln's concern about the album being made to appear to be a Bible thus seems to have existed apart from an understanding that the image would become one of the most famous and often-reproduced depictions of him.

11. Janet Neary reads Keckley's representation of Tad Lincoln's illiteracy as a savvy rewriting of traditional slave narrative conventions.

12. In particular, I am thinking of the well-known moments when the learned politician Mr. Sands fails correctly to "read" Harriet A. Jacobs when she is disguised as a darker-skinned male sailor (Jacobs 113) (as well as other moments of cross-dressing and disguise in other slave narratives), and when Douglass writes in the margins of white texts, learns to write in public from young white boys, and suggests that he might hide a pen in the cracks of his feet (Douglass, *Narrative* 35).

13. Jennifer Fleischner's *Mrs. Lincoln and Mrs. Keckly* is an engaging account of their relationship and of the intersections of nationalism and domesticity. Keckly's name was misspelled *Keckley* when her book was published; this spelling has persisted. Fleischner does not use it, as she is writing biography. I use the published spelling, *Keckley*, because I am more concerned with the authorial persona, rather than the historical person.

14. Christopher Castiglia has written about this scene in relation to the importance of the "dis-" or "misidentification[s]" (235) that happened when African Americans view portraits.

15. Gustavus Stadler's analysis of William Wells Brown's "produc[tion of] himself as a man of culture trafficking ideas among the great minds of Britain" (74) and Elisa Tamarkin's work on the sociability of an antislavery "Black Anglo-Saxonism" (231) are examples of recent work that places black writers into the broader conversations about art and cosmopolitanism that have long characterized the study of white writers from the era.

16. On the importance of the concept of "facing" to African American literary studies, see Kimberly W. Benston: "Here African American identity looks on an image of being at once external and internal to itself, an echo or reflection that it must revise in order better to see itself" (99–100). See also Henry Louis Gates Jr. Samuel Otter offers a reading of this scene as a commentary on Jacobs's literary self-creation: "Linda sees a kind of self-presentation that she has not seen before. Commissioned by those with means, preserving their visages, such portraits convey a status, a permanence, and a visual authority. In some ways, this is a self-reflexive passage describing Jacobs's own artistic effort: her book, which she hopes will grant her a durable presence" (103).

17. The film *Lincoln* (2012) (directed by Steven Spielberg) animates the famous photograph by showing the president reading a book with Tad on his lap. Allowing Tad a sort of visual literacy that the real Keckley did not, the film associates Tad with his father's abolitionist commitments by depicting the boy as obsessed with looking at glass plates of a series of well-known photographs of former slaves (the scarred back of "Gordon" is one prominent example). These images provide the film's only impetus for the discussion of slavery-as-lived-reality when Tad is spurred by the photographs to ask Keckley (played by Gloria Reuben) what slavery was like. Keckley's cuttingly matter-of-fact answer to Tad notwithstanding, this scene of well-meaning curiosity on the part of Tad Lincoln differs greatly from the historical Keckley's written depiction of Tad's manifestation of literacy and curiosity.

WORKS CITED

Behind the Seams; By a Nigger Woman Who Took in Work from Mrs. Lincoln and Mrs. Davis. New York: National News, 1868. Open Library. Web. 9 Aug. 2012.

Benston, Kimberly W. "Facing Tradition: Revisionary Scenes in African American Literature." *PMLA* 105.1 (1990): 98–109.

Berger, John. *Ways of Seeing.* 1972. New York: Penguin, 1990.

Best, Stephen. "Neither Lost nor Found: Slavery and the Visual Archive." *Representations* 113 (2011): 150–63.

Blassingame, John W. Introduction. "The Claims of the Negro Ethnologically Considered: An Address Delivered in Hudson, Ohio, on 12 July 1854." Douglass, *Frederick* 497–99.

Braddock, Alan C. *Thomas Eakins and the Cultures of Modernity.* Berkeley: University of California Press, 2009.

Castiglia, Christopher. "'I found a life of freedom all my fancy had pictured it to be': Hannah Crafts's Visual Speculation and the Inner Life of Slavery." *In Search of Hannah Crafts: Critical Essays on* The Bondwoman's Narrative. Ed. Henry Louis Gates Jr. and Hollis Robbins. New York: BasicCivitas, 2004. 231–53.

Chaney, Michael A. *Fugitive Vision: Slave Image and Black Identity in Antebellum Narrative.* Bloomington: Indiana University Press, 2008.

Crafts, Hannah. *The Bondwoman's Narrative.* c. 1853–1861. Ed. Henry Louis Gates Jr. New York: Warner, 2002.

Crary, Jonathan. *Techniques of the Observer: On Vision and Modernity in the Nineteenth Century.* Cambridge: MIT Press, 1992.

Dinius, Marcy J. *The Camera and the Press: American Visual and Print Culture in the Age of the Daguerreotype.* Philadelphia: University of Pennsylvania Press, 2012.

Douglass, Frederick. "The Claims of the Negro Ethnologically Considered: An Address Delivered in Hudson, Ohio, on 12 July 1854." 1854. Douglass, *Frederick* 499–525.

———. *The Frederick Douglass Papers. Series One: Speeches, Debates, and Interviews.* Vol. 2: 1847–54. Ed. John W. Blassingame. New Haven: Yale University Press, 1982.

———. *Narrative of the Life of Frederick Douglass.* 1845. New York: Penguin, 2013.

Farrington, Lisa E. *Creating Their Own Image: The History of African-American Women Artists.* New York: Oxford University Press, 2005.

Fleischner, Jennifer. *Mrs. Lincoln and Mrs. Keckly: The Remarkable Story of the Friendship between a First Lady and a Former Slave.* New York: Broadway, 2003.

Gates, Henry Louis Jr. "The Trope of a New Negro and the Reconstruction of the Image of the Black." *Representations* 24 (1988): 129–55.

Gundaker, Grey. *Signs of Diaspora/Diaspora of Signs: Literacies, Creolization, and Vernacular Practice in African America.* Oxford: Oxford University Press, 1998.

Hay, John. "Tad Lincoln." *New York Daily Tribune* 17 July 1871: 4.

Holzer, Harold. "Picturing Freedom: The Emancipation Proclamation in Art, Iconography, and Memory." *The Emancipation Proclamation: Three Views*. By Holzer, Edna Greene Medford, and Frank J. Williams. Baton Rouge: Louisiana State University Press, 2006. 83–136.

Jacobs, Harriet A. *Incidents in the Life of a Slave Girl: Written by Herself*. 1861. Ed. Jean Fagan Yellin. Cambridge: Harvard University Press, 1987.

Keckley, Elizabeth. *Behind the Scenes: or, Thirty Years a Slave, and Four Years in the White House*. 1868. Ed. William L. Andrews. New York: Penguin, 2005.

Lincoln. Dir. Steven Spielberg. Perf. Daniel Day-Lewis, Sally Field. DreamWorks Pictures, 2012. DVD.

Neary, Janet. "*Behind the Scenes* and Inside Out: Elizabeth Keckly's Revision of the Slave Narrative Form." 2012. TS.

Orvell, Miles. *The Real Thing: Imitation and Authenticity in American Culture, 1880–1940*. Chapel Hill: University of North Carolina Press, 1989.

Ostendorf, Lloyd, and Charles Hamilton. *Lincoln in Photographs: An Album of Every Known Pose*. Norman: University of Oklahoma Press, 1963.

Otter, Samuel. "Philadelphia Experiments." Rev. of *Rum Punch and Revolution: Taverngoing and Public Life in Eighteenth-Century Philadelphia*, by Peter Thompson; *These Fiery Frenchified Dames: Women and Political Culture in Early National Philadelphia*, by Susan Branson; *The American Manufactory: Art, Labor, and the World of Things in the Early Republic*, by Laura Rigal; *First City: Philadelphia and the Forging of Historical Memory*, by Gary B. Nash; and *The Elite of Our People: Joseph Wilson's Sketches of Black Upper-Class Life in Antebellum Philadelphia*, by Joseph Wilson. American Literary History 16.1 (2004): 103–16.

Stadler, Gustavus. *Troubling Minds: The Cultural Politics of Genius in the United States, 1840–1890*. Minneapolis: University of Minnesota Press, 2006.

Tamarkin, Elisa. *Anglophilia: Deference, Devotion, and Antebellum America*. Chicago: University of Chicago Press, 2007.

Trachtenberg, Alan. "Seeing and Believing: Hawthorne's Reflection on the Daguerreotype in *The House of the Seven Gables*." American Literary History 9.3 (1997): 460–81.

Wallace, Maurice O., and Shawn Michelle Smith. Introduction. *Pictures and Progress: Early Photography and the Making of African American Identity*. Ed. Wallace and Smith. Durham: Duke University Press, 2012. 1–17.

Wallace, Michele. "'Why Are There No Great Black Artists?' The Problem of Visuality in African-American Culture." Afterword. *Black Popular Culture*. Ed. Gina Dent. Seattle: Bay, 1992. 333–46.

Wilson, Michael L. "Visual Culture: A Useful Category of Historical Analysis?" *The Nineteenth-Century Visual Culture Reader*. Ed. Vanessa R. Schwartz and Jeannene M. Przyblyski. New York: Routledge, 2004. 26–33.

CHAPTER SIX

STEVE CRINITI

Thirty Years a Slave, and Four Years a Fairy Godmother
Dressmaking as Self-Making in Elizabeth Keckley's Autobiography

My clothes may express the dressmaker, but they don't express me.
—Henry James, *Portrait of a Lady* (183)

IN THIS EPIGRAPH FROM Henry James's *The Portrait of a Lady*, Isabel Archer argues with Madame Merle about whether clothing expresses the wearer. Isabel's retort is perhaps an unexpected one in light of the tradition in nineteenth-century fiction of clothing serving as an outward sign of a character's internal "selfhood." Madame Merle herself subscribes to this traditional idea admitting, "I know that a large part of myself is in the dresses I choose to wear" (181). In Edith Wharton's *The House of Mirth*, as Lily Bart lays her dresses reflectively across her bed, she notices, like Madame Merle, that "an association lurked in every fold: each fall of lace and gleam of embroidery was like a letter in the record of her past" (295). Not only do Lily's dresses express her inward self when she is wearing them, but they also tell the story of her past; they encapsulate the entire person of Lily Bart. Maria Susanna Cummins's *The Lamplighter* offers a poor orphaned Gerty, who also undergoes a Cinderella-like transformation. After Mrs. Sullivan appropriately cleans and dresses Gerty, "so completely did [Gerty] identify outward neatness and purity with inward peace" (25). Again, the outward appearance, the clothing, becomes a marker for what is "truly inside" a person. Finally, Horatio Alger's title character in *Ragged Dick* is not so ragged after all. Once he tries on the expensive suit he receives from Frank Whitney, Dick's inward gentleman cuts through the grime and rises to the surface. Dick even comments, "It reminds me of Cinderella . . . when she was changed into a fairy princess" (18).

All of these narratives feature variations on the well-known rags-to-riches story in which the honest and industrious protagonist achieves the American Dream through "luck and pluck." Ragged Dick is right to mention Cinderella, as she is the archetypal example of the good, humble, honest, and overall inwardly beautiful person whose goodness and diligence earn her the opportunity to transcend her life's lot. The rags-to-riches story lies at the core of the American Dream—anyone can be successful through honest hard work, or so the myth goes. Regardless of the form it takes—Cinderella the washerwoman-turned-princess, Gerty the rescued orphan, or Dick the industrious bootblack—the rags-to-riches story relies heavily on the "rags." In the case of these Cinderella stories, the outward appearance of the character, as the very label rags-to-riches tells us, becomes a signal for readers of the character's place on external social ladders as well as becoming an appropriate reflection of their already fully realized internal selves. As a result, we have an abundance of examples from nineteenth-century literature of authors using clothing in this symbolic way; however, as Isabel Archer suggests, the clothes might just be more expressive of the dressmaker than the character. Nonetheless, the dressmaker is rarely even mentioned much less featured in any significant way in these stories. Isabel Archer is perceptive to raise questions about the role of the dressmaker in the creation of the protagonist's image. In the rags-to-riches narrative—in which the role of the dressmaker is so crucial—why do we never hear the dressmaker's story?

Elizabeth Keckley does tell the dressmaker's story; it is her story. In her autobiography *Behind the Scenes: Or, Thirty Years a Slave, and Four Years in the White House*, Keckley relates the story of her rise from slave to dressmaker for and companion to Mary Todd Lincoln. While most scholars who have studied Keckley's book contextualize the work in relation to other slave narratives like those of Harriet Jacobs or Frederick Douglass, I would like to place the work in the rags-to-riches tradition described above using Alger's *Ragged Dick* as a representative example. As such, *Behind the Scenes* reads as essentially two intertwined Alger-esque rags-to-riches stories. In the first of these, Keckley herself earns respectability and, of course, freedom through her hard work and rise from slavery. However, what is more remarkable about Keckley's rise is her move from Cinderella to Fairy Godmother in the second rags-to-riches story in *Behind the Scenes*. The protagonist of the second such story is Mary Todd Lincoln, and Keckley serves, in some ways, as her "fairy Godmother." Not only, then, does Keckley achieve modest success as a result of her self-making, but she also has the opportunity to help make another. She moves from a self-made woman to the maker of another woman—a move that affords her control over the social communication and overall public image of the most prominent woman in the country. In reading Keckley's story in this way, I argue that Elizabeth Keckley executes the role of *dressmaker* in three key ways: (1) she *dresses* herself for success as a free Northerner via her own hard work and respectability; (2) she dresses and transforms Mary Todd, and in so doing occupies a unique position of unprecedented power; and (3) she *dresses* the narrative itself by telling her own story in her voice thereby furthering her own sense of agency, power, and personal success.

In placing Keckley's autobiography in the rags-to-riches context, it is first necessary to comment briefly on the "Alger Myth" using an early representative novel, *Ragged Dick*. Ragged Dick begins as a hardworking and plucky bootblack, who, on par with his profession, dresses in rags and "had no particular dislike to dirt" (4). The narrator, despite going out of his way to protest that Dick is not to be viewed as a model boy, does describe him as "frank and straight-forward, manly and self-reliant" (7). In first introducing us to Dick, the narrator makes an attempt to wipe away the dirt, so to speak: "But in spite of the dirt and rags, there was something about Dick that was attractive. *It was easy to see* that if he had been clean and well dressed he would have been decidedly good-looking" (4, my emphasis). Easy to see, indeed—the narrator makes it easy for readers to peer past the dirt and grime to Dick's interior character. Clearly the narrator has set the scene for the myth of the self-made man to play out, and almost immediately in the novel, Dick gets his big break to begin enacting the myth. Like the narrator, Mr. Whitney, too, is able to see through the dirt and grime, remarking, "He isn't exactly the sort of guide I would have picked out . . . . Still he looks honest. He has an open face, and I think can be depended on" (16). Again, Dick's honest look is highlighted, and it is matched to his outward appearance when Whitney provides a suit for Dick. Once in his new suit, the narrator remarks that "it was difficult to imagine that he was the same boy," and that he "might readily have been taken for a young gentleman" (18). Dick himself, then, makes the key reference to Cinderella becoming a fairy princess (18).

The implication here is that perhaps the clothes do not make the man, but they can certainly highlight who he already is underneath. Glenn Hendler offers a helpful paradigm for thinking about Dick's honest look: "In Alger's public sphere, the moral character of things and especially people is immediately legible to anyone trained in sympathetic observation" (418). For Hendler, Alger subscribes to "an ideal of transparent legibility," a legibility that makes Dick's interior honesty and goodness easy to see despite the dirt and rags in which he is clothed (418). Hendler further intimates that the task of the Alger novel is to unite the hero's inward self with his outward appearance. This conflation of interior and surface, as exemplified by Richard Hunter, esq. (née Ragged Dick), is at the heart of the Alger myth. "Good" people need to work to achieve a "good" position in society in order that their interiority and exteriority become indistinguishable.

However, the self-made man is almost always not entirely *self*-made. Aside from the requisite luck, the kindness of strangers is an equally important part of the myth. In short, every Cinderella needs a Fairy Godmother. Here again, legibility is key. If the hero is truly good and makes his interior goodness plain to see, those with means will "read" that goodness and offer to become patrons for the upward young man or woman, as both Whitney and Mr. Greyson do for Dick. In the end, Ragged Dick's luck places him squarely in the vicinity of ladders to success. However, his own pluck, his own honesty and hard work, are what drive him to climb these figurative ladders. In short, Dick represents the core of the myth: the fundamental—and easily legible—interior goodness and honesty and the striving to reconcile that interiority with a matching outward appearance and status.

In applying this Alger narrative—the American Dream myth—to Elizabeth Keckley's autobiography, it will be helpful to draw on some key distinctions established by Frances Smith Foster. In two separate essays, Foster goes to great lengths to compare antebellum slave narratives to postbellum slave narratives—of which she argues Elizabeth Keckley's is a prime example. Foster points out that the duty of antebellum slave narratives, like Jacobs's or Douglass's, was to bring to light the downright wickedness and brutality of the institution of slavery. The narrator of the antebellum slave narrative finds herself "working the emotions of a readership predominated by those who might sympathize but could never empathize" ("Autobiography" 50). Playing on this Northern sympathy and revealing the gruesome nature of plantation life were the essential modes of the antebellum slave narrative. After emancipation, however, the specific lot of slave narratives was "to convince their readers that the former slaves, especially those who had passively endured their bondage, were capable of assuming the responsibilities of freedom" ("Romance" 123). As an extension of this idea, Foster suggests that postbellum slave narratives often portray slavery as a kind of training for triumph ("Romance" 126). Freed slaves will be successful at assuming those responsibilities of freedom because their endurance of slavery has prepared them to triumph over the trials of reconstruction. Finally, Foster argues, "by moving from being property to becoming proprietors," the narrators of post-emancipation slave narratives "could be characterized as the epitome of the American Dream" ("Romance" 119). In short, postbellum slave narratives are essentially "rags-to-riches" stories of the highest order.

Foster extends her formulation to Keckley by noting that "the first part of her book is a success story designed to establish the narrator as an individual whose personal integrity and indomitable spirit resulted in remarkable achievements. . . . [S]he is portraying herself as a fellow participant in the American Myth" ("Autobiography" 50). Indeed, the first three chapters (of the fifteen total) of Keckley's *Behind the Scenes* are devoted to her own personal "rags-to-riches" rise from slavery. In this, the first "rags-to-riches" layer within *Behind the Scenes*, we see a hard-working, respectable girl who is confined to a low standing as chattel. Keckley is able to retain her pride and self-respect in the face of the beatings and other self-denying mistreatment associated with the institution of slavery. She describes her demeanor during one of the beatings she receives: "I did not scream; I was too proud to let my tormentor know what I was suffering" (21). Furthermore, Keckley shows unbelievable honesty and respect when she reveals to her master: "I can cross the river any day, as you know, and have frequently done so, but will never leave you in such a manner. By the laws of the land I am your slave—you are my master, and I will only be free by such means as the laws of the country provide" (31). It is clear that, like Ragged Dick, the young Keckley possesses the goodness and honesty necessary to become a self-made woman.[1]

Furthermore, like Dick, Keckley appears to be sufficiently legible as well. She is able to buy her own freedom and that of her son because she gains the emotional and monetary support of the St. Louis community who are able to read her internal character and agree to serve as her patrons. She is so internally principled, in fact, that she turns down the sixth necessary signature when she perceives that Mr. Farrow has lost faith in her. Keckley recognizes that Farrow is not equipped to appropriately read her clearly legible interior honesty, and she refuses to accept his money. In this act, her interior honesty becomes even more legible to readers, as she declares, "slavery, eternal slavery rather than be regarded with distrust by those whose respect I esteem" (34). Naturally, someone more equipped to view her interiority steps forward, the aptly named Mrs. Le Bourgois, to offer patronage to Keckley.

Thus, Keckley begins much like Ragged Dick. She possesses an upright interior constitution, clearly legible to trained viewers, and she seeks to match her external situation and status to her interiority. She is primed and ready to complete the myth. However, Keckley's constitution is even stronger and riper for future self-reliance than Dick's as a result of her enslavement. In a way, Keckley almost out-Algers Alger. She argues in the opening chapter of the book, "I had been raised in a hardy school—had been taught to rely upon myself and to prepare myself to render assistance to others. . . . Notwithstanding all the wrongs that slavery heaped upon me, I can bless it for one thing—youth's important lesson of self-reliance" (10). Here Keckley argues for one of what she repeatedly calls "the bright sides" of slavery—training in self-reliance and offering assistance to others in need. From the very first chapter, then, we can see the young Keckley as poised—and even schooled by slavery—to achieve the American Dream. As Foster has suggested, this view of slavery as training for triumph is one of the characteristics which makes postbellum slave narratives American Dream narratives. In many ways, the slave narrative is *the* American Dream narrative, a better American Dream narrative than any Horatio Alger could possibly dream up.[2]

It is further striking that this first "rags-to-riches" layer from *Behind the Scenes* is given so little attention (three chapters) relative to the rest of the book. In light of Foster's argument that postbellum slave narratives, relieved of the responsibility of making an argument for the insidiousness of slavery, are free to argue instead that freed slaves are prepared to participate productively in free American life, Keckley necessarily spends little time on the brutality of her slave experience and focuses, rather, on her successes and her contribution to Washington, DC, society. By spending the majority of her time on her life after slavery, Keckley is arguing that she, like other freed slaves, is prepared to accept the responsibilities of freedom. Lynn Domina goes a step further, arguing that Keckley, like other postbellum slave narrators, found it necessary to downplay the violence of slavery as a prerequisite for participation in the American Dream. This narrative of progress would need to include the moral progress of the South, and dwelling on the wrongs of the South would impede this progress (147). Domina goes on to set up Keckley's muting of slavery's brutality as an analogue to President Lincoln's speaking highly of General Lee or playing "Dixie" during his victory tour (147).

Indeed, as both Foster and Domina argue, Keckley's lack of attention to her enslaved self in the narrative is likely, at least partially, a political choice. If she is in the business of arguing for freedwomen's success and productivity, she necessarily spends her time displaying just that. However, this rhetorical choice may yet be another revelation of her interiority. Throughout the narrative—and as she promises in the preface—Keckley focuses her attentions not on herself but on others. In the first half of her preface, Keckley suggests that one of her tasks, as aforementioned, is to argue for the freed slave's ability to contribute. As such, she must spend time in the narrative highlighting her successes, but seemingly all in the name of her freed brothers and sisters. Furthermore, in the second half of the preface, she outlines one of her purposes as revealing to the world Mary Lincoln's true intentions and essentially clearing her name in the wake of the "Old Clothes Scandal."[3] Here again, the focus is not on Keckley's own personal story but on the reputation of her dear friend. Keckley arranges the narrative so as to downplay her own success story in favor of larger concerns. In short, the rhetorical choice to condense the story of her own rise from slavery can be read as an act of humility, a denial of herself in favor of others. In this way, the narrative structure mirrors Keckley's interior humility. Just as the "rags-to-riches" protagonist of the narrative seeks to equate her interiority with a matching outward appearance, the most outward appearance of all—the narrative structure itself—participates in this equation.

All in all, Keckley's own personal "rags-to-riches" story resides within these first three chapters of *Behind the Scenes*. In these chapters, she establishes herself as the prototypical self-made woman. She images her rise from the lowest of low conditions to a position of success and freedom—and she has her own fortitude, honesty, and industry to thank. As Foster puts it, Keckley characterizes herself as "the epitome of the American Dream" ("Romance" 119). In doing so, she figuratively calls upon her skill as dressmaker. Like Ragged Dick, she must "dress" herself for a successful rise; she must adorn herself with the qualities of honesty, diligence, and respect, and she must make her interiority legible by cloaking herself in an honest look. By figuratively dressing herself for success, Keckley manages to become the heroine of her own myth of self-made womanhood.

Keckley, in enacting her own "rags-to-riches" story, is a kind of figurative dressmaker creating an honest and industrious persona and clothing that persona in a legibly good look. Though, the much more obvious way that Keckley acts as dressmaker in *Behind the Scenes* is in her actual work as Mary Todd Lincoln's *modiste*. This unique position affords Keckley the opportunity to move from self-made woman to the "self"-maker of Mary Lincoln. If the first three chapters of the book relate Keckley's Cinderella story, the remainder of the book relates her Fairy Godmother story. Not only does she fashion her free self, but she also accepts the responsibility for fashioning the self of the wife of the Great Emancipator.

Before moving into Keckley's unique role as presidential dressmaker, however, it will be helpful to look briefly at the culture of dressmaking and history of seamstresses in literature. Erving Goffman in *The Presentation of Self in Everyday Life* states, "Regardless of the particular objective which the individual has in mind and of his motive for having this objective, it will be in his interests to control the conduct of the others, especially their responsive treatment of him" (3). Consciously or not, an individual carefully plans her self-presentation so as to control the way she is viewed, treated, and responded to. To this idea Goffman adds, "since the others are likely to be relatively unsuspicious of the presumably unguided aspect of the individual's conduct, he can gain much by controlling it" (8). Every individual, in some way, instructs her audience in the way they ought to view her, and it is advantageous for her to gain control over this transaction.

Clothing serves a social function. Not only does our clothing choice communicate to onlookers how we wish to be viewed and responded to, but it also, according to Eva Maria Stadler, works as "an encroachment of social norms upon the body's surface" (20). She goes on to point out that clothing can serve a variety of social functions: Clothing may "identify status or conceal identity," "embellish or disguise corporal traits," "mediate interpersonal and social relationships," "protect a woman's gendered space," "assert and assure a new social position," or "frame the inner psychic space" among others (20, 21,

22). Whereas Goffman highlights the way that clothing choice signifies from the self outward to society, Stadler points out how clothing choice simultaneously represents an affixing of social norms to the body.

It is reasonable, then, to formulate the dressmaker as an agent of culture. She participates in the interpersonal and social communication that clothing represents. As such, Kathryn E. Wilson recognizes that home dressmakers in the nineteenth century were, contrary to popular belief, "creative subjects possessing important cultural knowledge," and this position as cultural knower "was an important site of agency for women as producers and consumers" (142, 143). Seamstresses are an important vehicle in the creation of culture and a key component of the communication that takes place between wearer and onlooker, between individual and society. However, seamstresses were certainly not always viewed as important cultural agents. Work as a seamstress in the nineteenth century was typically frowned upon as low, menial work executed by women who failed to perform their "proper" domestic roles as wives and mothers. In literature of the nineteenth century, the seamstress became a sort of symbol for all working-class women and the ills that accompanied that lot. Amal Amireh points out, "for many middle-class women the seamstress became a cautionary tale. Those fighting for women's rights pointed to her as an embodiment of what is wrong with womanhood in general" (127). Amireh even goes so far as to argue that women writers, in order to justify their own existence as working women, presented seamstresses as fundamentally different from themselves; the seamstress became an Other (152). If not Othered, at the very least seamstresses were not recognized in the nineteenth century as cultural agents, producers, and communicators. Therefore, as a seamstress, and writing a seamstress's tale, Keckley faced not only prejudices associated with being a freed slave, but also prejudices associated with being a seamstress—the prototype for what was wrong with womanhood.[4]

To answer the question implied by the Isabel Archer epigraph at the head of this essay—why do we never hear the dressmaker's story—the answer is that we actually do. Lynn Alexander offers a representative list of literary works focused on the character of the seamstress in her essay on the seamstress in the Victorian novel. Some of the works she mentions are: W.M. Reynolds's *The Seamstress*, Charles Rowcroft's *Fanny, the Little Milliner*, Frances Trollope's *Jessie Phillips*, Elizabeth Stone's *The Young Milliner*, and Charlotte Elizabeth Tonna's "Milliners and Dressmakers," among others. Certainly we also see short scenes focused on seamstresses in some more prominent works such as Fanny Fern's *Ruth Hall*, Edith Wharton's *House of Mirth*, and Nathaniel Hawthorne's *The Scarlet Letter*, "The Procession of Life," and "The Christmas Banquet" (the short-story prototype for *The Blithedale Romance*) to name a few. Clearly, the seamstress's story is indeed told; however, the seamstress figures in these works are often less than flattering and even, as Amireh points out, used as object lessons for the education of "proper" girls. Keckley, however, takes it upon herself to tell the "real," behind-the-scenes story of the dressmaker—and through her privileged position behind the scenes of the most famous and important home in the country, we get the story of the dressmaker's role in helping to create the "image of a nation," so to speak.

In the second rags-to-riches layer in *Behind the Scenes*, Mary Todd Lincoln plays the Ragged Dick role. From her humble roots in Kentucky and her life as a frontierswoman in "the wilds of the west," the backward Mary Todd managed to land herself in the White House (Keckley 66). From Keckley's report we learn that "Mrs. Lincoln from her girlhood up had an ambition to be the wife of a president," and Keckley goes on to describe a young Mary Todd as "self-willed," "ambitious," "quite a belle," and one "who played her part quite well" (166). She had an ambition, and she achieved it, even rejecting the affections of Stephen A. Douglas because she felt Lincoln had a better shot at the White House. In many ways, Mary Todd's rise might be seen as a shining example of a rags-to-riches story. According to Keckley's reckoning, the young Mary Todd seemed to have had all the makings of a Ragged Dick figure—she was a self-reliant, ambitious, good-looking woman who worked hard to achieve her goal. However, once she reached the White House, she was hardly the polished, "finished product" that, say, Richard Hunter, esq., is by the end of *Ragged Dick*. Keckley's footnotes reveal that Mary Todd Lincoln was perceived to be "from the wilderness of Springfield, Illinois, [fueling] continual rumors that she was gauche and ill-prepared to be a first lady" (65).

Keckley herself admits that because she had heard "malicious report of [Mary Todd Lincoln's] low life, of her ignorance and vulgarity, I expected to see her embarrassed on this occasion [the inauguration party]" (64). However, in the very next breath, Keckley admits that she was wrong and that "no queen ... could have comported herself with more calmness and dignity than did the wife of the president" (64–65). What had changed? Mary Lincoln had changed—she changed at the hands of her Fairy Godmother Elizabeth Keckley.

Keckley produced the inauguration dress, arranged it on Mary Lincoln's body, and even dressed her hair. This moment just before the inauguration is the classic rags-to-riches, Cinderella moment: The gauche little wilderness girl from Kentucky is now magically transformed into a gleaming young woman fit to be the queen of a nation. Lincoln's rags-to-riches transformation is complete, with the help of Elizabeth Keckley, the dressmaker/Fairy Godmother. As a result, Keckley's own remarkable rise is even more than complete. She moves from being "just" Cinderella to becoming a Fairy Godmother; she moves from achieving the American Dream to *authoring* it.

A special kind of power accompanies Keckley's Fairy Godmother role—a power unique among freed slaves in nineteenth-century America. Lori Merish characterizes this power saying, "As a free woman, she turns the tables on the (ex-)masters, exercising the power to dictate the appearance of Anglo-Americans" (240). One potential way to view this power is through what both Frances Smith Foster and Katherine Adams (in slightly different terms) have recognized as the overall theme of the book: public vs. private, substance vs. appearance, or origin vs. surface. Returning briefly to the Alger paradigm, Ragged Dick, like other heroes of the American Dream story, is searching for a way to reconcile his interiority with the external situation charged with representing it. Once his outward appearance is equivalent to the honesty and virtue beneath it, he has made it; he is on the road to success, to achieving the American Dream. However, in the story of Mary Lincoln's rise from rags, Keckley is not searching to reconcile her own interiority and external appearance; she is working behind the scenes to provide substance for the First Lady's appearance. As the Fairy Godmother, she has even more control over this process of reconciling interior and exterior.

Keckley clearly states in her preface that "people knew nothing of the secret history of [Mary Lincoln's] transactions; therefore, they judged her by what was thrown to the surface" (5). The world is only acquainted with the surface appearance of the story, and as a result, Keckley feels it her duty to "[aid] in bringing a solemn truth to the surface *as a truth*" (5). She hopes to provide substance to the surface appearance. Foster locates this very theme in Keckley's book, and notes that the book is structured around the theme of "the pre-eminence of private substance over public appearance" (40). Katherine Adams takes Foster's theme a bit further, arguing that Keckley views herself as "a site of origination, located somewhere 'behind the scenes' and beneath a surface of meanings that stand as incomplete, vulnerable and incomprehensible without her" (63). Keckley is not only interested in providing the substance behind the surface appearance, but she is also interested in how that substance and appearance are constructed. Keckley's position as seer of both the "truth" and, even more importantly, the construction of that "truth" affords her a large measure of control.

First and foremost, Keckley is in control of the image of the First Lady. Not only does she serve as Lincoln's dressmaker, but she identifies herself even more as Lincoln's *modiste*. She is more than the menial, working-class laborer associated with the figure of the seamstress; her role as *modiste* requires that she be in tune with the larger theories and movements of fashion. As a result, and also as a result of the cultural implications of dress formulated above, Keckley not only crafts the First Lady's dresses; she articulates the larger social and interpersonal communication signified by the First Lady's choice of dress—a choice in which her *modiste* has a definite say. In this sense, Mary Lincoln's presentation of self is not a presentation of herself at all; it is Keckley's presentation of her. Isabel Archer is exactly correct: Her clothes do express the dressmaker; in fact, they express the dressmaker expressing her. In the case of the First Lady, it is Keckley, not Mary Lincoln, who decides how society views and responds to Lincoln. It is Keckley, not Mary Lincoln, who decides how Lincoln's wardrobe participates in the overall cultural communication and exchange associated with choice of dress. As dressmaker and *modiste* for the First Lady, Keckley has moved from being self-made to becoming a self-maker—and the self she makes belongs to Mary Todd Lincoln.

However, there is yet another way in which Keckley is able to act as figurative "dressmaker" to Mary Lincoln. Keckley further controls the image of the First Lady by virtue of her role as authoress of what was perceived as a "tell-all" book. Despite this public perception of *Behind the Scenes*, it does not appear, from her preface, that Keckley intended to write a sensational exposé. While we cannot be certain about Keckley's intentions in composing the text, she tells us via her preface that she would like the public to view Mary Todd Lincoln "free from the exaggeration of praise or scandal" (8). Clearly, if this is Keckley's stated intention, she would not intentionally publish a tell-all exposé—a form particularly susceptible to both exaggeration and scandal. Furthermore, it seems that in writing the book Keckley was responding directly to negative press Lincoln was receiving in the wake of the Old Clothes

Scandal. Again, someone attempting the reclaim the reputation of a friend would hardly choose an exposé form for such a task. Regardless of Keckley's intentions, we do know a bit about how the book was read and perceived. First, the letters appended to the book were to be edited so as to eliminate any overly personal information, but James Redpath, the editor for Keckley's publishing company Carleton & Company, printed them in their entirety. Second, Carleton & Company eventually advertised the book as *Behind the Scenes—The Great Sensational Disclosure by Mrs. Keckley*. Certainly by this point, Keckley's intentions were lost in the gears of the publishing machine, and the general public (including the Lincoln family) read the book as a sensational tell-all work—a threatening proposition from the likes of a hired (former slave) employee. In the end, due to the influence of Robert Lincoln, the book was ultimately suppressed—printing stopped, Keckley made little money from the publication and lost many of her dress-buying customers, and the figure of Elizabeth Keckley was soon forgotten.

It is clear from these notes on the publication's reception that, regardless of intention, the book was received as a public "undressing" of Mary Todd Lincoln, to borrow Lori Merish's turn of phrase (256). What, then, is ultimately the cause of all the concern about this book? Power. Through her work as Lincoln's dressmaker and unsolicited biographer, Keckley harnesses the power to dress and undress the First Lady as she sees fit. In her preface, Keckley claims, "I am not the special champion of the widow of our lamented president; . . . I have written with the utmost frankness in regard to her—have exposed her faults as well as given her credit for honest motives" (7–8). Merish argues that in this proclamation, as well as other similar claims from the preface, Keckley establishes her text as "the authoritative version of Mrs. Lincoln's life," and through this act, "Keckley controls the public image of the First Lady" (257). As authoress—just as in her dressmaking—Keckley has control over the manner in which Lincoln is viewed and responded to. Indeed, Foster points out that the narrative is written in the immediate wake of the Old Clothes Scandal, which was still hotly debated at the time of publication, and thus marks Keckley's attempt "to direct the final scene" of Mary Todd Lincoln's drama ("Autobiography" 56). Not only does Keckley control Lincoln's past life; she also attempts to control the public image-making that was still very much underway at the time of publication. The result is that Keckley carefully crafts the public image of Mary Lincoln in the same way that she carefully crafted an inauguration dress. She clothes Lincoln in fabric and in words. The implication here is that just as Keckley can magically transform the gauche little wilderness girl into Cinderella, she can turn the clock hand to midnight, undress her, and send her back to her life of low repute. Both literally and figuratively, Keckley controls the communication inherent in Mary Todd Lincoln's "choice" of dress and image. It is perhaps too strong to call upon the image of a puppet master here; nonetheless, the image of the First Lady and the resulting communicative act were indeed very much in Keckley's hands.

In the process of creating and controlling Mary Todd Lincoln's public image, Keckley also tries to create and dress herself as the authoress of her own story. When she switches the focus to Mary Lincoln for the last twelve chapters, she herself does not disappear from the narrative. Despite the focus on the Lincoln family, this text is still very much an autobiography.[5] In theorizing the performativity of autobiography, Sidonie Smith argues that "the interiority or self that is said to be prior to the autobiographical expression or reflection is an *effect* of autobiographical storytelling" (109). In essence, Smith argues that autobiographers write their "selves" into existence—interiority is a *result of* writing the exterior text. This takes us back, then, to the Alger hero looking for a way to reconcile interior and exterior. Through autobiographical writing, Keckley is afforded the opportunity, on a meta-textual level, to perform yet another "Alger-ian" success story. In her autobiography, then, we have the perfect matching of interior and exterior—in creating the exterior "dress" (i.e., the words, the text), the writer simultaneously creates the matching interior self. Once again, there is an extreme level of control that this process allows an autobiographer to possess. As autobiographer, Keckley controls not only the creation of the "dress," but the creation of the "body" beneath as well.

Keckley's use of a largely autobiographical mode to tell the dressmaker's tale is perhaps analogous to the dressmaker's wearing her own dress. Just as Keckley was able to exercise control over Mary Todd Lincoln's self-presentation and the communication accompanying that presentation, so too is Keckley able to dictate her own self-presentation—and even self-creation, as Smith would argue. Mary Jean Corbett puts it this way: "when one writes, prints, publishes, and markets an autobiography, one effectively sells oneself" (255). Not only, then, is Keckley presenting and creating herself, but she is selling the self she dresses up in text. The implication here is that in order to sell oneself, one must first *own* oneself. Having the ability and opportunity to publish an autobiographical text offers Keckley an almost unprecedented level of control and power over herself and the people she chooses "to dress." Therefore, the authoress is the ultimate dressmaker—she is charged with creating textual dresses for the characters in the story, creating textual dresses for her own self, and creating that very self as well.

In *Behind the Scenes: Or, Thirty Years a Slave, and Four Years in the White House*, Elizabeth Keckley performs a multilayered "Alger-esque" success story. As both character and writer, she is able to successfully meld her interiority with an appropriate external "dress." Perhaps even more important, her three-fold function as dressmaker—dressmaker as self-made woman, as maker of Mary Todd Lincoln, and as authoress of her own story—allows Keckley to exercise an almost unprecedented power and control over herself and the inhabitants of the most famous and important house in the country. Although, Isabel Archer is correct when she argues that her dress expresses not her but the dressmaker, she is only partially correct. The dress does not solely express the dressmaker, but the dress also expresses the dressmaker's expressing and controlling her. And like Isabel Archer, Mary Lincoln's public image—the outward representation of her very interiority—is placed firmly in the hands of her ex-slave *modiste* Elizabeth Keckley.

There is one final question deserving of brief consideration here: Was Keckley any good as a literal and figurative dressmaker? What follows will certainly not undercut the power assigned to Elizabeth Keckley in the argument above; however, it is rather striking that the general public did not really like any of the dresses, both literal and figurative, that Keckley crafted. In her account of the Old Clothes Scandal, Keckley admits that Keyes and Brady's room full of dresses-for-sale was often very populated; yet no one actually wanted to purchase the dresses. It appears that those in the room were really only there to *view* the pieces as having cultural value, but not worth an actual dime. When Keckley and Lincoln take the dresses "on the road" to try to sell to individual dealers, Keckley speaks of the hard bargains these dealers would drive: "the dealers wanted the goods for little or nothing" (211). What's more, even prior to the scandal while Lincoln was wearing the dresses herself, she was often criticized for their being too low-cut or too extravagant (Keckley 5). Yes, it was Lincoln's taste which compelled her to order low-cut and overly extravagant dresses, but as her *modiste* Keckley would have had some input into this matter of style. Finally, as aforementioned, we know that the book was not very well received. This is likely at least partially attributable to the threat that buyers perceived in the kind of power Keckley was able to wield via the narrative. Nonetheless, the newspapers which were so quick to criticize Lincoln before Keckley's book appeared were equally as quick to defend Lincoln against Keckley's "grossly and shamelessly indecent" sensational disclosure (Merish 258). In short, no one really liked *any* of Keckley's "dresses." Whether because of too much exposure of the breast or too much exposure of the truth, both the figurative and literal dresses were viewed as indecent.

Clearly people's dislike for Keckley's work as a dressmaker does not weaken the argument posited throughout this essay. If anything, it strengthens it. In both cases—with the dresses as well as with the book—she was praised early and often. In regard to her dressmaking abilities, it is clear from the number of referrals she received that people admired her work. One does not become dressmaker to the most powerful people in the country without having the appropriate skill and recommendations from reputable sources. Likewise, in regard to her writing skill, she was originally advertised as "a gifted and conscientious author" (Foster, "Autobiography" 39). It seems that her work was only criticized once people recognized the level of power and control she had actually achieved. The late nineteenth century was not ready for a black woman to be so successful and powerful—as both dressmaker (and White House image-maker) and writer. Keckley was keen in her perceptions when she wrote a letter in her own defense to the *New York Citizen*. In that letter, she asked: "Was it because 'my skin is dark and that I was once a slave' that I am being 'denounced?'" (Fleischner, *Mrs. Lincoln* 317). She goes on to ask again in that same letter: "As I was born to servitude, it was not fault of mine that I was a slave; and, as I honestly purchased my freedom, may I not be permitted to express, now and then, an opinion becoming a free woman?" (317–18). Clearly the answer at that time was "No." And in asking the stinging rhetorical question, Keckley's implied observation is accurate; she has "dressed" the sentiment perfectly, if you will. Yet again, she displays perfect control over the situation at hand. Now that we are finally able to appreciate Keckley's mastery and importance, it is becoming increasingly clear that, both literally and figuratively, Keckley is one of the greatest American dressmakers.

NOTES

1. Certainly it would be unfair to equate Ragged Dick's lot, as working class orphaned street boy, with young Keckley's lot as captive slave. Keckley begins her journey toward respectability from a much lower social standing than Dick ever could have. Keckley is not a member of the working class like Dick. In fact, she is *below* the working class; she is denied class and denied personhood by virtue of her enslavement. Despite the gross difference between the starting places of the two characters, the overall *pattern* of the characters' rise is similar.

2. Jennifer Fleischner argues that Keckley's self-reliance "is not the same as the American ideal of independence.... It referred to Lizzy's conscious awareness that there *was* no one for her to rely on but herself" (*Mrs. Lincoln* 83). Fleischner seems to be reading against Foster, William Andrews, and others who see postbellum slave narrators as heroes of the American Dream narrative. For Fleischner, Keckley's compulsory self-reliance is of a completely different nature than that of, say, Ragged Dick or other rags-to-riches heroes. While this is an astute point, it is perhaps insignificant to differentiate between "brands" of self-reliance. In the end, regardless of whether it is Dick's or Lizzy's brand of self-reliance, that self-reliance grows into the kind of success I describe in this study. Rather than accepting Keckley's notion that slavery schooled her for self-reliance and subsequent success, Fleischner seems to read this as the beginning of a process of assimilation. She argues that "with its lessons of hard work, slavery becomes a guarantee of the ex-slave's conformism" to white culture ("Objects" 94). Fleischner reads the ex-slave's self-reliance as that slave's telling whites, "we want to be like you" ("Objects" 94). Indeed, Fleischner has tapped into the inherent problem and possible contradiction of conflating a black writer's narrative with the white man's "Master Narrative" of the American Dream. However, as I discuss later in this study, the agency Keckley exercises throughout the events of this narrative and the privileged position of power she is able to obtain as a result can hardly be viewed as simple conformism. Fleischner is right to complicate the comparison that Foster, Andrews, and I myself make, but I want to give Keckley more credit than simply having a desire "to be like you whites."

3. "Mrs. Lincoln's Old Clothes Scandal" was the title given by newspaper columnists to Mary Lincoln's efforts to stave off poverty by selling much of her clothing and jewelry. After consulting with her friend Keckley, the two women decided to try to sell off—anonymously, due to Lincoln's shame regarding her financial situation—many of the ornate dresses and jewelry pieces for which Lincoln would no longer have use. They selected W.H. Brady & Co. as their broker, and William Brady and his associate Samuel Keyes ultimately convinced Lincoln to identify herself and publicize the event to the point that it became more spectacle than business venture. Perhaps the atmosphere of the event was best captured by one newspaper writer who, according to Fleischner, referred to Brady as "Showman Barnum" (*Mrs. Lincoln* 310). The ultimate result of the debacle was the rapid ruination of Lincoln's reputation.

Consequently, *Behind the Scenes* was published in the immediate wake of this scandal, and Keckley goes to great lengths in her prologue to establish as her purpose the restoration of Lincoln's good name. Fleischner is keen to point out that Keckley's own good name was inevitably tied to Lincoln's, as Keckley served as her primary advisor at the outset of the ill-conceived operation. Fleischner, therefore, argues that Keckley's "*primary* motive" was the reestablishment of her own character (315). Here I argue for Keckley's humility in focusing her story on the reclamation of her friend's reputation. In so doing, I do not deny Fleischner's seemingly contrary claim, as any *auto*biography is necessarily fueled, at least partly, by selfish motives (whether they be related to one's character or one's finances). Thus Fleischner is right to complicate Keckley's oversimplified posture of selflessness; however, I do not read Keckley's stated intention regarding Mary Lincoln as a wholly disingenuous one.

4. In this paragraph, I shift my terminology from "dressmaker" to "seamstress" in order to highlight the tradition of the seamstress-as-cautionary-tale in nineteenth-century fiction. However, I intend, in no way, to conflate the two social positions. It is clear from Kathryn Wilson's cited comments that the dressmaker would have been more highly respected than a "mere" seamstress. Also, I offer further clarification later in the essay when discussing Keckley's role as *modiste* as opposed to "mere" dressmaker.

5. In his introduction to the Schomburg Library edition of Keckley's narrative, James Olney prefers to call the narrative a memoir rather than an autobiography due to the fact that the narrative "does not focus on the personal element [but] describes instead external events and figures who occupy some important place in the affairs of the world" (xxxiii). However, Lynn Domina, I think rightly, reads against Olney and pulls the narrative back into the realm of autobiography explaining the apparent focus on the Lincoln family this way: "To the extent that Keckley's desired self is constituted through her interactions with the nationally powerful and famous, her public role permits her both to evade and establish revelations of a private self" (141). In other words, despite the focus on famous people, we never lose sight in the narrative of the role of, effects on, and changes to the autobiographical author's presented self. Keckley manages to keep her "self" central to the narrative despite its participation with famous people and events.

WORKS CITED

Adams, Katherine. "Freedom and Ballgowns: Elizabeth Keckley and the Work of Domesticity." *Arizona Quarterly* 57.4 (2001): 45–87.

Alexander, Lynn M. "Creating a Symbol: The Seamstress in Victorian Literature." *Tulsa Studies in Women's Literature* 18.1 (1999): 29–38.

Alger, Horatio, Jr. *Ragged Dick* and *Struggling Upward*. 1868, 1890. Ed. Carl Bode. New York: Penguin, 1985.

Amireh, Amal. "Domesticating Women: The Seamstress, the Factory Girl, and the Nineteenth-Century Woman Author." *The Factory Girl and the Seamstress: Imagining Gender and Class in Nineteenth-Century American Fiction*. New York: Garland, 2000. 111–56.

Corbett, Mary Jean. "Literary Domesticity and Women Writers' Subjectivities." *Women, Autobiography, Theory: A Reader*. Ed. Sidonie Smith and Julia Watson. Madison: University of Wisconsin Press, 1998. 255–63.

Cummins, Maria Susanna. *The Lamplighter*. 1854. Ed. Nina Baym. New Brunswick: Rutgers University Press, 1988.

Domina, Lynn. "I Was Re-Elected President: Elizabeth Keckley as Quintessential Patriot in Behind the Scenes, Or, Thirty Years a Slave and Four Years in the White House." *Women's Life Writing: Finding Voice/Building Community*. Ed. Linda S. Coleman. Bowling Green, Ohio: Bowling Green State University Popular Press, 1997. 139–51.

Fleischner, Jennifer. *Mrs. Lincoln and Mrs. Keckly: The Remarkable Story of the Friendship Between a First Lady and a Former Slave*. New York: Broadway Books, 2003.

———. "Objects of Mourning in Elizabeth Keckley's *Behind the Scenes*." *Mastering Slavery: Memory, Family, and Identity in Women's Slave Narratives*. New York: New York University Press, 1996. 93–132.

Foster, Frances Smith. "Autobiography After Emancipation: The Example of Elizabeth Keckley." *Multicultural Autobiography: American Lives*. Ed. James Robert Payne. Knoxville: University of Tennessee Press, 1992. 32–63.

———. "Romance and Scandal in a Postbellum Slave Narrative: Elizabeth Keckley's *Behind the Scenes*." *Written By Herself: Literary Production by African American Women 1746–1892*. Bloomington: Indiana University Press, 1993. 115–30.

Goffman, Erving. *The Presentation of Self in Everyday Life*. Garden City, NY: Doubleday, 1959.

Hendler, Glenn. "Pandering in the Public Sphere: Masculinity and the Market in Horatio Alger." *American Quarterly* 48.3 (1996): 415–38.

James, Henry. *The Portrait of a Lady*. 1881. New Riverside Editions. Ed. Jan Cohn. Boston: Houghton, 2001.

Keckley, Elizabeth. *Behind the Scenes: Or, Thirty Years a Slave, and Four Years in the White House*. Ed. Frances Smith Foster. Urbana: University of Illinois Press, 1998.

Merish, Lori. "Fashioning a Free Self: Consumption, Politics, and Power in the Writings of Elizabeth Keckley and Frances Harper." *Sentimental Materialism: Gender, Commodity Culture, and Nineteenth-Century American Literature*. Durham: Duke University Press, 2000. 229–69.

Olney, James. Introduction. *Behind the Scenes: Or, Thirty Years a Slave, and Four Years in the White House*. By Elizabeth Keckley. Ed. James Olney. New York: Oxford University Press, 1988. xvii–xxxvi.

Smith, Sidonie. "Performativity, Autobiographical Practice, Resistance." *Women, Autobiography, Theory: A Reader*. Ed. Sidonie Smith and Julia Watson. Madison: University of Wisconsin Press, 1998. 108–15.

Stadler, Eva Maria. "Addressing Social Boundaries: Dressing the Female Body in Early Realist Fiction." *Reconfigured Spheres: Feminist Explorations of Literary Space*. Ed. Margaret R. Higonnet and Joan Templeton. Amherst: University of Massachusetts Press, 1994. 20–36.

Wharton, Edith. *The House of Mirth*. 1905. Bedford Case Studies in Contemporary Criticism Series. Ed. Shari Benstock. Boston: Bedford, 1994.

Wilson, Kathryn E. "Commodified Craft, Creative Community: Women's Vernacular Dress in Nineteenth-Century Philadelphia." *The Culture of Sewing: Gender, Consumption, and Home Dressmaking*. Ed. Barbara Burman. Oxford: Berg, 1999. 141–56.

CHAPTER SEVEN

LISA SHAWN HOGAN

Exposing Mary Lincoln
Elizabeth Keckley and the Rhetoric of Intimate Disclosure

I have often been asked to write my life, as those who know me know
that it has been an eventful one. (xi)
—Elizabeth Keckley, *Behind the Scenes:*
  Or, Thirty Years a Slave, and Four Years in the White House

THREE YEARS AFTER THE assassination of her husband, Abraham Lincoln, Mary Lincoln was still grieving.[1] In a letter written in January of 1868 to her "dear friend," Elizabeth Keckley, Lincoln sounded almost suicidal, lamenting that she was "positively dying with a broken heart." "I am so miserable," she wrote, "that I feel like taking my own life." Only the love of her youngest son, Thomas "Tad" Lincoln, kept her from killing herself.[2] Just three days later, Lincoln again wrote Keckley, claiming that "[t]roubles and misfortune are fast overwhelming me; may the end come soon."[3]

Sadly, Lincoln's situation would only worsen by the spring, when her friend and former dressmaker, Elizabeth Keckley,[4] published a tell-all book about her life as a White House modiste and friend to the First Lady. Entitled *Behind the Scenes: Or, Thirty Years a Slave, and Four Years in the White House*,[5] the controversial book purportedly exposed Lincoln's most intimate feelings and thoughts. Keckley also claimed to reproduce verbatim intimate private conversations within the Lincoln family, and she even appended private letters written by Mary Lincoln. Although condemned at the time as "indecent" and an "outrage,"[6] many historians have accepted *Behind the Scenes* at face value. Some have even celebrated Keckley as a survivor who overcame the mental and physical abuses of slavery to become a well-respected entrepreneur, businesswoman, and friend to the First Lady.

This essay examines how *Behind the Scenes* functioned as a rhetoric of intimate disclosure, violating nineteenth-century standards of decorum and propriety, yet shaping later historical memories of Mary Lincoln and her time. Greeted with criticism, even ridicule at the time, the book disrupted prevailing rhetorical conventions about class, gender, and race and breeched the divide between the public and private sphere that historically had protected the reputations of well-known political figures like Mary Lincoln. More than a century later, however, historians reinterpreted the scandalous book as a conciliatory antebellum slave narrative, even a "rags-to-riches" success story, giving credence to Keckley's version of events. With its dramatically contrasting portraits of Keckley and Lincoln, *Behind the Scenes* not only fit the mold of later postbellum slave narratives, but also seemed to confirm historical memories of Mary Lincoln as petty, emotionally unstable, and politically ambitious. In short, Keckley's rhetoric of intimate disclosure may not have been persuasive in its own day, but it rang true in the context of later historical narratives.

I begin by recounting Keckley's remarkable life, primarily as she herself told it in *Behind the Scenes*. I analyze how her personal story about escaping from slavery and becoming a well-respected businesswoman positioned Keckley rhetorically as a Lincoln confidant and close personal friend. I also document the outrage and anger that first greeted publication of her book and, at the time, undermined Keckley's credibility. These reactions, I argue, were likely rooted in perceptions that Keckley violated prevailing standards of propriety, particularly race and gender expectations. In the second section of the essay, I show how later historians rehabilitated Keckley's reputation by celebrating her memoir as a story of achievement and success. Inspired by the changing racial attitudes of the civil rights era, these historians sought to recover Keckley's voice and her rightful place in history. I conclude by showing how, rhetorically, *Behind the Scenes* functioned not only as an autobiographical success story and as a typical postbellum slave narrative, but also as a rhetoric of intimate disclosure consistent with later historical memories of both Lincoln and her times. Despite violating nineteenth-century standards of decency and propriety, the book's contrasting portraits of Keckley and Mary fit neatly into later historical narratives about the lives of former slaves and the tragic life of Mary Lincoln.

From Slavery to Scandal

By all accounts, Elizabeth Keckley—born "Lizzy" Hobbes—was an impressive woman, who overcame seemingly insurmountable obstacles to become a self-sufficient and successful business woman. Keckely was an only child born into slavery in 1818 in Dinwiddie, Virginia. Her mother, Agnes, was the property of Armistead and Mary Burwell, a couple who also owned more than twenty other slaves on their family plantation.[7] Keckley would not discover the true identity of her father—Armistead himself—until she reached adulthood. By the standards of the Deep South, the Burwell plantation was small and, as biographer Jennifer Fleischner explained, the family suffered a "constant struggle to make ends meet."[8] As a result, Keckley was uprooted frequently and "loaned" to various family members as the need arose.

At the age of five, Keckley was given sole responsibility for Mary Burwell's infant daughter, Elizabeth.[9] Although this position provided Keckley greater privileges than other slaves, including "a better diet, better clothing, and exposure to opportunities for personal improvement,"[10] she was also subjected to physical, mental, and even sexual abuse. After once accidentally overturning the baby's cradle, for example, Keckley was viciously beaten—an experience she would remember for the rest of her life. As Keckley recalled the abuse in *Behind the Scenes*, this "was the first time I was punished in this cruel way, but not the last."[11] Keckley remembered how this experience destroyed her innocence and encouraged her to become a "self-willed girl," which was the "cause of much trouble to me."[12]

When she was fourteen, Keckley's master sent her to work for his eldest son, Robert, in Petersburg, Virginia, separating her from her mother.[13] Shortly thereafter, Keckley was raped by a neighbor, Alexander Kirkland, known to the locals as a hot-tempered drunk. This rape would result in the birth of Keckley's only child George, in 1838.[14] In the 1840s, Keckley was forced to move again when she was given to Armistead's daughter, Ann, and her husband Hugh Garland upon their marriage. In 1847 the Garlands took Keckley to St. Louis, where she would perfect her sewing skills and was often "hired out" to local dressmakers, who recognized her unique talent as a seamstress. According to Fleischner, this was an eye-opening experience for Keckley, as "St. Louis's free black communities were proud and active." This was "the kind of slave city," Fleischner noted, "that would have stirred reveries of freedom."[15]

Amid the sectionalist tensions of the 1850s, the Garland family struggled financially. Recognizing their pecuniary need, Keckley approached Hugh Garland with a proposal. She asked him what price he would accept to free her and her son, George. Garland agreed to the sum of $1200—an enormous sum for the time, but still not out of Keckley's reach. As Keckley recalled in *Behind the Scenes,* even the slightest possibility that she might someday buy her own freedom "gave a silver lining to the dark cloud of my life—faint, it is true, but still a silver lining."[16] In 1852 Elizabeth married James Keckley, but the marriage proved short-lived as James proved to be a "deceiving and dissipated husband," who tricked Keckley into believing he was a free man, when he was really a slave.[17] Yet Keckley persevered over this disappointment, and with the help of generous contributions from white friends and customers, she raised enough money to buy her own freedom. Shortly thereafter, Keckley moved with George to Washington DC, where she began a successful career as a dressmaker. Working for many prominent political families, she even entertained an offer from the wife of Senator Jefferson Davis to accompany her back to Mississippi after the election of Abraham Lincoln in 1860. Knowing that war was imminent, Keckley reasoned that such a move would be a mistake: "I preferred to cast my lot among the people of the North."[18]

For some time, Keckley had imagined herself a dressmaker for first ladies. "Ever since arriving in Washington," she wrote, "I had a great desire to work for the ladies of the White House, and to accomplish this end, I was ready to make almost any sacrifice consistent with propriety."[19] That opportunity arrived when one of Keckley's clients introduced her to Mary Lincoln in the spring of 1861. From that day forward, Keckley would serve as Lincoln's chief dressmaker, sewing at least fifteen dresses for the First Lady in the first four months alone.[20] More importantly, Keckley would become Lincoln's closest confidant and friend—at least according to Keckley's own account. That friendship would be irretrievably broken, however, by the publication of *Behind the Scenes.*

The details surrounding the publication of *Behind the Scenes* remain in dispute, but most historians believe that James Redpath, who would later found the Boston Lyceum Bureau and publish his own magazine,[21] played an important role in editing and finding a publisher for Keckley's memoir.[22] Already known as an "energetic propagandist and promoter," Redpath "must have seen the possibilities for sales in publishing this insider's view of the White House."[23]

Redpath's role in the writing of Keckley's memoir—whether he was her ghostwriter or merely her editor—remains unclear, but most historians agree that he played a major role in persuading Keckley to publish her book, which was completed in March of 1868.[24] Historians also agree that Redpath did not obtain Keckley's permission to publish twenty-one letters from Mary Lincoln as an appendix to *Behind the Scenes*. Without these letters, Frances Smith Foster, a scholar of African American literature has argued, *Behind the Scenes* would have been "interesting, but not scandalous," for the letters dramatically increased "the intrinsic interest" in Keckley's book.[25] Why Keckley gave Redpath access to her private letters in the first place remains something of a mystery, although John Washington, writing in 1942, suggested that Keckley gave the letters to Redpath in order to verify her story and boost her own credibility.[26]

The publisher of *Behind the Scenes*, Carlton & Company, was a "respectable and successful firm that was known for speedily producing books."[27] It published everything from travelogues, to comic books, to poetry and self-help manuals.[28] Carlton & Company even reprinted such literary classics as *Robinson Crusoe*, *Les Misérables*, and *Jane Eyre*, but it was new to publishing stories of personal intrigue and political scandal. Although Keckley maintained that the publication of her book was "prompted by the purest motives" and that her goal was simply to "place Mrs. Lincoln in a better light before the world,"[29] her publisher clearly had other ideas. Promoting the book as a "Literary Thunderbolt," advertisements for *Behind the Scenes* in the *New York Commercial Advertiser* promised readers an exposé of "startling nature, in regard to men and things in the White House."[30] Adding to the interest of the book, the newspaper insisted this was no work of fiction, but instead an "authentic and truthful" account of Keckley's life with the Lincolns.[31]

Not surprisingly, publication of *Behind the Scenes* inspired a huge public scandal. In an era of strict separation between the public and private spheres, the book seemed to cross the line of propriety, violating Victorian sensibilities regarding the disclosure of private, even intimate details—especially about the First Family. In nineteenth-century society, the home was considered a safe "haven," where the "spiritual and emotional needs of husband and children were met."[32] It was a place where even the most public of people could escape the troubles of the world and, as one nineteenth-century author put it, chase "away the gloom of the world."[33] Keckley's intrusion into this sacred and protected space provoked not only disapproval, but outrage. As a writer from the *Springfield Republican* in Massachusetts put it, Keckley had violated "the privacy" of the Lincolns' "family circle" by revealing their "private history," and she had done so for selfish reasons. "Scandal," the paper concluded, "is always a marketable commodity."[34]

The harsh criticism of *Behind the Scenes* came not only from the partisan press but from across the spectrum of newspapers, opinion journals, and literary reviews. For example, the *National Intelligencer,* a popular daily newspaper in Washington, DC, denounced the book as an "indecent volume," calling it an "atrocious invasion of private sanctity" and a "shameful" work that violated the "sacredness of the home." This "heartless and brutal assault" on the Lincolns was "coined out of the very blood and anguish of the hearts that compose the family." The *Intelligencer* proclaimed the book "outrageous," "wretched," and "miserable."[35] Similarly, the *Commercial Advertiser* exclaimed that the book should never have "seen the light" and dismissed it as "general rubbish."[36] *The Atlantic Monthly,* a popular literary magazine of the day, likewise proclaimed the book an "outrage," declaring that Keckley should be "ashamed" of herself,[37] while *Putnam's Magazine,* another well-respected monthly periodical on American literature, art, and politics, declared simply that the book "ought never to have been written or published." Now that it had been published, *Putnam's* urged its readers to avoid it, as the editors could not "conceive of any sensible person reading it with pleasure or profit."[38]

Reactions to *Behind the Scenes,* of course, reflected more than outrage over its violations of privacy. Reviews also were steeped in the racial and class prejudices of the day, for the book had been written not by a political rival, nor even by some arbiter of public taste and morality, but by a former slave and servant to the family. As historian Eric Foner has reminded us, long after the Civil War concluded, many whites still expected "deference" and "obedience" from African Americans and any violation from this unspoken social, economical, and racial hierarchy was considered an act of "insolence" and "insubordination."[39] It was more than just coincidence that the *National Intelligencer* refused to even mention Keckley's name until the end of its blistering critique, instead referring to her as a "treacherous black woman" or a "villainous creature" who should be "condemned and despised." When the paper finally did mention Keckley's name, it did so as part of a warning to its readers that Keckley's "treachery" might corrupt their own servants: "What family that has a servant may not, in fact, have its peace and happiness destroyed by such treacherous creatures as this Keckley woman."⁴⁰ Similarly, the *Atlantic Monthly* worried aloud that other servants of prominent public figures might follow Keckley's example, producing a string of unflattering exposés by the "cooks, lady's-maid, coachman, and footmen" of famous politicians and other public figures. The journal even imagined examples of such titles, including "Behind the Pantry Door" and "On the Kitchen Stairs; Sayings and Doings of Chief Justice Chase, reported by his former Cook."⁴¹

The racial undertones of the backlash against *Behind the Scenes* were most clearly evident in a parody that was published later that same year. Described by one contemporary critic as a work of "shocking venom," this pamphlet, entitled *Behind the Seams by a Nigger Woman Who Took in Work from Mrs. Lincoln and Mrs. Davis,* was written under the pseudonym D. Ottolengul and sold for ten cents in 1868.⁴² In just twenty-two pages (including an appendix with two letters parodying the appendix in Keckley's book), *Behind the Seams* ridiculed Keckley's account of her life in every way imaginable, and it also depicted her as a liar and a greedy money-grubber who did not care whom she hurt as long as she made a profit. "It's the blessed truth," the main character "Betsey Kickley" declared; "I'm not lying at all." The sarcasm continued as "Kickley's" brutal rape was dismissed as an "affair," and the author repeatedly transposed the word "modiste," or dressmaker, with "modest," in the process implying that the real Keckley was not in the least bit modest, but quite the opposite. Using the word "nigger" six times in just the first paragraph, the book was an obvious example of the racist backlash against *Behind the Scenes*. Yet, as Elizabeth Young has suggested, the parody also contributed to widespread skepticism about the truthfulness of Keckley's account, as it reproduced "each of the major events in Keckley's book" in a "violently" distorted form.⁴³

At the time, any damage that Keckley might have done to Mary Lincoln's reputation was thus mitigated by the fact that many dismissed *Behind the Scenes* as a "complete falsehood."⁴⁴ Condemned as a liar, a scandal-monger, and a greedy opportunist, Keckley had lost credibility and had little opportunity to respond to criticisms of her book. To make matters worse, Robert Todd Lincoln, Lincoln's eldest son, bought and destroyed as many copies of *Behind the Scenes* as he could and even persuaded the publisher to stop printing the book. As a respected lawyer and budding politician (not to mention the beloved son of the martyred president), Robert's opinion carried much weight in the court of public opinion, and his denunciation cost Keckley, who was still working as a seamstress, her reputation and thus many of her white customers.[45]

Even after Keckley's death, historians continued to question her motivations and truthfulness in writing *Behind the Scenes*. Indeed, some questioned whether she had written the book at all. In 1935, for example, an amateur Civil War historian named David R. Barbee reportedly "engaged in a close study of *Behind the Scenes*" and concluded that Jane Swisshelm, a Minnesota journalist, women's rights activist, and abolitionist, was the real author of the book. Comparing *Behind the Scenes* to Swisshelm's autobiography (written twelve years later), Barbee claimed to have found "indisputable similarities of style, with incidents of place and anecdote repeated in both." Reflecting the same racist assumptions that led her contemporaries to doubt Keckley's words, Barbee argued that "both the style and the incidents described were such" that no former slave could have written it.[46] Indeed, Barbee went so far as to claim that there was "no such person" as Elizabeth Keckley. In her "utter devotion to the antislavery cause," Barbee concluded, Swisshelm had simply "invented an ex-slave who made Mrs. Lincoln's dresses."[47] Barbee implied that Mary Lincoln would never have befriended a former slave and that Swisshelm had simply invented Keckley to support her views on racial equality.

Thus, Elizabeth Keckley—close personal confidante of Mary Lincoln and an inspirational story in her own right—was not only thoroughly discredited but, in effect, temporarily erased from the historical record. Keckley's reputation and career were destroyed, and the scandal over the book irretrievably broke her friendship and bond with the Lincoln family. It would remain for later historians to recover her voice and redeem her place in history by retelling the story of her relationship with the Lincolns. That retelling, of course, was a rhetorical construct as well—one that stood in sharp contrast to that which prevailed in Keckley's own day.

Recovering the Memory of Elizabeth Keckley

No one has contributed more to rehabilitating Elizabeth Keckley's historical reputation than historian Jennifer Fleischner. "I wanted to restore Elizabeth Keckley to her place in history, to give voice to her life and story," Fleischner wrote in her 2003 book on the friendship between Keckley and Mrs. Lincoln.[48] Lamenting that history has "neglected Elizabeth Keckly," Fleischner recalled the indignities Keckley suffered in both life and death, including the fact that after the scandal over her book some even disputed "her entire existence."[49] Even in death, Fleischner lamented, Keckley has been disrespected. In 1960, a developer paved over the Harmony Cemetery in Washington, DC, where Keckley had been buried. With no living relatives to claim her remains, Keckley was eventually reburied in Landover Cemetery in Maryland in an unmarked grave.[50]

The redemption of Keckley's historical memory has assumed familiar rhetorical forms. Most historians have placed Keckley's story in the tradition of the postbellum slave narrative, comparing *Behind the Scenes* to the better-known autobiographical works of Frederick Douglass and Harriet Jacobs.[51] As Smith Foster explained, postbellum slave narratives served a particular rhetorical function: "Unlike the antebellum slave narrators who downplayed their individual initiative and self-discipline to enhance their argument against the insidiousness of slavery as an institution, postbellum narrators needed to convince their readers that the former slaves, especially those who had passively endured their bondage, were capable of assuming responsibilities of freedom."[52] They accomplished this by emphasizing agency and empowerment through stories of hard work, determination, and self-sacrifice in the pursuit of success. The "mood of optimism" in such works functioned as politically expedient rhetorical strategies, designed to promote acceptance of free blacks and aid the "national healing process" in the Reconstruction era.[53] The early chapters of *Behind the Scenes* did, indeed, exhibit many of the thematic and stylistic markers of postbellum slave narratives, particularly their emphasis on reconciliation, forgiveness, and the economic mobility of former slaves.[54]

Fleischner has noted this tone of reconciliation and forgiveness in Keckley's tales of "inspirational uplift," her "lessons of hard work," and her adoption of a "non-threatening" posture.[55] Xiomara Santamarina likewise argued that Keckley's memoir showed the "possibility of racial reconciliation and national progress attainable through successful social and economic integration of freed blacks,"[56] while Katherine Adams contended that Keckley's "black agency" was evident in her story of personal triumph and demonstrated the potential for all freed slaves to succeed in the Reconstruction era.[57] Other scholars also have credited Keckley with creating an intellectual and social persona that disproved prevailing racial stereotypes, thus showing the potential for African American agency in a racist culture.[58]

The postbellum slave narrative is, in a larger sense, a version of that timeless American narrative, the "rags-to-riches" story.[59] Making that connection explicitly, Steve Criniti has compared *Behind the Scenes* to the popular series of post-Civil War novels by Horatio Alger, noting that Keckley's story of her rise from slavery to successful White House dressmaker epitomized the values taught by Alger's popular juvenile morality tales: hard-work, determination, courage, and high moral character. Like the characters in Alger's stories, Keckley had risen from poverty to middle-class respectability, confirming the promise of the American Dream and demonstrating that, in America, anybody who persevered and worked hard could "make it."[60]

While both the postbellum slave narrative and the "rags-to-riches" success story provided interpretive frameworks for redeeming Keckley's memory, they also functioned rhetorically to tarnish historical memories of Keckley's supposed close friend, Mary Lincoln. In trying to redeem Keckley's historical reputation, historians have accepted her story uncritically; few recall the public outrage and censure that greeted publication of *Behind the Scenes* in 1868. As I have argued, part of the explanation for these negative reactions no doubt lies in the racial and class prejudices of the day. Still, the sympathy for Mary Lincoln evident in those reactions is surprising, considering how unpopular she was as First Lady following her husband's assassination. Lincoln's tenure as First Lady was, of course, a time of great turmoil in the country, and Mary was often criticized by the Northern press for her Southern ancestry, her extravagant spending during the war, and even her "plump" figure. So the question remains: Why did public sentiment side with the unpopular First Lady, rather than the dressmaker and alleged friend who exposed intimate details of her life in the White House? At least part of the explanation may lie in the rhetorical character of *Behind the Scenes*. Specifically, I argue that the book's rhetoric of intimate disclosure not only violated nineteenth-century standards of decorum and propriety, but also disrupted prevailing hierarchies of class and race. That brought Keckley criticism, even ridicule, yet the book still helped shape a negative portrait of Mary Lincoln that persists to this day.

The Rhetoric of Intimate Disclosure

The political exposé is a common and often celebrated rhetorical form in the history of American public address. Typically designed to damage the credibility of some person or idea, as Dale Sullivan has argued, exposés are, by their very nature, a form of epideictic rhetoric, concerned with what is "praiseworthy or blameworthy in the present."[61] In epideictic exposés, revelations about wrongdoing are often used to "denigrate a person's credibility, or personal legitimacy, and thereby, dishonor or discredit the individual in the minds of auditors." Auditors are then asked to function as "judges," determining the "facticity of the charges against the individual" and rendering judgment.[62] According to Sullivan, the epideictic exposé establishes a "cultural consensus" not only about the "legitimacy of an individual," but also about larger "moral and doctrinal issues" for which the individual serves "as a synedochal representation." In this way, epideictic exposés are not just about particular people, but embody some larger persuasive purpose or "ideology."[63]

The rhetorical power of the exposé rests upon the dramatic "unveiling of secrets." By revealing secrets, the rhetor demystifies and disempowers the subject of the exposé, using rhetoric as a "weapon" to discredit and defame. The rhetor behind an exposé typically assumes the role of "translator," making sense out of otherwise mysterious statements or translating "words and experiences from one domain (friendly) to another (hostile)."[64] In order for an exposé to succeed, the secrets it reveals must have at least the semblance of truth and the audience must be "predisposed to believe the rhetor." In addition, the "revealing of secrets" must be accompanied by some effort to establish the rhetor's status as an insider privy to the truth.[65] Finally, rhetors must display moral outrage over their discoveries, dissociating themselves with the subject of the exposé and creating their own "self-definition as everything that the subject of the exposé is not."[66]

As an autobiographical narrative, *Behind the Scenes* functioned not only to discredit Mary Lincoln but to shape a positive persona for its author and to make larger moral pronouncements. It told the story of Keckley's own struggle to escape a life of slavery and to achieve the American Dream through hard work, perseverance, and good moral character. That rhetorical persona, then, contrasted sharply with Keckley's portrait of Mary Lincoln—a portrait of a woman who was selfish, overly ambitious (in an era when ambitious women were suspect), and emotionally unstable. At the time, Keckley's portrait of Lincoln may have confirmed what many of the First Lady's critics already believed. By revealing intimate secrets and disclosing private conversations and correspondence, she also breeched the divide between the public and the private spheres and violated nineteenth-century standards of propriety and decorum. In addition, Keckley defied prevailing attitudes toward race, class, and gender; she stepped beyond the bounds of proper behavior for female hired help and become what William E. Wiethoff has discussed in another context as "insolent."[67] Thus, *Behind the Scenes* invited the sort of backlash that did, in fact, greet the book. Nevertheless, the book's negative portrait of Mary Lincoln persists—at least in some measure—even to this day.

The Rhetorical Persona of Elizabeth Keckley

In *Behind the Scenes*, Elizabeth Keckley carefully crafted her own rhetorical persona. First and foremost, she portrayed herself as self-sufficient, self-disciplined, courageous, honest, and hard-working. Her story was clearly designed to boost her credibility and illustrate her many virtues, particularly in contrast to her employer, the mercurial Mrs. Lincoln. This persona fit within the genre of postbellum slave narratives, in which former slaves typically emphasized their individual initiative and ability to contribute to the postbellum economy. Yet, for all the attention that *Behind the Scenes* has received as a slave narrative, only the first three of fifteen chapters (75 of 371 pages) were devoted to Keckley's life as a slave. Instead, most of the book focused on what Keckley described as "the most important incidents which I believe influenced the moulding of my character."[68]

In this sense, Keckley's autobiography reflected the rhetorical conventions typical of nineteenth-century male autobiography.[69] Few women in the nineteenth century dared to write conventional autobiographies, for "self-exploration implied self-confidence" and "a sense of the writing self" that made women "uncomfortable." Grounded in an "individualist paradigm," nineteenth-century autobiographical conventions celebrated agency, control, power, and autonomy.[70] As literary theorist Valerie Sanders explains, nineteenth-century women were "ashamed of writing about themselves," and thus those who did "frequently pretended they were doing something other than telling the story of their lives."[71] Consistent with societal expectations, women of this era typically portrayed themselves as intuitive, nurturing, or passive, but rarely as accomplished or heroic. The heroic, "how-I-succeeded" self-portrait was the domain of the middle- or upper-class white male.

Keckley's self-portrait was a clear exception to this rule. Depicting herself as a self-reliant, precocious, and a courageous child, she chronicled how she had persevered through a lifetime of adversity to become a strong, successful woman. In the type of self-reflection more typical of the male autobiography, she explained, "I had been taught to rely upon myself, and to prepare myself to render assistance to others." She emphasized how, through hardship and abuse, she had developed "principles of character" that enabled her to "triumph" over "many difficulties."[72] Throughout these early passages, Keckley spent very little time recounting her own private thoughts or feelings. Instead, she adopted the persona of a dispassionate observer.

Two anecdotes in particular illustrate this persona. In the first, Keckley recounted how, at the age of seven, she witnessed her first slave auction. The family cook's son, known affectionately as "Little Joe," was ripped from his mother's arms and taken to the slave auction. Keckley described the horrific event in a matter-of-fact tone: "He came in with a bright face, was placed on the scales, and was sold." Meanwhile, according to Keckley, his mother was "kept in ignorance of the transaction," even though "her suspicions were aroused."[73] Although Keckley relayed the tragic nature of the event, lamenting that "the mother went down to the grave without ever seeing her child again," she revealed little of her own feelings about witnessing a child of her own age being ripped from his family and sold like an animal.[74]

In the second anecdote, Keckley recalled the story of her uncle's suicide. After losing a pair of plows, Keckley's uncle hung himself rather than "meet the displeasure of his master.... Rather than be punished the way Colonel Burwell punished his servants," Keckley relayed in a matter-of-fact tone, "he took his own life." Again, Keckley communicated very little emotion—no horror, not even grief—over this horrible event, which likely would have been even more devastating for a young child. Instead, Keckley reflected dispassionately on the lesson to be learned from the tragic episode: "Slavery had its dark side as well as its bright side."[75]

The "bright side" of slavery, Keckley suggested, were the lessons she learned from the beatings and other abuse she endured as a slave. These experiences, she maintained, encouraged her to become courageous, strong, and self-sufficient. When her unscrupulous owner beat her in an effort to break her "stubborn pride,"[76] she would end up "sore and bleeding" but ultimately emerge "strong and defiant."[77] Although this abuse must have been traumatizing—both physically and mentally—Keckley rarely recalled her own emotions and instead distanced herself from such events by reflecting on how others must have perceived her treatment. Relating the story of one particularly cruel and undeserved beating, Keckley recalled how her brutal master became the "talk of the town and neighborhood," which ultimately hurt him more than the beating hurt her: "I flatter myself that the actions of those who had conspired against me were not viewed in a light to reflect much credit upon them."[78] For Keckley, it seemed, even beatings and betrayals only served to make her stronger and dramatize the contrast between her principled opposition to slavery and the treachery and brutality of her oppressors.

Keckley's dispassionate and detached tone continued through her chapter about her escape from slavery, entitled "How I gained my Freedom." Nearly half of this twenty-page chapter consisted of legal contracts, court papers, and bills of sale. The language of the contracts may have been dehumanizing, listing Keckley and her son as personal property of the Burwell family. Yet Keckley herself never said as much, instead treating her own escape from slavery as if it were just another business transaction. Documenting the sale and thanking those friends and supporters who helped her raise the money to make it possible, she expressed emotion only when finally describing her moment of liberation in the summer of 1855: "Free, Free, what a glorious ring to the word. Free! The bitter heart-struggle was over!"[79]

As others have noted, Keckley's tendency to minimize the horrors of slavery and her emphasis on self-reliance were typical of postbellum slave narratives. Emancipated slaves were concerned less with conveying the evils of slavery and more with demonstrating how they might contribute to the new social order of the post-war era. Stories of individual initiative and self-discipline were common in slave narratives, as many former slaves sounded themes of self-reliance and personal achievement. Yet Keckley's story was different; she was a first-hand eyewitness to history, a friend and confidant of the First Lady. As Mary Lincoln's dressmaker, she claimed familiarity with the most intimate details of the First Lady's life. Devoting the bulk of the book to her life in Washington, Keckley portrayed herself as a uniquely determined, hard-working, and morally upright woman, who tolerated the mercurial Mary Lincoln with patience and devotion.

Contrasting her own attitude with those of "emancipated blacks" who "pined for the old associations of slavery, and refused to help themselves," Keckley cast the story of her success in Washington as an object lesson in how to succeed in life. While recalling her early days working for Senator Jefferson Davis's wife, Varina, she remembered toiling for long hours, with her head "aching" and "no rest for my busy fingers."[80] Yet Keckley "persevered," and eventually she earned enough money to pay off all her debts—including the $1,200 that friends had loaned her to help buy her freedom. Keckley displayed no bitterness about these tough times in her life, declaring simply that "fortune, fickle dame," had not yet "smiled upon me" during this time.[81]

Perhaps anticipating charges of disloyalty and betrayal, Keckley took pains to emphasize her devotion and faithfulness to Mary Lincoln. She recalled how she initially had agreed to work for Mrs. Lincoln at a very modest salary, presumably out of respect for the First Family. As "soon as it was known that I was the modiste of Mrs. Lincoln," however, the challenge became greater, as "parties crowded around and affected friendship for me, hoping to induce me to betray the secrets of the domestic circle."[82] One particularly unscrupulous woman even promised Keckley "several thousand dollars" for access to the First Family.[83] Yet Keckley resisted these temptations and remained loyal to Lincoln, insisting that she would sooner "throw myself into the Potomac river" than "betray the trust of a friend."[84] Keckley would later discover that the woman who had attempted to bribe her planned to "enter the White House as a servant, learn its secrets, and then publish a scandal to the world."[85] The irony of this statement appeared lost on Keckley.

This theme of loyalty was further emphasized in Keckley's recollections of her reconciliation with her former slave masters. In a chapter entitled "Old Friends"—a title that, in itself, might have caused readers to pause—Keckley described her joyful and affectionate reunion with the Garland family of Virginia in 1866. Showing no bitterness nor resentment toward her former masters, Keckley instead focused on the affectionate bonds of friendship that remained after the Civil War. As in previous chapters, Keckley's account lacked emotion, and she used the letters and conversations of others to express her own feelings. Keckley's conciliatory and magnanimous tone were typical of postbellum slave narratives, yet they also helped shape Keckley's authorial persona as a loving, forgiving person.

Even Keckley's former owners provided testimony to support the persona she cultivated in *Behind the Scenes*. Ann Garland, who by all accounts caused Keckley much emotional and physical pain when she was a slave, was quoted as saying, "love is too strong to be blown away like gossamer threads. The chain is strong enough to bind life even to the world beyond the grave."[86] One of the children Keckley cared for, Maggie Garland, proclaimed her love for her former slave in even stronger terms: "I love Lizzie next to mother. She has been a mother to us all."[87] Keckley also included two letters from the Garland family in the appendix to the book, both further testifying to the Garland family's great affection for Keckley and their desire to see her again. "I shall always love you," concluded one letter written by Maggie Garland; "No one can take your place in my heart."[88] In effect these letters showed that even in slavery Keckley never evidenced any sort of vindictive personality and the testimony of Keckley's former owners provided the final proof of her gracious, loving spirit.

Hysterical Grief, Peculiar Constitution

In contrast to the self-portrait Keckley created in telling her story, *Behind the Scenes* depicted Mary Lincoln as an overly emotional, often hysterical woman who could barely cope with the daily challenges of everyday life. Historian Carroll Smith-Rosenberg has reminded us that hysteria was "one of the classic diseases of the nineteenth century, associated primarily with overly indulged, white, middle-class women."[89] In an era of primitive medical practices, definitions of hysteria varied, but most physicians attached the label *hysterical* to "idle, self-indulgent, [and] deceitful" women "who craved sympathy."[90] In other words, the hysterical woman was the epitome of a bad wife and mother. By describing Lincoln in these gendered ways, Keckley not only exposed her weaknesses, but more importantly, she questioned Lincoln's feminine virtue.

In the preface to *Behind the Scenes,* Keckley anticipated the charge that "I have written too freely on some questions, especially in regard to Mrs. Lincoln." In response, Keckley insisted that "Mrs. Lincoln, by her own acts," had "forced herself into notoriety" and declared that the "veil of mystery must be drawn aside."[91] Referring to the First Lady informally as "Mrs. L," Keckley claimed to reproduce actual conversations (complete with quotations marks), as she stylistically reinforced her claim that she was "intimately associated" with the First Lady during the "most eventful periods of her life."[92] Insisting that everything she wrote was "strictly true" and that "nothing had been exaggerated," Keckley professed only the "purest motive" in going public with her story. She even promised to show the "good side as well as the bad side" of Mrs. Lincoln.[93]

Readers of *Behind the Scenes*, however, would have been hard pressed to find the "good side" of Mary Lincoln. Indeed, the portrait of Mary Lincoln that emerged from the book was so thoroughly negative that, even for critics of Mary Lincoln, it may have failed the test of narrative fidelity, or that quality of "ringing true" in light of the auditor's own knowledge and experiences.[94] In Chapter Thirteen, "The Origin of the Rivalry between Mr. Douglas and Mr. Lincoln," for example, Keckley recounted conversations that would have occurred four decades before Keckley even met Mary,[95] while elsewhere in the book she reconstructed long conversations between Mary and her maternal grandmother—when Mary was but a child. Keckley even went so far as to describe Mary as a "petted child" and a young girl "fond of flirting."[96] She also claimed insight into Mrs. Lincoln's deepest thoughts and motivations, including even her choice of a husband. In discussing Mary's decision to marry Abraham Lincoln rather than her other prominent suitor, Stephen A. Douglas, Keckley not only implied that she had access to Mrs. Lincoln's most private thoughts, but also opined that Mary's sole motivation for marrying Lincoln was to "become Mrs. President."[97] Of course, all of this took place decades before Keckley had even met Mrs. Lincoln.

Keckley intruded even further into the private life of Mrs. Lincoln in describing Mary's reactions to the death of her eleven-year-old son, "Willie," in 1862. In an era of exaggerated sentiment, as historian Karen Halttunen has noted, one "of the most significant expressions of the sentimental culture was the cult of mourning."[98] Mourning loved ones was considered an intensely private matter, and "public displays of grief" were "regarded with distaste."[99] In an era of high infant mortality and primitive medical care, women were expected to "face severe bodily pain, disease and death—and still serve as the emotional support and strength of the family."[100] In *Behind the Scenes*, however, Keckley not only exposed Lincoln's private grief for the world to see, but cast her as obsessive, even hysterical in her mourning. Although the "capacity to experience deep grief" generally "demonstrated true gentility" in nineteenth-century culture,[101] Mary Lincoln's grief went beyond the pale, as she become "inconsolable," according to Keckley. The very mention of her son "threw her into convulsions," and she erupted into "paroxysms" so severe that her husband worried that she might end up in a "lunatic asylum."[102] Keckley concluded that the death of Willie had left Mary an "altered woman."[103] And she went into great detail in describing the depths of Mary's hysterical grief.

Sometimes, when in her room, with no one present but myself, the mere mention of Willie's name would excite her emotion, and any trifling memento that recalled him would move her to tears. She could not bear to look upon his picture; and after his death she never crossed the threshold of the Guest Room in which he died, or the Green Room in which he was embalmed. There was something supernatural in her dread of these things, and something she could not explain.[104]

Keckley acknowledged that she herself had lost her only son, George, in the Civil War, and she conceded that this had been "a sad blow to me."[105] But her sadness over her child's death stood in sharp contrast to Mary Lincoln's hysterical grief, as did Abraham Lincoln's acceptance of Willie's death as part of God's plan. Again claiming to have been privy to the family's most private motives, Keckley quoted Mr. Lincoln as saying: "My poor boy, he was too good for this earth. God has called him home."[106] In contrast to his wife, Abraham Lincoln found solace in his faith and, while sad, mourned in private while carrying on with his day-to-day duties. Mary, however, was distraught and hysterical, with her "fits of hysterics" even inspiring suicidal thoughts. I should like to live for my sons," Keckley recalled Mary saying, "but life is so full of misery that I would rather die."[107]

Keckley's portrait of Mrs. Lincoln was even more disparaging in a cultural context in which women were expected to be the spiritual leaders of their families. As Barbara Welter has argued, "[r]eligion or piety was the core of woman's virtue, the source of her strength" in nineteenth-century culture.[108] Religion "belonged" to the woman "by divine right, a gift of God and nature."[109] Infant and child mortality rates remained high in the 1860s,[110] and Willie Lincoln had died from a common cause, typhoid fever.[111] Since the loss of a child was quite common at the time, a virtuous woman was expected to understand death in a spiritual context, recognizing that the child was in a better place with God. In one popular lady's manual of the day, the *Lady's Token,* women were encouraged to "Trust in God" when a child died, and although tears were appropriate, the author advised against "weeping."[112] Women were considered naturally pious and virtuous, and Mrs. Lincoln's inability to accept the death of her child as part of God's plan pointed to a lack of virtue.

In addition to being hysterical, Mrs. Lincoln was portrayed by Keckley as a "peculiarly constituted woman." By that she meant not merely that Lincoln had quirky personality traits or that she was eccentric, but that she lacked feminine virtues. "Search the world over," Keckley wrote, "and you will not find her counterpart."[113] While other nineteenth-century women embraced the virtues of "True Womanhood"—piety, purity, submissiveness, and domesticity[114]—Mary actively participated in politics, advised her husband on political matters, and made public her views on Lincoln's political appointments. According to Keckley, Mary frequently gave her husband unsolicited and often unwelcomed advice and would break down in "jealous freaks" if he refused her counsel or made decisions with which she disagreed. In one chapter, "Candid Opinions," Keckley recalled Mary expressing strong judgments about almost every member of Lincoln's cabinet—and even about their wives. "Suspicious" of those around her husband, Mary expressed "very bitter" hostility toward her husband's Secretary of the Treasury, Salmon P. Chase, calling him "a selfish politician instead of a true patriot" and urging her husband not to "trust him too far."[115] Mary was even harder on William Seward, Lincoln's Secretary of State, for whom she had "especially severe" criticism, rarely passing up an opportunity "to say an unkind word of him."[116] Again re-creating private conversations between Abraham and Mary, Keckley quoted Mary calling Seward a man without "principle," a "disappointed, ambitious politician," and even a "hypocrite."[117]

In *Behind the Scenes,* Mary's criticisms were not limited to her husband's cabinet. Keckley also recalled her labeling Vice President Andrew Johnson a "demagogue," dismissing General McClellan's opinions as "humbug," and calling General Ulysses S. Grant a "butcher" who was "not fit to be at the head of any army."[118] As Keckley reconstructed conversations between Mary and her husband, she again feigned objectivity and detachment by attributing all judgments of Mary's interventions to Abraham Lincoln himself. "[Y]our prejudices are so violent," Keckley recalled Lincoln saying to his wife, "that you do not stop to reason."[119] While the president was thus portrayed as careful, reflective, kind, honest, and spiritual, Mary was portrayed as "crazy with anxiety" and animated by her irrational, "excited moods."[120] In contrast to the hysterical, harshly judgmental Mary, Keckley celebrated the president as a "demi-god" and the savior "of my race."[121]

Keckley's account of what came to be known as the "Old Clothes Scandal" was perhaps the most scandalous chapter in *Behind the Scenes*. In the fall of 1867, a year before *Behind the Scenes* was published and two years after Lincoln's assassination, Mary Lincoln had entrusted two unscrupulous New York businessmen, W.H. Brady and Samuel Keyes, to sell some of her jewelry and clothing. Panicked that she was running out of money and in debt (Lincoln died intestate and his affairs were not yet settled),[122] Mary hoped this would be a quick and easy way to raise needed cash. In the male-dominated society of the 1860s, as historian Jean Baker has pointed out, women had few opportunities for economic independence, and this was especially true for a pampered Southern widow who had never worked a day in her life.[123] Nevertheless, Lincoln's "conduct and her character came under intense scrutiny" because of her decision to sell some of her own possessions.[124] As Baker explained, "what might have been a legitimate business enterprise" instead became an "unseemly sideshow."[125] The press attacks "were more brutal" than those in the "bleakest days" of the Civil War,[126] when Mary had been accused of being a Confederate spy. Keckley would reprint twenty-one letters from Mary during the five-month period from October 1867 to February 1868, providing documentary proof of Mary's complete mental breakdown. In one letter, dated October 6, 1867, Mary wrote that she was suffering from a "sleepless night of great mental suffering."[127] In another letter, she admitted to great "suffering" and "anguish" and even prayed for death.[128] Throughout the affair, Mary seemed to be worrying herself sick, writing in yet another letter that "[e]very other day, for the past week, I have had a chill, brought on by the excitement and suffering of mind."[129] Mary's letters also reflected wild mood swings; one day she was "nervous and miserable," while six days later she was angry, praying that God would exact just "retribution" on her tormentors.[130]

As verbatim transcripts of Mary's personal letters,[131] the appended correspondence in *Behind the Scenes* reinforced Keckley's credibility as both an intimate friend of Mary's and a truth-teller. Yet in publishing personal correspondence from the First Lady, Keckley once again violated prevailing standards of propriety and decorum. In an era of separation between the public and private, Mary's decision to sell her own clothing was understandably scandalous (unlike today, when celebrities often auction off personal items for charity).[132] The Victorian era demanded modesty, and a public exhibition and sale of one's clothing and other personal items no doubt violated standards of female respectability and decorum.[133] Yet Keckley committed an even greater sin in the context of nineteenth-century standards of propriety and decency: She had betrayed the personal confidences of a presumably trusted friend and, perhaps more importantly, disrupted the racial, social, and economic hierarchy that defined the Reconstruction era.

Although Brady and Keyes had promised Lincoln at least $10,000 for her personal effects, the sale failed to raise enough to pay even the auctioneers for their services. In reporting on the sad story, the *New York Herald* gave voice to many Americans who viewed the "Old Clothes Saga" as the low point in Mrs. Lincoln's already controversial life. "We regret, as every sensible American must regret, that the private affairs of Mrs. Lincoln" were "brought before the public," the story began. But that did not absolve Mrs. Lincoln of blame for the scandal, as she should have known that such a sale could not help "but lead to gossip and disagreeable discussions."[134] However desperate the circumstances, a Victorian lady did not sell her private effects for profit.

The Historical Legacy of *Behind the Scenes*

However badly the Old Clothes Scandal reflected on Mary Lincoln, the scandal paled—at least at the time—in comparison to the outrage ignited by Keckley's book. *Behind the Scenes* damaged Keckley's reputation, and during her lifetime she never recovered from the controversy. Not only did Keckley fail to profit from publication of her book, but she also lost most of her best customers. By all accounts, Keckley's final years were spent in abject poverty and disgrace. Living on a twelve-dollar monthly pension passed down from her son George, who died for the Union cause in the Civil War, Keckley eventually ended up in a Home for Destitute Women and Children, where she died alone in 1907.[135]

Yet despite being thoroughly discredited in her own day, Keckley has been redeemed by contemporary historians who have treated *Behind the Scenes* not only as an accurate historical account, but also as an inspirational tale of a former slave who overcame great obstacles to become a successful entrepreneur. In her well-received *Mrs. Lincoln and Mrs. Keckly,* for example, Fleischner largely accepts Keckley's self-portrait as a hardworking, virtuous, and selfless friend to Mary Lincoln. Fleischner even praised Keckley as being "[e]ver loyal to Mary."[136] This positive portrait of Keckley is especially common in contemporary juvenile literature, where Keckley's story is celebrated as a case study in African American achievement. For example, Becky Rutberg's illustrated biography for children and young adults, *Mary Lincoln's Dressmaker,* described

Keckley as "strikingly beautiful" and "tall and lean," especially in contrast to Mary Lincoln, who was "inclined to stoutness."[137] The contrast between the two women is even more striking in Lynda Jones's book for middle-school children, *Mrs. Lincoln's Dressmaker*, which contrasted the pampered and demanding Mary, whom Jones labeled the "Kentucky Belle," (with all its connotations of privilege) with the self-reliant and hard-working "Slave Girl."[138] Finally, Ann Rinaldi's fictionalized account for sixth-to-ninth-grade children, *An Unlikely Friendship*, celebrated Keckley as a hard-working, resilient survivor, while Mary is again portrayed as a petty, child-like, and overly ambitious woman obsessed with "fame and power."[139] In all of these books, of course, there is no mention of the outrage and skepticism that greeted *Behind the Scenes*, and many of the events and even the conversations recounted in Keckley's memoir are treated as historical fact.

Thus, it comes as little surprise our historical memories of Mary Lincoln remain less than positive. Portrayed in the historical literature as "high-strung," "hard to please," "unpredictable," "jealous," "irrational" and "arrogant,"[140] Mary Lincoln "remains America's most provocative First Lady,"[141] as Baker has noted; indeed, she "ranks among the most detested public women in American history."[142] Polls of historians seem to confirm this assessment. In a Watson Presidential Scholar poll in 1997, Lincoln was rated as the "Least Successful First Lady."[143] In a similar poll, Lincoln was deemed the worst First Lady, second only to Anna Harrison, who served as First Lady for a mere thirty days.[144] Baker has tried to resuscitate Mary's reputation by resisting the "unbalanced view" of Mary Lincoln.[145] Baker has even called Mary a "victim of bias" and a woman "ahead of her time," a woman "battered by personal adversity and trapped by destructive conventions of Victorian domesticity."[146] Yet the negative memories remain, and historians still rely heavily upon Keckley's book as an authoritative account of Mary Lincoln and her time.

As someone who overcame slavery to became a successful entrepreneur, Elizabeth Keckley's accomplishments may well be worthy of celebration. But so too does Mary Lincoln deserve her due, for she too was a victim of the prejudices and stereotypes of the Victorian era. After the publication of *Behind the Scenes*, neither Mary Lincoln, nor any of the rest of the Lincoln family, would ever again speak to Elizabeth Keckley—or even mention her name. Keckley would outlive Mary by more than two decades, but both would die in relative obscurity—Mary isolated at her sister's house in Springfield, Illinois, and Keckley in a home for destitute women in Washington, DC. There is no indication that Mary ever forgave Keckley, nor did she talk about her again in letters—except in one passing and disparaging reference in 1868 to that "colored historian."[147] This too, is part of the sad legacy of *Behind the Scenes*.

NOTES

1. Most contemporary historians refer to the wife of Abraham Lincoln as "Mary Todd Lincoln," although she never used the name "Todd" after her 1842 marriage. Although she signed her name in a dozen different ways, she never once used "Mary Todd Lincoln" or even "Mary T. Lincoln." Mary had a strained relationship with most of her Todd relatives, many of whom supported the Confederate cause during the Civil War, and she often tried to distance herself from their name and influence. For these reasons I will be referring to her only as Mary Lincoln. I will use "Lincoln," unless there is some confusion as to whether I am referring to her or her husband. In that case, I use "Mary." I also use "Mary" when referring to her life before she married Abraham. For more information see, *Abraham Lincoln Presidential Library and Museum* (blog), by James Cornelius, "Mary Lincoln. Period," 15 November 2010. http://www.alplm.org/blog/2010/11/15/.

2. Mary Lincoln to Elizabeth Keckley, 12 January 1868, *Mary Todd Lincoln: Her Life and Letters*, ed. Justin G. Turner and Linda Levitt Turner (New York: Alfred A. Knopf, 1972), 468.

3. Ibid., 15 January 1868, 469.

4. There is some dispute about the proper spelling of Keckley's name. The original 1868 publication of *Behind the Scenes* listed her name as "Keckley," so I will follow that convention, although some historians argue that her name was actually spelled "Keckly." See Jennifer Fleischner, *Mrs. Lincoln and Mrs. Keckly: The Remarkable Story of the Friendship Between a First Lady and a Former Slave* (New York: Broadway Books, 2003), 7.

5. Elizabeth Keckley, *Behind the Scenes: Or, Thirty Years a Slave, and Four Years in the White House* (1868; reprint, New York: Oxford University Press, 1988).

6. "A Book of Scandal," *National Intelligencer*," 25 April 1868.

7. Fleischner, 28–29.

8. Ibid., 35.

9. Ibid., 38.

10. Ibid., 39.

11. Keckley, *Behind the Scenes*, 21.

12. Ibid., 21.

13. Fleischner, *Mrs. Lincoln and Mrs. Keckly*, 66.

14. Ibid., 85.

15. Ibid., 126–27.

16. Keckley, *Behind the Scenes*, 49.

17. Yet Elizabeth would keep Keckley's surname for the rest of her life. Fleischner, *Mrs. Lincoln and Mrs. Keckly*, 142.

18. Keckley, *Behind the Scenes*, 73.

19. Ibid., 76.

20. Fleischner, *Mrs. Lincoln and Mrs. Keckly*, 207.

21. Angela G. Ray, *The Lyceum and Public Culture in the Nineteenth-Century United States* (East Lansing: Michigan State University Press, 2005), 39–40.

22. Fleischner, *Mrs. Lincoln and Mrs. Keckly*, 319; John E. Washington, *They Knew Lincoln* (New York: E.P. Dutton and Company, 1942), 238.

23. Fleischner, *Mrs. Lincoln and Mrs. Keckly*, 316.

24. Catherine Clinton, *Mrs. Lincoln: A Life* (New York: HarperCollins, 2009), 208.

25. Frances Smith Foster, *Written by Herself: Literary Production by African American Women, 1746–1892* (Bloomington: Indiana University Press, 1993), 128.

26. Washington, 239.

27. Fleischner, *Mrs. Lincoln and Mrs. Keckly*, 316.

28. In the "New Books" and "New Editions" section, Carleton & Co. included such titles as *The Habits of Good Society, The Art of Conversation, The Art of Amusing, The Artist in Cuba*, and *The Artist in Peru*. See appendix to *Behind the Scenes*.

29. Keckley, xiii, xiv.

30. Washington, 232–33.

31. "A Literary Thunderbolt," *New York Commercial Advertiser* (New York City), 4 April 1868.

32. Karlyn Kohrs Campbell, ed., *Man Cannot Speak for Her: A Critical Study of Early Feminist Rhetoric* Vol. 1 (New York: Praeger, 1989), 10.

33. Cotesworth Pinckney, ed., *The Lady's Token: Gift of Friendship* (Boston: J. Buffum, 1848), 116.

34. "A Fresh Book of Scandal," *Springfield Republican* (MA), 22 April 1868.

35. "A book of Scandal," *National Intelligencer* (Washington, DC), 25 April 1868.

36. "Behind the Scenes," *Commercial Advertiser*, 16 April 1868.

37. "Review of *Behind the Scenes*," *Atlantic Monthly*, July 1868, 128.

38. "Review of *Behind the Scenes*," *Putnam's Magazine*, July 1868, 116.

39. Eric Foner, *Reconstruction: America's Unfinished Revolution, 1863–1877* (New York: Harper and Row Publishers, 1988), 79.

40. "A Book of Scandal," *National Intelligencer* (Washington, DC), 25 April 1868.

41. "Review of *Behind the Scenes*," *Atlantic Monthly*, July 1868, 128.

42. Elizabeth Young, "Black Woman, White House: Race and Redress in Elizabeth Keckley's *Behind the Scenes*," in *Disarming the Nation: Women's Writing and the American Civil War* (Chicago: University of Chicago Press, 1999), 143; D. Ottolengul (pseud.) *Behind the Seams; by a Nigger Woman who took in work from Mrs. Lincoln and Mrs. Davis* (New York: National News Company, 1868).

43. Young, 143.

44. "A Book of Scandal," *National Intelligencer* (Washington, DC), 25 April 1868.

45. Steve Criniti, "Thirty Years a Slave and Four Years a Fairy Godmother: Dressmaking as Self-Making in Elizabeth Keckley's Autobiography," *American Transcendental Quarterly* 22 (2008): 320.

46. *St. Cloud Sentinel,* 14 November 1935. Newspaper clipping from the Minnesota Historical Society Library, St. Paul.

47. *Washington Star,* 11 November 1935. Newspaper clipping from the Minnesota Historical Society Library, St. Paul.

48. Fleischner, *Mrs. Lincoln and Mrs. Keckly*, 5.

49. Ibid., 319.

50. Ibid., 325.

51. Criniti, 310.

52. Frances Smith Foster, *Written by Herself,* 123.

53. William L. Andrews, "Reunion in the Postbellum Slave Narrative: Frederick Douglass and Elizabeth Keckley," *Black American Literature Forum* 23 (Spring 1989): 8.

54. Sylvia D. Hoffert, "Jane Grey Swisshelm, Elizabeth Keckley, and the Significance of Race Consciousness in American Women's History," *Journal of Women's History* 12 (2001): 14.

55. Jennifer Fleischner, *Mastering Slavery: Memory, Family, and Identity in Women's Slave Narratives* (New York: New York University Press, 1996), 94.

56. Xiomara Santamarina, "Behind the Scenes of Black Labor: Elizabeth Keckley and the Scandal of Publicity," *Feminist Studies* 28 (2002): 516.

57. Katherine Adams, "Freedom and Ballgowns: Elizabeth Keckley and the Work of Domesticity," *Arizona Quarterly* 57 (Winter 2001): 67.

58. Michael Berthold, "Not 'Altogether' the 'History of Myself': Autobiographical impersonality in Elizabeth Keckley's *Behind the Scenes: Or, Thirty Years a Slave, and Four Years in the White House," Transcendental Quarterly* 13 (June 1999), 105–19.

59. Criniti, 310.

60. See a similar argument in Lori Merish, "Fashioning a Free Self: Consumption, Politics, and Power in the Writings of Elizabeth Keckley and Frances Harper," in *Sentimental Materialism: Gender Commodity Culture and Nineteenth Century American Literature* (Durham: Duke University Press), 229–69.

61. Dale L. Sullivan, "Identification and Dissociation in Rhetorical Exposé: An Analysis of St. Irenaeus's 'Against Heresies,'" *Rhetoric Society Quarterly* 29 (Winter 1999): 50.

62. Susan Schultz Huxman and Wil A. Linkugel, "Accusations and Apologies from a General, a Senator, and a Priest," in *Oratorical Encounters: Selected Studies and Sources of Twentieth Century Political Accusations and Apologies,* ed. Halford R. Ryan (Westport: 1988), 31.

63. Sullivan, 51.

64. Ibid., 54.
65. Ibid., 55.
66. Ibid., 70.
67. William E. Wiethoff, *The Insolent Slave* (Columbia: University of South Carolina Press, 2002).
68. Keckley, 18.
69. Susan Standford Friedman, "Women's Autobiographical Selves: Theory and Practice," in *The Private Self: Theory and Practice of Women's Autobiographical Writing*, ed. Shari Benstock (Chapel Hill: University of North Carolina Press, 1988), 36.
70. Joanne Schattock, "Victorian Women as Writers and Readers of (Auto)biography," in *Mortal Pages, Literary Lives: Studies in Nineteenth-Century Autobiography*, ed. Vincent Newey and Philip Shaw (Tuscaloosa: University of Alabama Press, 1991), 142.
71. Valerie Sanders, "'Father's Daughters': Three Victorian Anti-Feminist Women Autobiographers," in *Mortal Pages, Literary Lives: Studies in Nineteenth-Century Autobiography*, ed. Vincent Newey and Philip Shaw (Tuscaloosa: University of Alabama Press, 1991), 152.
72. Keckley, 19.
73. Ibid., 28.
74. Ibid., 29.
75. Ibid., 30.
76. Ibid., 36.
77. Ibid., 37.
78. Ibid., 38.
79. Ibid., 55.
80. Ibid., 67.
81. Ibid., 330.
82. Ibid., 92.
83. Ibid., 94.
84. Ibid., 94.
85. Ibid., 95.
86. Ibid., 257.
87. Ibid., 259.
88. Ibid., 266.
89. Carroll Smith-Rosenberg, "The Hysterical Woman: Sex Roles and Role Conflict in Nineteenth-Century America," *Social Research* 39 (Winter 1972): 652.
90. Smith-Rosenberg, "The Hysterical Woman," 667.
91. Keckley, xiii–xiv.
92. Ibid., xiv.
93. Ibid., xv.
94. Walter R. Fisher, "Narration as a human communication paradigm: The case of public moral argument," *Communication Monographs* 51.1 (1984): 1–22.

95. Keckley, 230.
96. Ibid., 229.
97. Ibid., 230.
98. Karen Halttunen, *Confidence Men and Painted Women: A Study of Middle Class Culture in America, 1830–1870* (New Haven: Yale University Press, 1982), 124.
99. Halttunen, 132.
100. Smith-Rosenberg, "The Hysterical Woman," 657.
101. Halttunen, 144.
102. Keckley, 104. Keckley re-created a dialogue between Mary and Abraham whereby Abraham points to an insane asylum and warns Mary that she might soon be headed there. Jean Baker doubts that this conversation ever occurred, as one could not see the new million-dollar Governmental Hospital for the Insane from the White House. Jean Baker, *Mary Todd Lincoln: A Biography*, 2nd ed. (New York: Norton, 2008), 213.
103. Keckley, 116.
104. Ibid., 117.
105. Ibid., 105.
106. Ibid., 103.
107. Ibid., 200.
108. Welter, 21.
109. Ibid., 22.
110. Clifton D. Bryant, *Handbook of Death and Dying* Volume 1 (Thousand Oaks, CA: Sage Publications, 2003), 189.
111. Baker, 208.
112. Pinckney, 100–101.
113. Keckley, 182.
114. Welter, 21.
115. Keckley, 128.
116. Ibid., 130.
117. Ibid., 131.
118. Ibid., 133.
119. Ibid., 131.
120. Ibid., 151.
121. Ibid., 269.
122. Jason Emerson estimated that Mary owed approximately $70,000 at the time of her husband's death. At the time of the Old Clothes Scandal, Mary was living on the interest of the Lincoln estate which was approximately $1500 a month. Emerson claimed that even in the 1860s, that was considered a "modest" sum. Jason Emerson, *The Dark Days of Abraham Lincoln's Widow: As Revealed in her Own Letters*, ed. Myra Helmer and Jason Emerson (Carbondale, IL: Southern Illinois University Press, 2011), 43.

123. Baker, 278.
124. Clinton, 275.
125. Baker, 275.
126. Clinton, 275.
127. Keckley, 332.
128. Ibid., 333.
129. Ibid., 338.
130. Ibid., 349.
131. These letters are reprinted verbatim in Turner and Turner, *Mary Lincoln*.
132. See, for example, William D. Montalbano, "Lady Diana's Evening Gowns to be Auctioned for Charity," *Los Angeles Times*, 30 January 1997, 8:1; and Michelle Green, Maria Speidel, Nancy Jo Sales, and Marisa Salcines, "Objects of Desire," *People*, 1 April 1996, 74–78.
133. Baker, 278.
134. "Mrs. Lincoln and her Wardrobe," *New York Herald*, 4 October 1867.
135. Washington, 213.
136. Fleischner, 295.
137. Becky Rutberg, *Mary Lincoln's Dressmaker: Elizabeth Keckley's Remarkable Rise from Slave to White House Confidante* (New York: Walker and Company, 1995): 14, 3.
138. Lynda Jones, *Mrs. Lincoln's Dressmaker: The Unlikely Friendship of Elizabeth Keckley and Mary Todd Lincoln* (Washington, DC: National Geographic, 2009).
139. Ann Rinaldi, *An Unlikely Friendship: A Novel of Mary Todd Lincoln and Elizabeth Keckley* (Orlando: Harcourt Publishers, 2007), 126.
140. Rutberg 47, 48 53, 83, 85, 102.
141. Baker, xi.
142. Ibid., xxi.
143. Robert P. Watson, *The Presidents' Wives: Reassessing the Office of First Lady* (Boulder: Lynne Rienner Publishers, 2000), 188.
144. Watson, 189.
145. Baker, xiv.
146. Ibid., xiii–xxiii.
147. Mary Lincoln to Rhoda White, May 2, 1868, *Mary Todd Lincoln: Her Life and Letters*, ed. Justin G. Turner and Linda Levitt Turner (New York: Alfred A. Knopf, 1972), 476.

VOLUME 2: ARTISTRY, COMMERCE & CULTURE

DRAMA

CHAPTER EIGHT

TAZWELL THOMPSON

Mary T. & Lizzy K.

Characters:

Mary Todd Lincoln
Elizabeth Keckly
Ivy
Abraham Lincoln

Setting: A white room. Grand. Yet intimate. Elegant. Yet deteriorating. Faded glory. Classical and profane. The white walls, painted white over and over—a pentimento—cannot hide a history of secrets and broken promises in them. Etched scrawls and desperate scratchings of former inhabitants. There are doors and windows that seem forever sealed, painted over in white. The room contains the scattered remains and memories that span the life of Mary Todd Lincoln; furniture and props: chairs, settee, cradle, baby carriage, toys, trunks, hatboxes, vanity, and chandelier. Etc. There is one chair—Lizzy's chair—that has a place of prominence in the room. Beside the chair is an overstuffed carpetbag filled with fabric pieces, sewing materials, a notebook, and a book or folder of newspaper clippings and receipts.

Time: Nineteenth century.

(*To us. Through the lighted scrim.*)

MARY: I woke up this morning. That's an achievement. The people need to see me. I am sitting for: My frozen moment. To be captured. By: Matthew Brady. The people need to remember me. I put on my strawberry dress. See? Attached my pearls. A row of roses. In my hair. Kid gloves. I am clutching. This spring bouquet. In my lap. Flowers. A nice parenthesis. Between my face. And hands.

(*To Lizzy*)

Lizzy? Your gloves. Working them. Again. Like clockwork.

LIZZY (*Lights up on Lizzy. She is repairing/adding on to her own soft blue gloves that she crocheted in memory of her son.*)

To mark the death. Of my boy. On the battlefield. It was September. I claimed him. His body. Pulled from me. I couldn't. Wouldn't. Let go. I held on. To my child. By his sweater. I knit for him. It unraveled. In my hands. Here it is. Once a ball of. Blue wool. Now a string of wool. Woven into gloves. Was a time. I wouldn't wear gloves. No matter the weather. No matter the work. Wanted to: Reach out. And touch. And feel. And grab. The world. Long denied me. Head on. With both bare hands. Not even thimbles. Would cover. My fingertips. Now. Never without them. These gloves? Unfinished. Like my child. Each month: A crocheted ring is added. A commemorative wreath. For my son.

MARY: Oh. Here goes. Mr. Brady is ready. Breathe in. Mary. And. Hold.

(*The sound of a shutter. Mary's picture is taken.*)

(*The scrim falls to the floor.*)

(*Music. Lights shift. A visit.*)

Assassinated. Over and over. Every time someone buys your book. And turns a page. What is this need to know? To dig? To hunt? My life is not yours to excavate. And you. Failed. Out there on your own. Failed as a book author. Had you thought of something else?

LIZZY: I make dresses. I love what I do. I have a few orders from those who remember me. I'm working on something new now.

MARY: What is it?

LIZZY: A baby's baptismal gown.

MARY: How could you afford the material?

LIZZY: I tore it out from one of my petticoats.

MARY: Had you the money. All those years: What were you planning to do with it?

LIZZY: I wanted to have a classroom.

MARY: I never knew this.

LIZZY: To teach young girls what I know.

MARY: Like Ivy?

LIZZY: Yes.

MARY: I had no idea.

LIZZY: Yes.

MARY: Since when?

LIZZY: Always.

MARY: Always?

LIZZY: Since when I came.

MARY: Why didn't you tell?

LIZZY: Came to work for you in the White House.

MARY: But you still could've.

LIZZY: The work for you was all-consuming.

MARY: You had other clients.

LIZZY: No. Not really. Not after you took me on.

MARY: Still. You could've informed me.

LIZZY: With you I was on call. I became more than just your dressmaker. I became . . .

MARY: We: Became friends.

LIZZY: And even if I had the time. Which I never did.

MARY: You must have had some time.

LIZZY: Putting a school together requires . . .

MARY: I can't imagine that I commanded.

LIZZY: Demanded.

MARY: All your attention.

LIZZY: My time.

MARY: Your time.

LIZZY: Day and . . .

MARY: Did I?

LIZZY: You did. Day and night.

MARY: But still. Lizzy.

LIZZY: Putting a school together.

MARY: I mean.

LIZZY: Requires.

MARY: You could've alerted me.

LIZZY: Materials.

MARY: You should've made it clear to me.

LIZZY: Endless supplies.

MARY: Forced me to understand just how important this was to you.

LIZZY: (*Tumbles out.*)

Spools of thread. A pressing iron. Worktables. Fabric. Measuring tools. Scissors. A dye vat. Buttons. Hooks. Pins. Space. Room. Sponsors. For students.

MARY: How was I to know? You seemed happy. Content. To work for me. I just couldn't: Pull out of the sky. What you were feeling. You needed to: Tell me. That Lizzy needs extra fulfillment! That Lizzy needs more gratification! That Lizzy needs.

LIZZY: To be paid!

MARY: There's no denying that money. Can ease the skids when: Bad health. Or loss of work. Or other drastic misfortunes. Are driving you downhill. It cannot ever replace: The loss of loyalty. True love. An eternal bond. Sisterhood. What advantage is money then?

LIZZY: That's one of the myths. You can console yourself with. Only the arrogance of the privileged. Would say such a thing. I've lost my home. My workspace. My credit. As a reliable dressmaker. I'm losing my hair. I am now relegated: To southwest Washington. In a run down. Flop house. Disguised as a tenement. Dust stagnant in the hallways. Screams. Cats in heat. Fist fights. Smell of urine and old fish. A constant stink of cabbage. I stay awake: Sweeping mice. Cockroaches. From the doorway. I've worked too hard. All my life. To have: Nothing. Put aside. Nothing. To show: For the work. And to have my future. My survival. Tied up in what you owe me.

MARY: You were working for Mary Todd Lincoln! The First Lady of the land! Mrs. President! An invaluable calling card! Wasn't that payment enough? You cannot wish for better reference. Or greater collateral. You had the world stage of the White House as your platform. To display your clothes. And you took it. You took my trust. And my friendship. And warped it into a book.

LIZZY: And what did I have that you didn't take from me? Sucked up: All my energies. Stole away every extra precious time I had. You sent White House messengers. In wartime! In the middle of the night! You were having: Second thoughts. On the cut. Of a certain piece of fabric. Or. I'm unable to sleep. Lizzy. Having nightmares. Come at once! If you should pass Center Market. On your way. Have my man wake up the proprietor. And purchase something soothing. For us to eat.

MARY: (*Amused. Laughing.*)

Oh. Lizzy! I know. I'm impossible. But you have told me. More than once. That you are always up. Working. Burning the midnight oil. Sewing to meet a deadline.

LIZZY: My deadline! My schedule! My time! Not yours to commandeer. Certainly not up to you to take complete advantage. Of every fiber of my physical being.

MARY: Explain.

LIZZY: The territory of my lap. For instance. Where you assume: That it is always there. My lap! For your convenience. At your selfish disposal. And whim. To make a comfortable nest in! My constant and available shoulder: For you to cry on! And my nipple: For you to drain dry!

MARY: An unfortunate exaggeration.

(*Silence.*)

Lizzy. Remember we once tried to sell my clothes? I can laugh at it now. Brady & Keyes. 609 Broadway. New York City. The curious. The enemies. Picking. Sniffing through my things. Dozens and dozens of items. And nothing sold. I myself had forgotten. That I had treasury notes. Government bonds. And jewelry. Tucked. And sewn. In the hems. And petticoats. All safe when the clothes were returned. Do you remember my jewelry?

LIZZY: All. Everything.

(*The following is very playful.*)

MARY: Blue agate earrings.

LIZZY: Gold and tortoise-shell hair comb.

MARY: Necklace.

MARY & LIZZY: In Byzantine revival style.

MARY: Necklace.

LIZZY: With gold ivy leaves.

MARY: Wheat and star motif cut steel necklace.

LIZZY: And pendant. Silver pin.

MARY & LIZZY: In Greek revival style.

LIZZY: With matching bracelet and earrings.

MARY: Punched up with red.

LIZZY: Cranberry seed–size rubies.

MARY: My bangles.

MARY & LIZZY: In French renaissance style.

MARY: With Limoges enamel inset.

LIZZY: That gold pendant with the tiny emerald cherub.

MARY: And my prize: a pin.

LIZZY: A clip.

MARY: A brooch.

LIZZY: A medallion is more like it.

MARY: In the shape of a starfish.

LIZZY: (*Correcting.*)

A starburst.

MARY: Sunburst.

LIZZY: Some kind of burst.

MARY: It had five fresh-water pearls at the center.

LIZZY: With dazzling gold flames.

MARY: Shooting out from all sides.

LIZZY: Like the sun.

MARY: And the eye-of-a-needle size diamonds at the tip of each flame. You had me wear it atop of my shoulder.

MARY & LIZZY: Military style.

MARY: Women would tip on their toes to get the full picture of this jewel.

LIZZY: Men would bow their heads in homage looking down at this dazzler.

MARY: So beautiful.

LIZZY: Exquisite.

MARY: My favorite.

(*Mary reaches underneath the hem of her uniform. She exposes a purse sewn into the inside hem. She takes out the prized brooch from the purse and places it in Lizzy's hand.*)

Now it's yours. Minus: A few stones. A couple of pearls. Used for bribes. Still precious to me. As you are.

LIZZY: (*Overcome. Lizzy's face crumbles. She cries. Then.*)

And the book?

MARY: What's done. Is done. It cannot be undone. As Mr. Lincoln. Was fond of saying. We had him for a while. Didn't we. Lizzy? My husband.

LIZZY: For a time. Yes.

MARY: They said in the papers: He belongs to the ages.

LIZZY: Yes.

MARY: That President Grant: Is in the mold. Of Mr. Lincoln. That there are others. In the House and Senate. Being compared to my husband. Only a matter of time. They say. Before we have another.

LIZZY: He must first learn to walk on water. He must first find a way. To put the thunder back. He must: Recall a roll call of the saints. For surely. He needs to find his name in that number. No. There will never be: Another Mr. Lincoln. He could be: The King of Bombay. With gold coins. Spillin' from his eyes and ears. Dozens of white doves. Spoutin' from his mouth. The King of Bombay! Flying in on a red carpet. Made real from a fairytale book. And he. Beside Mr. Lincoln. Would appear cheap and derelict. I don't care who he is. Or what he is. Or who he was. Or who. Or what he thinks he might be. Or become. There will never be: Another Mr. Lincoln.

CHAPTER NINE

Maureen Quilligan with Michael Malone

Behind the Scenes
A Meeting between Anna Burwell and Elizabeth Keckly

Front porch and grounds of the Burwell School, 1870, late afternoon.

SCENE I

Mrs. Anna Burwell, 60, sits with a closed book in a rocking chair on the porch, a quilt around her. She wears a plain but beautifully fitted black dress with a cap. She is "a majestic, imposing woman— nearly six feet tall—with a handsome, kindly face; a decided flair for efficient organization and management."

We should get the impression we're seeing her reflections on the book she's been reading . . .

Young Lizzy, 14–16, a teenaged slave, beautiful and intense, sits in a simple white dress, on the porch step huddled over a book, scribbling on a piece of paper. Young Anna, 25–27, comes impatiently out of the house. Lizzy jumps up, starts to hide the paper in her pocket then defiantly takes it back out.

YOUNG ANNA: Lizzy! That stove's as cold as ice! *(grabs the book)* Mathematics? How many times have I said it? Stay out of that schoolroom. You're here to work. I can't do everything myself.

YOUNG LIZZY *(stubborn)*: I want to get the right answer.

YOUNG ANNA: *(snatches paper, looks at it)* The right answer's, "Fire up that stove." 549 minus 212 equals 337. (*She hits Lizzy in the face with the rolled up paper.*) Your answer to the problem is incorrect because of a careless error in subtraction.

Brusque, she thrusts the paper back at Lizzy and hurries her inside. As they go...

YOUNG ANNA (*begrudgingly*): Otherwise you were on the right track.

SCENE II

Anna Burwell puts down the book, troubled, then settles with the quilt, as if she were going to nap.

 A distinguished African American woman very well dressed, early 50s, walks up to the porch and stands a diffident measure away. She is Lizzy Keckly.

LIZZY: (*She is surprised, expecting the Collins.*) Is that Miz. Burwell?

ANNA (*locating her glasses so she can focus on the woman*): I'm Anna Burwell. How may I help you?

LIZZY: It's Lizzy. Where are the Collins'?"

ANNA: Who, dear? (*stands up; a flicker of recognition*)

LIZZY: (*comes closer*) Lizzy Keckly. Lizzy Hobbs. I used to work here at the school.

ANNA (*standing up, hiding her book under her quilt*): Come up on the porch; my eyesight's not what it was.

(*Lizzie goes up to her.*)

Ah yes. I recognize you. I remember you and I did not agree on things. I'm surprised to see you down here in Hillsborough. What brings you after all these years?

LIZZY: You're right. We did not agree. I came down to get something from the Collins'. I suppose I also came down to see where my son was born, where I was a slave. I'm surprised to see you here.

ANNA: *(after a long and awkward pause)* You haven't changed at all.

LIZZY: Oh yes I have. But this house hasn't changed much. Is Mr. Burwell here?

ANNA: No. . . . You were lucky to find me here. We live in Charlotte now. We started another school, a university.

LIZZY: I heard that. A women's college.

ANNA: We did. The Collins asked me to check on it while they were out west visiting their children. Where are you staying?

LIZZY: I'm not. I walked up from the train station. I'll walk back. The town hasn't changed much. Richmond was ruined when we came down with President Lincoln on the train right after it fell. I was shocked to see it a field of broken bricks. They are starting to rebuild now. But nothing seems to have happened here. President Lincoln said that Sherman decided to spare North Carolina because early on it voted not to enter the war.

ANNA: *(stiff)* North Carolina was the last state to surrender. Months after Appomattox. The war ended not ten miles from this house. *(awkward pause)*

LIZZY: May I sit down? *(Anna nods. Lizzy sits.)*

ANNA *(sitting down herself)*: It seems you've gotten to be quite famous. In the newspapers.

LIZZY: I teach. I raise money for those in need.

ANNA: Yes. And you write. Mrs. Lincoln's "friend."

LIZZY: That's not how I would like to be famous.

ANNA: Really? *(snorting a bit)* How would you *like* to be famous?

LIZZY: I'm a working woman, good at my craft, the clothes I make. I try to make a difference.

ANNA: Well, you did do that. The *modiste*. Newspaper pictures of those dresses you made for Mrs Lincoln called too much attention to themselves, I'd say. I saw them. *(gestures)* But *your* costume is . . . tasteful.

LIZZY *(ironic)*: Thank you for that compliment. My own tastes are plain. You may not realize that Mrs. Lincoln had to dress for an international audience as well as a national one.

ANNA: *(matches her)* Thank you for correcting my provincial opinions. Well, sad to say, now you're famous for betraying your friend . . . although how you became Mrs. Lincoln's friend, I can only guess.

LIZZY: I need to ask you something.

ANNA: *(ignoring)* I can think how it might have happened. I saw you making friends with some of the students here, by sewing them dresses when you should have been working for me. Always climbing and never minding. Always ambitious. And then there you were, in the White House.

LIZZY: *(comes back at her)* I did the work of three slaves here!

ANNA: *(rises)* And I did the work of six!! While you took an hour to fetch a bucket of water, I slaughtered and butchered a whole hog, then I taught a school of 30 girls, taught them physics and French and poetry. Did you work like that? Did you give birth to twelve children?

LIZZY: No. I gave birth to one. (*Accusingly, shaking a finger:*) And not by choice. . . . *(Anna starts to reply but closes her mouth firmly)* And I salted all those chopped up hog parts of yours, I wrapped them, I cleaned up so you could go teach. Teaching's a pleasure.

ANNA: I think you should just leave! Why did you even come here? What do you want from me? Parading around in your smart clothes.

LIZZY: I left a cloak here when I was sent back to Virginia. I would like to have it, if I may. I didn't expect I would have to ask you for it.

ANNA: A cloak? A cloak of yours wouldn't be here.

LIZZY: It's upstairs, hidden under some boards in the back of the attic.

ANNA: What?? What kind of cloak?

LIZZY: A blue velvet cloak with epaulets at the shoulder. I was making it for Lorelei Kanter. She bought the fabric. But she died before I finished it.

ANNA: So you stole it.

LIZZY: No. she gave it to me the day she died. She was kind.

ANNA: *(memory stops her)* . . . Influenza. We lost three girls. My husband thought we would have to close down the school. Fortunately, I did not have to do that. Yes, Lori was a kind girl. . . . Not a smart one.

LIZZY: May I go look for that cloak?

ANNA: Will you pay me for it? It would have belonged to me.

LIZZY: As I belonged to you and Mr. Burwell? *(Takes money from her purse.)* It took a long time but I bought myself. I bought my son. So I can buy a little cloak. Here.

ANNA: *(Takes the money but doesn't look at it.)* Before I go climbing to the attic, I'd like a glass of tea.

Lizzy closes her purse with an audible and resistant snap.

ANNA: Could you get it for me? I think there are still some cups in the cupboard and there's a kettle on the stove. Where everything used to be, you remember.

Lizzy puts her purse back in her bodice, then stands for a very long time.

ANNA: You don't have to do it. It's your choice now. That must feel good. I am more than a decade older than you are. And not in my best health.

LIZZY: Eleven years is not that much difference in a hard life. *(Taking off her hat and cape, she opens the door.)* Do you have milk?

ANNA: Yes. And maybe some cookies? They are on the sideboard. I made them this morning.

Lizzy starts inside. Anna finds the book under the quilt and looking around nervously for a new place to hide, and finding none, hides it more securely. Lizzy turns and watches her do it (from the front door), then goes. Anna sits back in her chair, pulls the quilt around her.

SCENE III

Young Anna comes out, pulling on a simple but handsome polka-dotted short cape. Lizzy follows her.

YOUNG LIZZY: It's not finished. (*She grabs the shawl off Young Anna and starts quickly sewing a last small bit.*)

YOUNG ANNA *(impatient and embarrassed)*: It's fine, Lizzy. It's perfect. I'm not going to a fancy ball. I'm going to church.

YOUNG LIZZY: You think God that makes all your pretty roses and all your big beans and carrots and squash can't see the difference in good stitching and bad? Here.

(*She puts the cloak around Young Anna's shoulders.*) Now it's perfect.

YOUNG ANNA: "Let another man praise thee and not thine own mouth." Proverbs 27:2. Go tell the family to hurry up. Don't dawdle.

She hurries off, tying the cape with a jerk. Young Lizzy watches the cape's movements, then returns to the house.

VOLUME 2: ARTISTRY, COMMERCE & CULTURE

POETRY

CHAPTER 10

JAKI SHELTON GREEN

a feast of whispers

~

elizabeth keckley was nobody's back woods *whisper* She knew that even the clothes-pins sparrow feathers blue glass all *whispered* in the night like the spider unlacing a full moon web She gathered the very blood line of cotton damask silk linen She worked inside of the stillness of the night Knowing that this stillness was deeper than death waiting She becoming more of the notion of free.

~

each stitch prick between torch flight and night's light knew how to measure a sky of neck hips wrists thighs each stitch taught her how to tell rock from bone each stitch *whispering* bone hangs close to the needle rock pushes slices color pattern like the soles of her feet out racing the notion of freedom.

~

the unrecognizable sound of her own voice crying for the loss of her son's skin weaves into the dancing sleeve of a white woman on the brink of *becoming* more of the notion of free like birds who fight the shadows of their own wings.

~

soft dawn *whispers* crown a morning that pushes back the blush of shimmering thread against the paleness of a dancing southern mistress stupefied elegance stretched across drowned indigo-stamped chemise soaked in a music that erases the gentility of surrender.

~

mary todd lincoln prayed for rain clouds against a bloodstained horizon that would not bend Her only salvation in the hands of her *modiste lizzie* slave bonded as confidante Her words carrying empty potions unrecognizable as the taste of *Her* own bondage.

~

the master's tools will not dismantle the master's house... lizzie offered a prayer for the prayers unanswered for the torched scorched torn damned soul of her captor Her womb soothed a thousand lashes that wounded the sky the grass the river the fire of her breath.

~

as the story unfolds beneath her cloth She holds the few strands of what remains of another story hushed folded unwritten like the path from arrival to departure from hem to bodice She sews glass buttons in between the hours that grow inside the desert of her unrecognizable heart.

~

two women hold back sinister nights drink from the same cup that spills disintegrating the only blank canvas between them They reach for the same light one hand burned the other holds heat so close it frays the lace the landscape of her whiteness so close it becomes an airborne divination.

~

face to face silhouette to silhouette They feel each other's breath but too many years have stripped them bare of any notion of the freedom they stole from each other They are the reflection of the same offering to a hungry god.

~

conjuring new skirts for new dancers the prick of the thumb unleashes more than blood stained seams unleashes more than the shrouded dance floors of slaves in unmarked cemeteries more than the unbearable notion of unrecognizable freedom crawling through the very eye of Her needle.

~

mary todd wears weary well like an undressed sunrise bulging with veins of poverty throbbing beckoning with the unraveling voice of fallen petals It becomes her well She steps out of her skin for an unmeasurable fitting of her soul.

~

one last lift of muted organza that hugs the waist perfect SHE becomes her own *modiste* dressing for the dance of freedom dressing for all the denied dances of her mother dressing for all the denied slaves whispering from her unrecognizable voice.

~

from a rooftop She imagined she saw him but then she never could decipher between bone and stone the smell of her abe lincoln still lingering in the bloody fabric pressed hard against her chest flooding parched untamed rivers weighing more than her drooping breasts.

~

each stitch taught her how to tell taught her how to measure the heaviness of her own war each stitch created a forbidden game a forbidden weapon She learned to dress and undress the shadows of her own ladies-in-waiting the shadows of quivering stardust hanging from shackled branches.

CHAPTER ELEVEN

ZELDA LOCKHART

Posthumous

December 16, 2015

Dear Black Woman—"I have been intending to write to you for a long time, but numerous things have prevented, and for that reason you must excuse me."

If I said I died with no regrets, I'd be lying, so I need to tell you some things that are explained in my book, but people don't pay much attention to. I thought to get people to read the book and the atrocity there, that I should write a book of what people seemed most interested in, the inside of the White House during the Civil War. My story and this story I paint together, but my story doesn't seem to be the focus of what got left behind as your map.

I spent all my life thinking that if I was owned by the right person, had the right amount of money or said the right thing that I could somehow turn the truth into a key that would equal my freedom, but every time I side-stepped the truth for the sake of my survival like marrying somebody I didn't love, or telling the world that slavery was bad but not at the fault of the currently living, or telling somebody else's truth instead of my own, I stood just off-center of the truth hoping it would make me free, but all it made me was what I was in the first place a negro woman. I came in to the world through a negro woman and left as a negro woman. In the end, she died broken and without a tomb stone to remember her and I died broken having lived long, when I would have rather been whole, having lived short.

I want you to know that there is a long list of side-steppers, who have strategized to survive that way and a long list of bad assess who looked death in the eyes and told the truth with straight precision. The later, is the better.

My plan for survival was always, just tell the part of the truth that won't raise any dust, won't rile any feathers. When I was a child in Virginia, I wish I'd done both. I used to listen to my little Elizabeth Burwell go on and on talking about the expedition of Lewis and Clark and how they marched off westward from Missouri, just repeating what she heard her father say. I would dream a plan to follow the caves from Missouri straight across in the wagon tracks of Lewis and Clark, maybe find my father there out West, but then I'd get the horror thoughts in my head, like the image of my uncle hanging in the tree by his own hands to keep Mr. Burwell from beating him, and I'd hear the woman's voice hollering for her son that Burwell sold. I'd hear her son somewhere beyond everywhere hollering back and none of us could holler to him unless we'd get the same flogging his mother got. All those lives and voices beaten out and snubbed to silence, so for survival sake I stopped thinking about the wagon wheels of Lewis and Clark and even when I told the truth about slavery, I still tagged on lies of survival like, "Slavery had its dark side as well as its bright side."

When I moved to Hillsboro, North Carolina, the worst of it all began, between young Mr. Burwell and the reverend beating me regularly within an inch of my life, all for being a black woman with pride, who knew to walk with her head up. When I think of those days, I fear for you. There are white men who will use their power and station in life to make sure you feel and look small to the world, for if you look small they might look tall. There are white women who will be so hurt by the world that they won't feel whole unless you are almost dead with pain. Mind you, they don't want you dead, just in a pain that's worse than their pain, because if there is a pain greater than theirs, then they can feel alive and powerful over something. And only in my death have I been able to call rape, rape. There was the man in Hillsboro who violated me regularly with no one saying a thing about it and with me having no defense. He made me feel like no more than a piece of meat in this world.

I fear for you, because there are men, sick men, who will see the power that other white men have beaten out of you and the pain that white women have built themselves atop of, and seeing you way down there and small, they will use the sacredness of the sex God has given them and rather than making life, will take the last of yours and leave you the walking dead.

Faith in humans regardless of their station in life, regardless of their pain, regardless of their belief was my flaw. Humans, man and women alike, are the same as any other animal but more cunning. It they have to save their own hide and they see that you have fur on your back, they'll cut it loose from your body and leave you to bleed. When I got to go work for Anne and Mr. Garland in St. Louis, I thought all was good, because of how often they said I was a good woman, a trusted woman, hard working. But, when poverty looked them in the eyes, they looked at me and sent my hide out to work to support all eleven people of their house: *Don't just feed us, make us rich white people again.* One day in St. Louis when Mr. Garland tempted me with a dollar and told me that if I was so displeased then take my son and run away. I should have taken it, rather than thinking I'd be better off following the rules of freedom that said I was only free if I had a piece of paper that said not only had I supported this man's family and brought them out of poverty, but I had also made enough to buy myself and my son. You can't buy what you already own. There I was, like a fool, working my fingers to the bone to buy, me.

And I did, but free didn't mean that I couldn't be made small by the beatings of white men, or made the height of pain for the pained white woman, or raped by the ill-minded white male predator. All it meant was that now wherever I went, a group of white people had to look at my papers and agree that they were true, even though white men from Mississippi all the way to Missouri had signed sheets of paper saying they weren't supposed to treat me that way anymore, but the law they lived by, was signed almost 100 years before my freedom papers and also didn't mean much.

Why am I telling you all this? Because I need to deliver the message that is codified in my book, but remove all of that side-stepping and just give you the lessons straight so that you don't keep thinking that the lesson has to do with being in the White House, or with how friendly a person can be with their ex-masters and ex-bosses. I want you to do some things different while you are here living:

Work for yourself.

Do not wait for those who stole your liberty to reinstate it.

Do not invest in the praise of your oppressors. You are only good in their eyes as long as your actions serve them. The minute you do for yourself and it don't serve them, you go from good loyal worker, friend, to foe.

Dance. I never told any body of this, because the occasion set me to dance once and never again. I didn't know my body could be so free until the night I sat by poor Willie Lincoln's bedside and downstairs the music of the reception played lively and strong. I felt something in my heart beat with the Marine drum and something in my blood go metallic with the symbols, that and the rhythm of the rain clacking on the glass, and the dark of the night, and I started moving my body. I stopped when I heard Mrs. Lincoln come up the stairs and down the hall and Willie was close to death. I will always think that something about the spirit coming and the spirit going brings the body to dance, but I never told anybody about that. It was a moment between me and my body and everything in the world. It was a moment that wasn't focused on white people and negro people and war. It just had to do with me and my body not other people owning it, putting it to work or violating it, just me celebrating that I was alive. So, dance.

Grow some food. When those times come that white men are fighting over white men's rules, you can eat out of the ground, because the ground doesn't care anything about what color you are, what sex you are, it is just growing you something to eat, because you are alive.

Write it down. That's the best thing I ever did. Even though I skipped some painful things and made nice over some wrongful things, and drew attention to some things that weren't the point, write it down. If you gone write it, write it true, don't leave anything out and don't worry who is gonna get offended by seeing themselves in the mirror of your words. Worse thing could happen is that they kill you, but you gonna die anyway, or they can turn you out and denounce your friendship, but you came in this world alone and will leave alone, a few bouts of loneliness in the middle won't hurt. If you don't tell what it was like for YOU to live this life then the only thing left behind for other black women will be road maps made by white men like Lewis and Clark. Or worse, road maps with tributaries about the famous white people, and people will forget your story and follow the tributaries. Write it, and write it true, that'll make me feel like the mistakes I made in my strategy of trying to smooth feathers will all be rectified and the road maps made clear again.

Run. If people tell you that you are their prisoner, and they start proving all the ways that they have power over you, run. Take heed of when people pretend you have a choice, but then say that they won't take no for an answer. When you run. Don't take a lot of stuff with you, because you came into this world naked and if you gonna get to the next place in life, you might have to swim or blend in with the trees with your skin as camouflage, you might have to show up at your next station in life naked too, but you're better off free for real than fake-free by the laws of white men.

I think that's all I have to say. Now, wake up black woman, wake up, and get to telling your truth and doing whatever you came here to do. You don't have time to waste being polite and doubting yourself, those are white men's rules for your thinking. Think, but not with the mind made up on their rules that tells you there is a protocol to speaking and being heard, or that a protest is a good idea. It ain't. That's a trick that stands you in the town square squealing like a pig and making it clear to the predator where you are located, just outside his den.

One more thing, don't just write and tell the truth, seek out the written and spoken truth. Sometimes, people try to roll the truth up in some truth that they feel people are hungry for, some good celebrity gossip, but what they forget, well, what I forgot is that people chase after the celebrity and forget about the trampled life of the dressmaker, they forget about it so much so, that they will dig up your grave and run the new train right through the place where your dead body lay.

Look for the truth in the written and spoken word. It is the echo that will keep you company on a sometimes-tedious journey and might steer you away from death in an unmarked grave.

Farewell, darling Black Woman,
Elizabeth Hobbs (Keckley)

CHAPTER TWELVE

GIDEON YOUNG

what it is i hide from myself

what is it i hide from myself when i say the bright side of slavery[1]
to avoid sweeping all southerners into the muck
i both deny myself and excuse myself—
i am black and must rail against the dark
i am black and must hasten the glad day of deliverance[2]
i am white and see my face in the crowds
i am white and do not want to call myself devil
i am brown and a bug under America's boot
i am brown and the hope of what might be
i am brown and loved and spread my arms to the sun
i am brown and black and white and slave and free
i am so new upon this earth my voice is one of creation
i am swirling up from the ether i must make my own way

NOTES

1. Preface excerpt from *Behind the Scenes,* the autobiography of Elizabeth Keckley, 1818–1907. A mixed-race former slave, who purchased her freedom for $1200, Elizabeth philosophized that slavery must run its course before being destroyed, describing slavery as "a curse" and "evil."

2. Appendix excerpt from Frederick Douglass's *Narrative of the Life of Frederick Douglass, 1818–1895.* An escaped slave, Frederick was entirely opposed to slavery and slaveholders, citing "No Compromise!" and declaring abolishment a "sacred cause."

CHAPTER THIRTEEN

L. TERESA CHURCH

Woman of the Cloth
(for Elizabeth Keckley, Dressmaker)

Vicious as hell-hound-teeth, the lash
spoils your flesh but spares your hands,
nimble fingers that knot, needle silk threads
like slave passes tucked into bolted cloths:
silks, satins, cottons, velvet, brocade, organza, lace,
yardage fitted special to each client's request.
Every dress, every stitch secures your freedom

CHAPTER FOURTEEN

MELVIN E. LEWIS

The Modiste *in Séance*
For the Spiritualist in Elizabeth Hobbs Keckley

The medium lit one candle before we heard her skirts sweep past:
    My parents and their ancestors worked for people who lacked spirits & courage
        chains and abuse our passport & registration
    White men chained Africans as long as it took redwoods to grow, taught & reached the Gospel
        beat me, but I would not break
    My father was sold away when I was a child, mother never saw her husband again
    That bucka raped me for four years, men who lacked spirits and courage did not defend me
        Sometimes, I dreamt of using large needles, weapons to quell his loins.
    There's George—my son is in his Union Army uniform. My son's father, a white man
    On a plantation you learn to make your own tools, clothes survive
        In my fingers I saw colors, designs comforting ladies of means, imagination emancipates
    I sewed for people who came to my apartment, only the best designer to entrust their desires
    Made me famous, then turned their backs on me.
        I refuse their dismemory, rework my own body, soul and spirit. The blood from nails have sealed buttons.

          ***

The wind blow between the gates of a second floor set of chimes.

    In the afterworld, I saw your father. My grandfather taught me woodwork. We craved a long chair. At daybreak, the sun warms it.

How are my grandmothers? In a purple quilt, I have a corner for their favorite dresses, flowers and fruit.

They felt jewels. The men dug stones for them to polish and they share them, as well as kept a few for sticks in their African and grey hair.

Child, my son and love, what are the sounds of the next challenge, the steps to the new world?

Mama, we will see you when the wheat is dry and blue dye has dried on the hands of people near the *Sierra* Pond. The boards to turn clothes are still.

Baby, it's cold by the fire, in the winter?

Mama, it's hollow here and I've listened to stories in languages, I heard freshwater Africans whisper among themselves. Now, I understand them. Drawings of doors and scars are common on the frames of window seals. Pain beyond screams, lava on their skin and volcanoes destroying their villages at night, are the memories of people of color in the Americas. They know the eyes of bucka and have heard them speak of their blond God. We worship our ancestors and leave foreigners on the rocky side of the river. They are not invited to our ring shouts.

People speak in tongues when they're not in church. The winds from the North and West African deserts, cross the *Sahel*, cross the Atlantic Ocean—fall currents bring empty merchant and slave ships. Desert eagles are on the masks. The ugly vessels are burnt and the nails turned inside to make circles. I have a needle of yours. As the cow bells ring, I think of you and found a blue bottle. It whistles. It cries on your birthdays. It is getting cold . . .

Son, Baby I want to hear your laughter and think of the sounds of your steps on muddy porches.

CHAPTER FIFTEEN

DIANE JUDGE

Needlework and Names

Lizzie, Mrs. Lincoln's dressmaker, you call me, and I once was.
Four years I wore that label. Now sewn into the fabric
of my history, it cannot diminish me. Nothing has.
Savage whippings started when I was put to work
at four. Separation from the man I thought my father
when his owners took him West. The truth my mother
whispered on her deathbed: Our master sired me.
Bondage to my half-brother when I was fourteen.
Beatings by a schoolteacher my brother's wife tasked
with breaking me. Rape by a neighbor who thought
his white skin made my virginity his to steal.
A disappointing marriage to a dissipated man.
Patrons like the wives of Robert E. Lee
and Jefferson Davis whose husbands warred to keep
my kin in chains. To re-enslave me. Instead, I stitched
an armor forged in steel. I am not your Lizzie.
Call me Mrs. Keckley.

CHAPTER SIXTEEN

LENARD D. MOORE

Dear Elizabeth Keckley

Are you captured
on somebody's glass-plated negative
permanent as the sky,
stars of your eyes infinite
and glittering?

What was the shadow-hour like
when you witnessed Richmond's ruins,
shells of buildings
so fragile and broken,
ghost-stunned?

How did you wear seamstress
as life, as existence,
in which you were steady
like a needle
eyeing your thread of freedom?

Do you still walk
the White House
when the North Star winks
while crickets intensely sing
as if they, too, were human?

ELIZABETH HOBBS KECKLEY TIMELINE

1818   Elizabeth Hobbs (Keckley) is born in February in Dinwiddie County, Virginia.

1832   At fourteen, Elizabeth Keckley is given by Armistead Burwell to his oldest son, Robert. She lives with the Robert Burwell family in Chesterfield County, Virginia.

1835   The Robert Burwell family and Elizabeth Keckley move to Hillsborough, North Carolina, where Robert becomes minister of Hillsborough Presbyterian Church.

Harriet Jacobs escapes to her grandmother's attic in Edenton, North Carolina, where she will hide for seven years.

1836   The Burwells arrange for Elizabeth Keckley to be beaten by local schoolmaster William J. Bingham to correct her "stubborn pride."

1837   Anna Burwell opens the Burwell Academy for Young Ladies.

1839   Elizabeth Keckley gives birth to son, George, the result of repeated rapes by Alexander Kirkland, son of a prominent local merchant and planter in Hillsborough; Keckley names the baby George Pleasant Hobbs for her mother's husband and the man she knew as her father.

Keckley is returned to Virginia.

1847   Frederick Douglass begins publication of *The North Star*.

Keckley, her son, and her mother are held by Anne Burwell Garland and her husband Hugh; the Garland family moves to St. Louis.

1849   Harriet Tubman escapes slavery.

1850   Fugitive Slave Act passes.

1852   Elizabeth Keckley marries James Keckley.

After Elizabeth Keckley's repeated requests, the Garlands set the price of her freedom and that of her son's at $1,200 in November.

Harriet Beecher Stowe publishes *Uncle Tom's Cabin*.

1853   Stowe publishes *A Key to Uncle Tom's Cabin*.

1855	Elizabeth Keckley purchases her and her son's freedom from the Garland family.
	Frederick Douglass publishes *My Bondage and My Freedom*.
1857	*Dred Scott v. Sandford* is decided by the U.S. Supreme Court, declaring that African Americans, freed or enslaved, are not U.S. citizens, and the federal government has no power to regulate slavery. Elizabeth Keckley's former owner Hugh Garland had been a defense attorney early in the case.
1859	16 October: John Brown leads the attack on the arsenal at Harpers Ferry, Virginia.
	Georgia passes a law forbidding owners from manumitting slaves in their wills.
	Harriet Wilson publishes *Our Nig: Or, Sketches from the Life of a Free Black*.
1860	Elizabeth Keckley's son, George, enrolls in Wilberforce University.
	Keckley moves to Baltimore, then to Washington, DC.
1861	Elizabeth Keckley meets Mary Todd Lincoln on March 4, 1861, the day after Lincoln's first inauguration. Elizabeth Keckley will go on to make approximately sixteen dresses for her in four months.
	April 12: Attack on Fort Sumter off the coast of Charleston, South Carolina, signals the beginning of the Civil War.
	August 10: Keckley's son, George, is killed in the Battle of Wilson's Creek, Missouri.
	Harriet Jacobs publishes *Incidents in the Life of a Slave Girl*.
1862	Elizabeth Keckley founds of the Contraband Relief Association (CRA).
1863	According to the *Christian Recorder*, the CRA's receipts were "$838.68 the first year and $1,228.43 the second year."
	January 1: Lincoln issues the Emancipation Proclamation.
	November 19: Lincoln delivers the Gettysburg Address.
1865	Thirteenth Amendment passes.
	14 April: Lincoln is shot by John Wilkes Booth at Ford's Theatre and dies the following day.
1867	September 18: Old Clothes Scandal begins; Elizabeth Keckley joins Mary Todd Lincoln in New York.

Elizabeth Hobbs Keckley Timeline | 249

1868   *Behind the Scenes: Or, Thirty Years a Slave, and Four Years in the White House* is published.

1875   Civil Rights Act of 1875 passes.

1881   *Life and Times of Frederick Douglass* is published.

Tuskegee Institute is founded by Booker T. Washington.

1890   Elizabeth Keckley sells twenty-six of the Lincolns' articles to a collector for $250.

1892   Elizabeth Keckley accepts a position at Wilberforce University.

Anna Julia Cooper publishes *A Voice of the South: By a Woman from the South*.

1893   Elizabeth Keckley organizes a dress exhibit at the World's Columbian Exposition, also known as the Chicago World Fair.

1897   Harriet Jacobs dies and is eulogized by Francis Grimké, as Keckley will be a decade later.

1898   Wilmington, North Carolina, Race Riot.

1890s   Elizabeth Keckley suffers a stroke and moves back to Washington, DC.

1907   Elizabeth Keckley dies of a stroke at the Home for Destitute Colored Women and Children, Washington, DC; is buried at the Columbian Harmony Cemetery.

1960   Elizabeth Keckley's remains are transferred to the National Harmony Memorial Park in Landover, Maryland.

2010   Elizabeth Keckley's unmarked grave is located and a marker is placed in her honor. It reads,

Elizabeth Keckly
1818–1907
Enslaved. Modiste. Confidante.

FURTHER READING

Adams, Katherine. *Owning Up: Privacy, Property, and Belonging in U.S. Women's Life Writing.* New York: Oxford University Press, 2009.
Ames, Mary Clemmer. "Life in Washington: Stories of the Late Slaves." *Evening Post* 18 April 1862: 1.
———. *Ten Years in Washington: Life and Scenes in the National Capital, as a Woman Sees Them.* Hartford: A.D. Worthington, 1873.
Amireh, Amal. *The Factory Girl and the Seamstress: Imagining Gender and Class in Nineteenth Century American Fiction.* New York: Routledge, 2015 (reprint edition).
Andrews, William L. "The Changing Moral Discourse of Nineteenth-Century African American Women's Autobiography: Harriet Jacobs and Elizabeth Keckley." *De/Colonizing the Subject: The Politics of Gender in Women's Autobiography.* Eds. Sidonie Smith and Julia Watson. Minneapolis: University of Minnesota Press, 1992. 225–41.
Berlin, Ira. *Slaves without Masters: The Free Negro in the Antebellum South.* New York: Pantheon Books, 1974.
Brennan, Charlie. *Amazing St. Louis: 250 Years of Great Tales and Curiosities.* St. Louis: Reedy Press, 2013.
Brown, Elsa Barkley. "African-American Women's Quilting: A Framework for Conceptualizing and Teaching African-American Women's History." *SIGNS Journal of Women in Culture and Society* 14.4 (1989): 921–29.
Carby, Hazel V. *Reconstructing Womanhood: The Emergence of the Afro-American Woman Novelist.* New York: Oxford University Press, 1987.
Chiaverini, Jennifer. *Mrs. Lincoln's Dressmaker.* New York: Dutton, 2013.
Crowston, Clare Haru. *Fabricating Women: The Seamstresses of Old Regime France, 1675–1791.* Durham: Duke University Press, 2001.
Domina, Lynn. "I Was Re-Elected President: Elizabeth Keckley as Quintessential Patriot in *Behind the Scenes: Or, Thirty Years a Slave, and Four Years in the White House*." *Women's Life-Writing: Finding Voice/Building Community.* Ed. Linda Coleman. Bowling Green: Bowling Green State University Popular Press, 1997. 139–51.
Fleischner, Jennifer. *Mastering Slavery: Memory, Family, and Identity in Women's Slave Narratives.* New York: New York University Press, 1996.
———. *Mrs. Lincoln and Mrs. Keckly: The Remarkable Story of the Friendship between a First Lady and a Former Slave.* New York: Broadway Books, 2003.
Foley, Barbara. "History, Fiction, and the Ground Between: The Uses of the Documentary Mode in Black Literature." *PMLA* 95.3 (May 1980): 389–403.

Foster, Frances Smith. "Romance and Scandal in a Postbellum Slave Narrative: Elizabeth Keckley's *Behind the Scenes*." *Written by Herself: Literary Production by African American Women, 1746–1892*. Bloomington: Indiana University Press, 1993. 117–30.

Gimeno Pahissa, Laura. "Former Slaves on the Move: The Plantation Household, the White House, and the Postwar South as Spaces of Transit in Elizabeth Keckley's *Behind the Scenes*." *Revista Alicantina de Estudios Ingleses*. 25: 335–49.

Hoffert, Sylvia. *When Hens Crow: The Woman's Rights Movement in Antebellum America*. Bloomington: Indiana University Press, 2002.

Hutchison, C. "Elizabeth Keckley." *American Literary History*. 19.3: 603–28.

Jones, Lynda. *Mrs. Lincoln's Dressmaker: The Unlikely Friendship of Elizabeth Keckley and Mary Todd Lincoln*. National Geographic Children's Book, 2009.

Karwatka, Dennis. "Elizabeth Keckley and Dressmaking Innovation." *Tech Directions*. 68.4: 12.

Keckley, Elizabeth. *Behind the Scenes: Or, Thirty Years a Slave, and Four Years in the White House*. (1868) Introduction by Dolen Perkins-Valdez. Hillsborough, N.C.: Eno Publishers, 2016.

Keckley, Elizabeth. *Behind the Scenes: Or, Thirty Years a Slave, and Four Years in the White House*. (1868) Ed. Frances Smith Foster. Urbana: University of Illinois Press, 2001.

Lewis, Catherine, and J. Richard. *Women and Slavery in America: A Documentary History*. Fayetteville: University of Arkansas Press, 2011.

Litwack, Leon F. *Been in the Storm So Long: The Aftermath of Slavery*. New York: Random House, 1979.

Lusane, Clarence. *The Black History of the White House*. San Francisco: City Lights Publishers, 2011.

Painter, Nell. *Sojourner Truth: A Life, a Symbol*. New York: W.W. Norton, 1996.

Petrino, Elizabeth. "Disarming the Nation: Women's Writing and the American Civil War." *Legacy*. 18.1: 112–14.

Rinaldi, Ann. *An Unlikely Friendship: A Novel of Mary Todd Lincoln and Elizabeth Keckley*. New York: HMH Books, 2008.

Roberts, Cokie. *Capital Dames: The Civil War and the Women of Washington, 1848–1868*. New York: HarperCollins, 2015.

Rutberg, Becky. *Mary Lincoln's Dressmaker: Elizabeth Keckley's Remarkable Rise from Slave to White House Confidante*. New York: Walker, 1995.

Schwalm, Leslie A. "'Agonizing Groans of Mothers' and 'Slave-Scarred Veteran': The Commemoration of Slavery and Emancipation." *American Nineteenth Century History*. 9.3: 289–304.

Silber, Nina. "Intemperate Men, Spiteful Women, and Jefferson Davis: Northern Views of the Defeated South." *American Quarterly* 41.4 (December 1989): 614–35.

Smith, Sidonie, and Julia Watson. *De/Colonizing the Subject: The Politics of Gender in Women's Autobiography*. Minneapolis: University of Minnesota Press, 1992.

Smith McKoy, Sheila, ed. *The Elizabeth Keckley Reader: Volume 1—Writing Self, Writing Nation*. Hillsborough, N.C.: Eno Publishers, 2016.

Steadman, Jennifer Bernhardt, et al. "Archive Survival Guide: Practical and Theoretical Approaches for the Next Century of Women's Studies Research." *Legacy.* 19.2: 230–40.

Sten, Christopher, ed. *Literary Capital: A Washington Reader.* University of Georgia Press, 2011.

Sterling, Dorothy, ed. *We Are Your Sisters: Black Women in the Nineteenth Century.* New York: W.W. Norton, 1984.

Stover, Johnnie M. "African American 'Mother Tongue' Resistance in Nineteenth-Century Postbellum Black Women's Autobiography: Elizabeth Keckley and Susie King Taylor." *A/B: Auto/Biography Studies,* 2003, Volume 18, Issue: 117–44.

Turner, Justin G., and Linda Levitt. *Mary Todd Lincoln: Her Life and Letters.* New York: Alfred A. Knopf, 1972.

Vidal, Gore. *Lincoln: A Novel.* New York: Ballantine Books, 1984.

Way, Elizabeth. "Elizabeth Keckly and Ann Lowe: Recovering an African American Fashion Legacy That Clothed the American Elite." *Fashion Theory* 19, Issue 1 (2015): 115–41.

Williams, Susan S. "Contractual Authorship: Elizabeth Keckley and Mary Abigail Dodge." *Reclaiming Authorship: Literary Women in America, 1850–1900.* Philadelphia: University of Pennsylvania Press, 2006.

Young, Elizabeth. "Black Woman, White House: Race and Redress in Elizabeth Keckley's *Behind the Scenes.*" *Disarming the Nation: Women's Writing and the American Civil War*. Chicago: University of Chicago Press, 1999.

Zafar, Rafia. "Dressing Up and Dressing Down: Elizabeth Keckley's *Behind the Scenes* at the White House and Eliza Potter's *A Hairdresser's Experience in High Life.*" *We Wear the Mask: African Americans Write American Literature, 1760–1870.* New York: Columbia University Press, 1997.

EDITOR'S BIOGRAPHY

Dr. Sheila Smith McKoy is chair of the English Department at Kennesaw State University, and former associate professor of English at North Carolina State University. Smith McKoy holds a BA from North Carolina State University, an MA from the University of North Carolina at Chapel Hill and a PhD from Duke University. She is the first African American to receive a PhD from Duke's English Department. She is editor of *The Elizabeth Keckley Reader* series, published by Eno Publishers. A poet, literary critic, and fiction writer, Smith McKoy's work has appeared in numerous publications including the critically acclaimed Schomburg series *African American Women Writers 1910–1940, Callaloo, Contours, Journal of Ethnic American Literature, Mythium, Obsidian: Literature in the African Diaspora, Research for African Literatures,* and *Valley Voices.* Her book, *When Whites Riot: Writing Race and Violence in American and South African Cultures* (University of Wisconsin Press, 2001) received critical attention. She has recently completed a book of poetry.

Dr. Smith McKoy has worked extensively in the fields of African, African American, Afro-Caribbean, and other African-descent literatures. She focuses on the relationships between Africa and African diaspora counties and cultures, and also on indigenous knowledge, especially as it relates to issues related to health and healing rituals. Her global engagement work has enabled her to contribute widely to projects nationally and internationally.

ABOUT THE CONTRIBUTORS

Katherine Adams is Associate Professor of English and Kimmerling Chair in Women's Literature at Tulane University. Her research and teaching focus on nineteenth-century U.S. literature and culture, women's writing, African American literature, and gender and race theory. She is the author of *Owning Up: Privacy, Property, and Belonging in U.S. Women's Life Writing* (Oxford 2009), editor of *U.S. Women Writing Race, A Special Issue of Tulsa Studies in Women's Literature* (2009), and co-editor of *Recovering Alice Dunbar-Nelson for the Twenty-First Century: A Special Issue of Legacy: A Journal of American Women Writers* (2016).

Sarah Blackwood researches and teaches American literature, culture, and art with a particular focus on nineteenth-century visual culture, African American literature, and the history of inner life. She is currently working on a monograph about nineteenth-century portraiture and the invention of inner life, is co-founder and co-editor of the web magazine *Avidly*, and co-editor of the book series *Avidly Reads* (NYU Press). She writes literary and cultural criticism regularly for national outlets.

L. Teresa Church is a member of the Carolina African American Writers' Collective and serves as Membership Chairperson and Archivist for this organization. She penned her first poem at age sixteen. Her writings have appeared in publications such as *Simply Haiku*, *The Heron's Nest*, *Obsidian: Literature in the African Diaspora*, *Solo Café*, *Nocturnes: (Re)view of the Literary Arts*, and *African American Review*.

Tyree Daye, a native of Youngsville, N.C., is an MFA candidate at North Carolina State University. His chapbook entitled *Sea Island Blues* was published by Backbone Press in 2014. He is the author of *What You and The Devil Do to Stay Warm*, a chapbook published with Blue Horse Press in 2015. An award-winning poet, Daye won the Amy Clampitt Residency for 2018 and the Glenna Luschei Prairie Schooner Award. Most recently, he won the prestigious American Poetry Review 2017 Honickman Poetry Prize for his forthcoming poetry collection, *River* Hymns. He is a Cave Canem fellow.

Lisa Shawn Hogan studies nineteenth-century political rhetoric, with an emphasis on how gender constrained the rhetoric of suffrage activists and other outspoken women. She earned her PhD in communication and women's studies from Indiana University-Bloomington and has taught at Eastern Illinois University and the Pennsylvania State University. Her published work appears in *Gender Studies, Women's Studies, Rhetoric and Public Affairs,* and several other journals specializing in rhetoric and gender studies.

Diane Judge is a member of the Carolina African American Writers' Collective. Her work has been published in *Black Magnolias Literary Journal, Backbone Poetry Journal, 34th Parallel, Obsidian: Literature in the African Diaspora, Frogpond,* and *Poetry South*. She has contributed to two anthologies, *Remembrances of Wars Past,* edited by Henry Tonn, and *Black Gold: An Anthology of Black Poetry,* edited by Ja A. Jahannes. Her flash fiction story, "Dear in the Headlights," is online www.kalyanimagazine.com.

Jeffrey Allen Langley attends North Carolina State University, where he is majoring in Arts Application with a concentration in visual art and culture. During his years there, he developed a great appreciation for the musical and physical arts. As a graphic designer, artist, and web designer, Langley uses his talents to teach through various artistic and physical lenses.

Melvin E. Lewis is the Director of Emergency Management/Environmental Health and Safety at Fayetteville State University. His articles and radio programs on jazz, fine art, horticulture, and adverse weather preparedness have been broadcasted on 107.7 FM as well as published *in City View NC, Fayetteville Observer Fayetteville Press, Ex Umbra, Port-of-Harlem, The World and I, Up and Coming Weekly,* and *Pluck! Journal of Affrilachian Arts*. His poetry has been published nationally and internationally in the *Afro-Hispanic Review, Antietam Review, Black American Literature Forum, The Black Panther Newspaper, The Black Scholar, Gargoyle, NOMMO, Obsidian: Literature of the African Diaspora, OBA Songs, Pen International, Wasafiri, Presence Africaine, Isivivane, Mother Tongues* and *Possibilitiis*. Lewis is the recipient of the Red Rock Tribal poetry prize in South Africa.

Zelda Lockhart is currently pursuing a PhD in Expressive Art Therapies at Lesley University, and holds an MA in literature from Old Dominion University and a BA in English from Norfolk State University. She is author of *The Soul of the Full-Length Manuscript: Turning Life's Wounds Into the Gift of Literary Fiction, Memoir or Poetry,* and the award-winning novels *Fifth Born, Cold Running Creek,* and *Fifth Born II: The Hundredth Turtle.* Her other works of fiction, poetry and essays can be found in anthologies and journals. A resident of Hillsborough, N.C., she is director of LaVenson Press Studios and travels and lectures regularly. www.zeldalockhart.com, www.LaVensonPressStudios.com.

Michael Malone is the author of twelve internationally acclaimed novels, including the classic *Handling Sin, Dingley Falls,* and *The Last Noel. The Four Corners of the Sky* was his latest national bestseller. He is currently at work on *Dark Winter,* the fourth in a "Hillston" quartet of novels, all set in a town much like Hillsborough, N.C., where he lives with his wife, Maureen Quilligan. His television writing credits include network shows for ABC, NBC, and Fox. His stories, essays, and critical writings have appeared in publications such as the *Wilson Quarterly, Mademoiselle, Harper's,* the *New York Times,* and *The Nation*. He's also written plays, musicals, and film scripts. Among his prizes are the O Henry, the Edgar, the Writers Guild Award, and the Emmy for ABC's "One Life to Live," where he was head-writer for nearly a decade. He has taught at Yale, the University of Pennsylvania, Swarthmore, and Duke.

Carme Manuel is professor of English in the Department de Filologia Anglesa i Alemanya at the Universitat de València. Her interests lie in African American studies and genre studies and she has published and lectured widely on nineteenth- and twentieth-century American and African American women writing. Among other publications, she has edited and is the author of the first Spanish translations of *Our Nig* (Harriet E. Wilson), *Incidents in the Life of a Slave Girl* (Harriet A. Jacobs), *Behind the Scenes* (Elizabeth Keckley), and *Contending Forces* (Pauline Hopkins). She is the author of the first anthology published in Catalan of eighteenth- and nineteenth-century African American women poets. In 2002 she founded the independent scholarly collection Biblioteca Javier Coy d'estudis nord-americans at the Universitat de València, Spain (PUV), devoted to publishing work on American studies. BJC has published 108 volumes to date by Spanish, American and European scholars. She has been vice president of the Spanish Association for American Studies (SAAS) since March 2012. She is completing a book on late nineteenth-century black women's life writing. In 2013 she published her first novel, *Llanceu la creu*.

Lenard D. Moore, founder and executive director of the Carolina African American Writers' Collective and co-founder of the Washington Street Writers Group, is a U.S. Army veteran. He is the author, editor, and co-editor of several books, including the 30th anniversary edition of his poetry book, *The Open Eye*, published by Mountains and Rivers Press. His poetry has been translated into several languages. Recipient of the Margaret Walker Creative Writing Award (CLA, 1997) and numerous other awards, he teaches African American Literature and Advanced Poetry Writing at the University of Mount Olive.

Maureen Quilligan was the R. Florence Brinkley Professor of English Emerita at Duke University before her retirement in 2015. She taught Renaissance literature at Yale University, University of Pennsylvania, and Duke University for forty-three years. She lives in Hillsborough, North Carolina, where she was a commissioner of the Burwell School.

Xiomara Santamarina is an associate professor of English at the University of Michigan. Her primary areas of interest include nineteenth-century African American literatures with a primary focus on autobiography and slave narratives; antebellum fiction and prose; economic criticism; theories of value, race and labor. Santamarina is author of *Belabored Professions: Narratives of African American Working Womanhood* (University of North Carolina Press, 2005).

Jaki Shelton Green, 2016 Lenoir-Rhyne University writer-in-residence, teaches poetry at Duke University Center for Documentary Studies. She is the recipient of numerous awards including the 2014 Pushcart Prize Nominee, 2010 Fine Arts Emerald Award, 2009 N.C. Piedmont Laureate, 2007 Sam Ragan Award for Contributions to the Fine Arts of N.C., the North Carolina Award for Literature; she was inducted into the North Caroliniana Society and the N.C. Literary Hall of Fame. Shelton Green's poetry collections include *Dead on Arrival and New Poems, Masks, Conjure Blues, singing a tree into dance, breath of the song,* and *Feeding the Light.* She is the author of the play *Blue Opal* and co-editor of two anthologies: *Poets for Peace* and *Immigration Emigration and Diversity.* She is the owner of *SistaWRITE* providing writing retreats and travel excursions for women writers.

Carolyn Sorisio is a professor of English at West Chester University of Pennsylvania specializing in nineteenth-century U.S. literature. Her publications include *The Newspaper Warrior: Sarah Winnemucca Hopkins's Campaign for American Indian Rights* (co-editor, University of Nebraska Press) and *Fleshing Out America: Race, Gender and the Politics of the Body in American Literature, 1833–1879* (Georgia University Press). She has guest-edited special issues of *ESQ: A Journal of the American Renaissance* ("Native Americans: Writing and Written," 2006) and *MELUS* ("Cross-Racial and Cross-ethnic Collaboration and Scholarship: Contexts, Criticism, and Challenges," 2013) and has published essays in the *African American Review, Legacy: A Journal of American Women Writers,* and *Modern Language Studies.*

Tazewell Thompson is the award-winning author of the plays: *Mary T & Lizzy K*; *Constant Star,* about the life of Ida B. Wells; *Jubilee* about the Fisk Jubilee Singers; *Jam & Spice*, an adaptation of the music of Kurt Weill and *A Christmas Carol.* He is the internationally acclaimed director of opera and theater with productions in Europe, Japan, Canada, and Africa, as well as nationally in California, Kentucky, Indiana, Minnesota, Illinois, Pennsylvania, Virginia, Florida, Washington, DC, and New York.

Gideon Young is a member of the Carolina African-American Writers' Collective and the Haiku Society of America. His poetry has appeared in *Backbone Press, Carve Magazine, Obsidian: Literature in the African Diaspora, Spillway, The Long River Review, The White Elephant,* and *Black Gold: an Anthology of Black Poetry.* He has an MA in elementary education and teaching from North Carolina State University and a BA in Literature from the University of Connecticut. He is a Title 1 elementary reading teacher and literacy specialist in Efland, North Carolina.

PERMISSIONS & ACKNOWLEDGMENTS

"Mary T. & Lizzy K.," by Tazewell Thompson (copyright ©2013 by Tazewell Thompson), is reprinted here with permission from Tazewell Thompson and the Barbara Hogenson Agency, Inc. All rights reserved.

Lisa Shawn Hogan's essay "Exposing Mary Lincoln: Elizabeth Keckley and the Rhetoric of Disclosure" originally appeared in *Southern Communication Journal* 78 (5): 405–26, and appears her with permission from Southern State Communication Association (http://www.ssca.net).

Steve Criniti's essay "Thirty Years a Slave, and Four Years a Fairy Godmother: Dressmaking as Self-Making in Elizabeth Keckley's Autobiography" appears in this volume with permission from *Transcendental Quarterly,* where his piece was published in 1999.

Katherine Adams's essay "Freedom and Ballgowns: Elizabeth Keckley and the Work of Domesticity" was originally published in issue 57.4 of the *Arizona Quarterly* (2001).

Carme Manuel's essay "Elizabeth Keckley's Behind the Scenes; or, the 'Colored Historian' Resistance to the Technologies of Power of Postwar America" first appeared in *African American Review* 44.1–2 (Spring-Summer/2011).

Carolyn Sorisio's essay "Unmasking the Genteel Performer: Elizabeth Keckley's behind the Scenes and the Politics of Public Wrath" first appeared in *African American Review* 33:19–38 (Spring 2000).

Sarah Blackwood's essay "'Making Good Use of Our Eyes': Nineteenth Century African Americans Write Visual Culture" first appeared as in *MELUS* 39.2 (2014): 42–65.

Xiomara Santamarina's essay "Behind the Scenes of Black Labor: Elizabeth Keckley and the Scandal of Publicity" appears here courtesy of *Feminist Studies,* where it first was published in Vol. 28, No. 3 (Autumn 2002): 514–37.

INDEX

abolitionist(s), 9, 83, 90, 93
Adams, Katherine, 71, 177, 195
African American(s), 1, 3, 4, 5, 8, 22, 26, 61, 74, 134, 141, 142, 143, 149, 152; African American literature, 115, 116, 142, 144, 156; African American writers, 13, 19, 20, 68, 142, 144, 155, 158, 161, 162; labor, 27
African American men, 74
African American women, 2, 3, 5, 7, 9, 13, 28, 43, 44, 50, 53, 65, 66
Alexander, Lynn, 175
Alger, Horatio: *Ragged Dick*, 168, 169, 170
American Dream, 44–45, 170, 172, 177, 196
American First Ladies, xii
American history, 5, 26
Ames, Mary Clemmer, 23, 24, 36, 37
Amireh, Amal, 175
Andrews, William, 20, 92, 136
antebellum era, 8, 20, 45, 46, 50, 188, 195, 196
Asbury, Herbert: *Gangs of New York*, 11
autobiography, 22, 75, 82, 90, 93, 131, 170, 194, 197, 198

Baker, Jean H., 206
Baltimore, 3
Barbee, David R., 194
Barthes, Roland, 7, 26, 30
Behind the Scenes, x, 45, 67, 76, 93, 100, 115, 148, 193. *See also* Keckley, Elizabeth
Berlant, Lauren, 95, 96
Berlin, Ira, 2

Black America, 10
Black American(s), 9; community, 4, 7; women, 8. *See also* African Americans, African American women
black body, 76, 84, 85, 89, 91; female body, xiii
black codes, 84
black tax, xi
Blackwood, Sarah, 141
bondage, 67
Boorstin, Daniel J., 80
Brady, Mathew, 8, 9, 10, 30, 217
Brown, Gillian, 74
Burwell, Anne, 225
Burwell, Armistead, 19

Carlton & Company, 191
Chaney, Michael A., 141–42
Child, Lydia Maria, 53
Church, Teresa, 242
Civil War, ix, 4, 5, 42, 98, 192, 201, 204, 236
Cleveland Daily Plain Dealer, 57, 59
Confederacy, 12, 17, 19, 21, 23, 32, 34, 35, 98, 99, 206, 209; Confederate Army, 20; Confederate leaders, 21. *See also* Davis, Jefferson; Lee, Robert E.
Confederate-Union Divide, xi
Constitution (U.S.), 4
Contraband Relief Organization (Association), 4, 12, 22, 62
Corbitt, Mary Jean, 180
Criniti, Stephen, 167
Crowston, Clare Haru, 2
cult of true womanhood, 54–55
cultural hybridity, xi, xii

Davis, Jefferson, 17, 34, 97
Davis, Varina Howell, 114
Daye, Tyree: "Coined: Sonnet for Elizabeth Keckley," ii
Democrat, 77, 98
Democratic party, 73
Dinius, Marcy J., 141
Dobson, Joanne, 63
Douglas, Ann, 74
Douglas, Mrs. Stephen Douglas (née Adele Cutts), ix
Douglass, Frederick, 12, 13, 33, 90, 92, 93, 116, 141, 144, 154, 160, 161, 162; *My Bondage and My Freedom*, 90; *Narrative of the Life of Frederick Douglass*, 241
Dred Scott case, 20

Emancipation, 5, 13, 200
Emancipation Proclamation, 13, 23
enslaved female body, 118
enslaved labor, 76, 87, 123, 126
enslaved mother, x, 158
enslaved people, 87, 88, 89, 92, 100, 106, 156, 157, 158

female labor, 118, 120
Fifteenth Street Presbyterian Church, 22, 35, 247
Fleischner, Jennifer, 11, 23, 32, 61, 63, 64, 65, 68, 139, 140, 156, 164, 182, 183, 184, 189, 194, 195, 207, 209, 210, 211, 214
Foner, Eric, 4, 26, 28, 35, 103, 104, 105, 135, 192
Foster, Frances Smith, 19, 20, 26, 30, 42, 43, 44, 103, 106, 115, 116, 136, 137, 138, 139, 170, 171, 172, 173, 177, 179, 182, 183, 191, 195, 210, 211
Foucault, Michel, 5, 6
Fourteenth Amendment, 1, 4, 5, 103
Fox-Genovese, Elizabeth, 138

Free Negros, 2, 3, 31
free labor, 83, 84, 87, 92, 93, 96, 97, 99, 104, 105, 107, 113, 135
Freedman's Bureau, 94, 104
Fry, Smith D., ix

Garland, Anne Burwell, 201, 247
Garland, Bettie, 20
Garland, Hugh, 19–20, 136, 189–90, 248
Garnet, Henry Highland, 22, 35, 133, 161
gender, 35, 54, 64, 74, 75, 77, 116, 118, 119, 120, 125, 134, 135, 137, 188, 198
Genovese, Eugene, 8, 36, 105, 138
Goffman, Erving, 55, 174, 175
Green, Jaki Shelton, 233
Haiti, 32

Halttunen, Karen, 43, 45, 51, 52, 54, 55, 56, 57, 60, 61, 63, 65–66, 203
Harper's Weekly, 13, 15, 21, 24, 25, 27, 32, 34, 86, 99, 145, 147
Harris, Leslie, 11–12
Hay, John, 147
Hobbs, Agnes, 20
Hogan, Lisa Shawn, 187

interracial marriage, 19, 71, 72, 73, 74, 85, 102, 105

Jacobs, Harriet, 29, 36, 46, 47, 52, 53, 56, 93, 95, 96, 105, 106, 107, 116, 118, 119, 136, 138, 139, 158, 159, 163, 168, 195, 247, 249
Johnson, Andrew, 29, 48, 71, 72, 73, 83, 92, 94, 104, 105
Judge, Diane, 245

Keckley (Keckly), Elizabeth: audience, 19, 22, 28, 47, 119; beatings, 53, 189, 243; *Behind the Scenes*, ix, x, 1, 2, 3, 4, 5, 6, 7, 8, 9, 10, 12, 13, 20, 21, 22, 23, 24,

26, 27, 28, 29, 31, 33, 34, 41, 42, 43, 44, 52, 56, 57, 58, 60, 62, 63, 64, 67, 75, 76, 82, 85, 92, 97, 107, 113, 114, 116, 117, 119, 120, 121, 122, 128, 129, 131, 134, 135, 142, 147, 168, 171, 172, 173, 174, 178, 181, 187, 188, 189, 190, 191, 192, 193, 194, 197, 198, 201, 202, 203, 205, 206, 207, 208–9, 241; business owner, x, xi, 2, 43, 45, 47, 75, 114, 118, 124, 127, 133, 218; colored historian, 1, 8, 20, 42, 209; death of, x, 194; dressmaker for Mary Todd Lincoln, 8, 23, 36, 75, 99, 169, 178, 187, 200, 219, 244; freedom, purchase of, xi, 3; husband, 190; letters, 67, 179, 191, 206; literacy, 149, 225; memoir, xi, 144, 147, 149; modiste, 2, 4, 8, 26, 28, 115, 174, 178, 187, 227, 233, 235, 243; relationship with Jefferson Davis, 21–22; son (*see* Kirkland, George [Hobbs]), death of, 10, 42, 59, 204, 218. *See also* Lincoln, Abraham, relationship with Elizabeth Keckley; Lincoln, Mary Todd, relationship with Elizabeth Keckley

Keyes, Samuel, 76, 77, 181, 183, 206, 207, 222

Kirkland, Alexander, 19, 189, 247

Kirkland, George (Hobbs), x, 11, 19, 102, 107, 108, 189, 190, 204, 207, 242, 243, 247

Langley, Jeffrey. "Coined. Sonnet for Elizabeth Keckley," ii

Lee, Robert E., 17, 21, 35, 132, 173, 243

Lefort, Claude, 78

Lewis, Melvin E., 243

Lincoln, Abraham: anti-slavery position, 32; assassination, 15, 16, 128, 145, 147, 148, 187, 196; Brady image, 10; Douglass, Frederick, meeting, 10, 12, 22, 33; emancipation of slaves, 16; glove (*see* mementos of), 100; Keckley memoir, 1; *Lincoln* (film), 164; mementos of, 63; relationship with Elizabeth Keckley, 43; relationship with wife, 49, 205; upbringing, 56. *See also* Emancipation Proclamation

Lincoln, Mary Todd: behavior, 63, 67, 68; death of son Willie, 11, 59, 62, 63–64, 203; Confederate spy, 206; death of husband, 1, 59, 128, 187, 224; financial problems, 48, 49, 50, 77; Keckley, letters to, x, 77; Keckley memoir, 53, 56, 57, 65, 130, 131; Old Clothes Scandal, x, 1, 27, 75, 82; relationship with children, 91; relationship with husband, 127; relationship with Elizabeth Keckley, ix, 1, 2, 4, 9, 28, 42, 43, 50, 58, 59, 93, 113, 126–27, 129; reputation, 25, 193; upbringing, 176, 177

Lincoln, Robert, 42, 61, 76, 153, 155, 179

Lincoln, Tad, 32, 61, 91, 92, 98, 142, 145, 146, 147, 149, 150, 152, 153, 154, 155, 156, 161, 163, 164, 187; illiteracy, 151, 152, 153, 154, 156

Lincoln White House, ix, 75, 114, 115

Lincoln, William "Willie," 11, 59, 60, 61, 62, 63, 64, 80, 97, 107, 127, 203, 204, 238–39

Litwack, Leon F., 2

Lively, James, 9, 17

Lockhart, Zelda, 236

Longstreet, Bettie (née Garland) 20,

Longstreet, James A., 20, 34–35

Lott, Eric, 101

Lutz, Catherine, 138

Lutz, Tom, 16–17

Malone, Michael, 225

miscegenation, 9, 10, 12, 18, 31, 72, 73, 74, 85, 87, 102

Moore, Lenard D., 246

Nast, Thomas, 13, 15, 21, 24, 25, 27, 34, 84, 85
New York Citizen, 43, 130, 131, 136, 137, 138, 182
New York Commercial Advertiser, 191, 210
New York Draft Riots, 10–11
New York Evening News, 29, 63
New York Evening Post, 23
New York Herald, 207, 214
New York, NY, 31, 41, 46, 67, 76, 114, 206, 222
New York Times, 41, 67, 70, 258
New York Tribune, 8, 32, 33, 147
New York World, 129
nineteenth century, xiii, 7, 20, 28, 54, 60, 145, 152, 154, 191, 203, 205, 217; Americans, 6, 43, 45
North Carolina, 158, 227, 237, 247, 249

Old Clothes Scandal, x, 1, 41, 75, 77, 78, 79, 82, 85, 88, 114, 129, 173, 181, 205
Ottolengul, Daniel, 100, 101, 107, 148, 194; *Behind the Seams: by a Nigger Woman Who Took in Work form Mrs. Lincoln and Mrs. Davis*, 40, 45, 67, 69, 76, 93, 100, 110, 115, 136, 148, 165, 193, 194, 210

Painter, Nell, 22, 30, 35, 36, 138
Panama, 32
Payne, Daniel A., 22
Payne, Robert, 138
postbellum, 44, 48, 50, 64, 84, 85, 87, 120; post-war, 5, 7, 9, 10, 15, 19, 26, 27, 28, 47, 200
Putnam's Magazine, 40, 41, 192, 210

Quilligan, Maureen, 225

racial identity, 72, 117
racial relationships, 10, 84, 120

racism, 71, 75, 102, 149, 189
rape, xii, 73, 102, 189, 193, 237, 238, 243, 243, 247
Reconstruction, 1, 4, 5, 10, 19, 26, 27, 28, 29, 31, 32, 34, 35, 37, 44, 48, 52, 68, 72, 74, 75, 82, 83, 93, 101, 103, 104, 109, 134, 135, 171, 195, 207, 210
Redpath, James, 67, 107, 179, 190, 191
Republican party, 4, 23, 27, 29, 30, 31, 32, 67, 71, 72, 77, 83, 87, 106, 129
Romero, Lora, 74
Rudisill, Richard, 7
Rutberg, Becky, 9, 12, 30, 36, 207–8, 214

Sánchez-Eppler, Karen, 90, 105
Santamarina, Xiomara, 34, 113, 136, 195, 211
slave codes, 8
slave narratives, 13, 23, 121, 150, 171, 173, 188, 195, 196, 198
Smith McKoy, Sheila, xiii, ix, xi, xiv
Sorisio, Carolyn, 41
South, 2, 8, 20, 23, 29, 84, 97
South Carolina, Slave Code of 1740, 8
St. Louis, MO, xi, 3, 20, 46, 47, 114, 125, 126, 127, 171, 189, 237, 238, 247
Stadler, Eva Maria, 174, 175
Stadler, Gustavus, 164
Stampp, Kenneth, 10, 20, 29, 31, 32, 35
Stewart, Maria W., 3, 35
Stowe, Harriet Beecher, 37, 46, 62, 247; *Uncle Tom's Cabin*, 37, 46, 62, 68, 105, 247
Swisshelm, Jane, 194, 211

Tagg, John, 5, 6, 7, 8, 26, 30, 36
Thompson, Tazwell, 217
Tompkins, Jane, 68, 74, 103
Trachtenberg, Alan, 7, 8, 9, 29–30, 157
Truth, Sojourner, 22, 35

Union Army, 11, 12, 29, 32, 108, 242

Victorian novel, 176
Victorian era, 191, 206, 207, 208
Virginia, xv, 19, 201, 228, 235, 247, 248; Dinwiddie, VA, 189

Wallace, Maurice O., 142
Washington, Augustus, 143
Washington, Booker T., 6, 116, 134–35, 249
Washington, D.C., 2, 4, 24, 25, 35, 43, 49, 67, 93, 126, 190
Washington, John E., 128, 210
white body, 73, 103; female body, 74, 85, 120

White, Deborah Gray, 69, 137
White House, 12, 16, 25, 33, 48, 57, 63, 64, 75–76, 77, 78, 79, 80, 88, 114, 190, 221
Wilberforce University, 63, 108, 135, 248, 249
Wilson, Kathryn E., 175, 184
womanhood, true, 50, 54, 55, 67, 81, 107, 119, 205

Young, Elizabeth, 16, 18, 34, 193, 210
Young, Gideon, 241

Zafar, Rafia, 11, 26, 28, 52, 53, 60, 68, 87, 103, 106, 107

ALSO AVAILABLE FROM ENO PUBLISHERS

Behind the Scenes
Or Thirty Years a Slave, and Four Years in the White House
Elizabeth Hobbs Keckley
With an introduction by Dolen Perkins-Valdez
Paperback
$10
ISBN: 978-0-9896092-7-2
Also available as an ebook

The Elizabeth Keckley Reader
Volume One: Writing Self, Writing Nation
Edited by Dr. Sheila Smith McKoy
Paperback
$15.95
ISBN: 978-0-9896092-5-8

The Elizabeth Keckley Reader
Volume Two: Artistry, Culture & Commerce
Edited by Dr. Sheila Smith McKoy
Paperback
$17.50
ISBN: 978-0-9973144-4-1

www.ingramcontent.com/pod-product-compliance
Lightning Source LLC
Chambersburg PA
CBHW020609300426
44113CB00007B/573